A Designed Life

Contemporary
American Textiles, Wallpapers,
and Containers & Packaging,
1951–54

Edited by Margaret Re

Center for Art,
Design and Visual Culture
UMBC

Photographs of the exhibition as presented at UMBC's Center for Art, Design and Visual Culture.

Photo credit: Dan Meyers Photography

They come day after day, night after night. Eight millions of them have knocked upon the gates already, and have been admitted.

Tapeten in USA

Eine Ausstellung
der Amerikahäuser
in Deutschland

Entwurf: Tom Lee

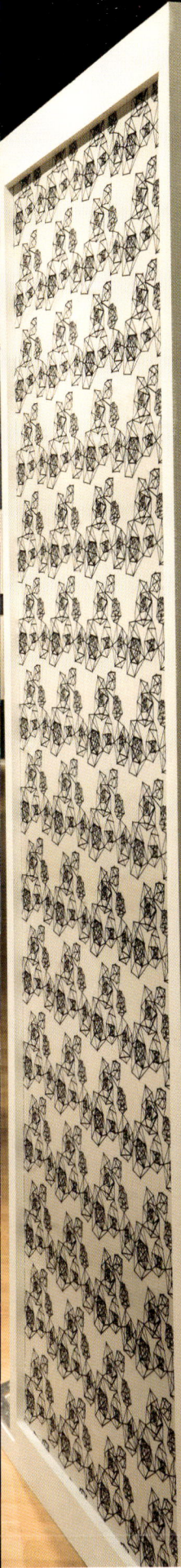

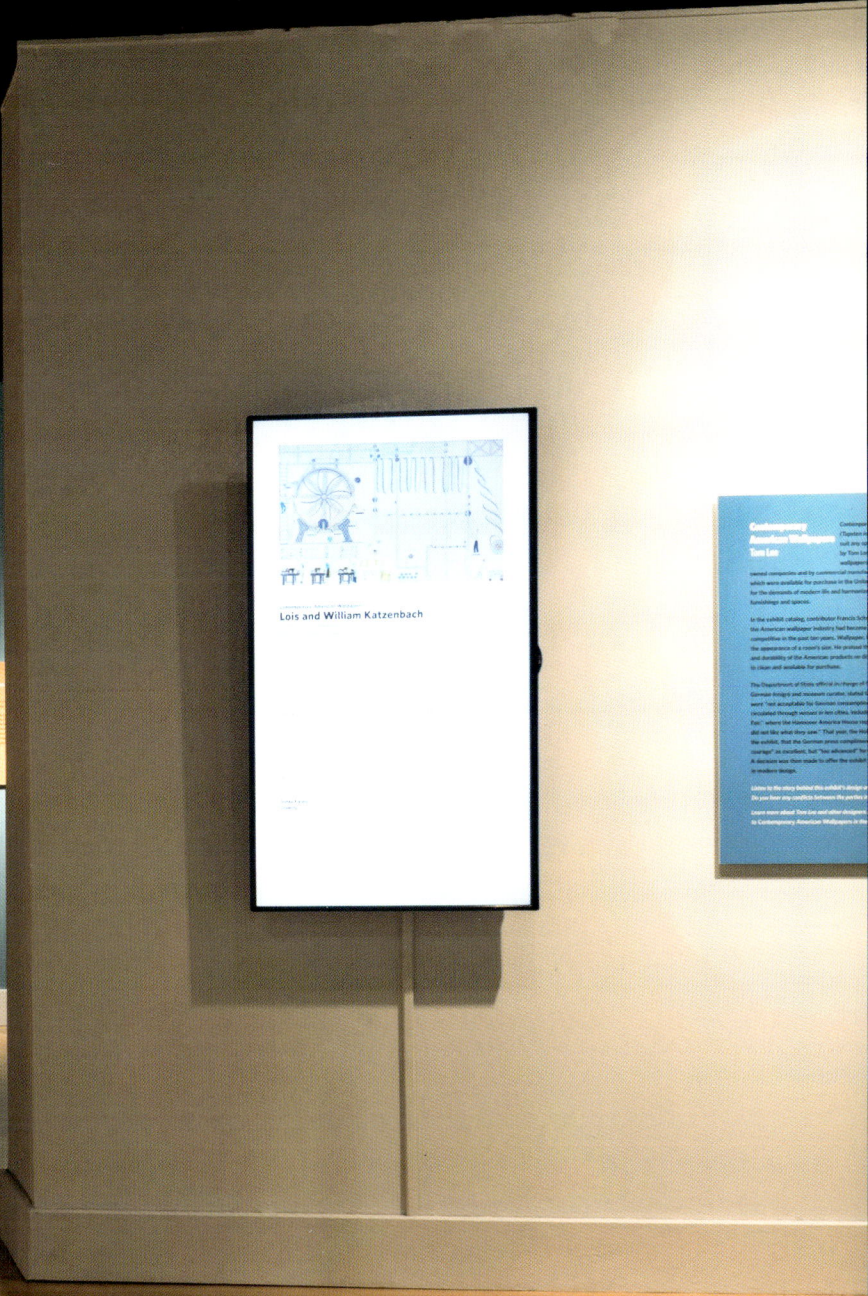

Lois and William Katzenbach

The presentation of "A Designed Life: Contemporary American Textiles, Wallpapers, and Containers & Packaging" at UMBC and this accompanying publication were made possible by generous support from The Coby Foundation, the National Endowment for the Arts, and Knoll Inc. Support was also provided by the Maryland State Arts Council, an agency funded by the State of Maryland and the National Endowment for the Arts; and the Baltimore County Commission on Arts and Sciences.

A Designed Life: Contemporary American Textiles, Wallpapers, and Containers & Packaging is published in conjunction with an eponymous traveling exhibition curated by Margaret Re and organized by the Center for Art, Design and Visual Culture, University of Maryland, Baltimore County.

Center for Art, Design and Culture,
University of Maryland, Baltimore County
        September 13–December 8, 2018
Center for Architecture, Sarasota, Florida
        February 7–April 30, 2019

Library of Congress Control Number 2019939169
ISBN 978-0-9600885-0-8

The photographers, sources of visual material other than the owners indicated in the captions, and copyright owners are listed next to each image. Every reasonable effort has been made to supply complete and correct credits; if there are errors or omissions, please contact the Center for Art, Design and Visual Culture so that corrections can be addressed in any subsequent edition. Material in copy is reprinted by permission of copyright holders or under fair use.

UMBC
Center for Art, Design and Visual Culture
1000 Hilltop Circle
Baltimore, MD 21250
cadvc.umbc.org

Editor: Charles Gute
Design and Typography: Margaret Re
Exhibition Photography: Dan Meyers
Printed by PBtisk

FOREWORD

On behalf of the Center for Art, Design and Visual Culture (CADVC), I would like to extend our congratulations to Associate Professor Margaret Re on the publication of her book *A Designed Life: Contemporary American Textiles, Wallpapers, and Containers & Packaging, 1951–54*. The book accompanies her noteworthy traveling exhibition of the same name, which premiered at the CADVC in the fall of 2018 and has subsequently traveled, in the spring of 2019, to the Center for Architecture in Sarasota, Florida.

"A Designed Life" represents the first time the CADVC has presented a design exhibition inspired by military events on a global scale. Shortly after World War II, the US Department of State commissioned noted designers Florence Knoll, Tom Lee, and Will Burtin to create design structures that would travel throughout Germany and Austria for the express purpose of influencing their citizens regarding the benefits of democracy through consumerism. Knoll's "Contemporary American Textiles," Lee's "Contemporary American Wallpaper," and Burtin's "Containers & Packaging" were instrumental in allowing European audiences to evaluate the comingling between the modernist aesthetic and American capitalism.

Although we have written and photographic documentation of the traveling exhibitions as they were successfully presented at multiple venues, the original design structures themselves remain unaccounted for. It is a testament to Professor Re's commitment and resourcefulness that all three design structures have been rebuilt to their original specifications and are once again available to new generations so they can directly experience the visual environment of this innovative diplomatic effort.

The organization and presentation of "A Designed Life" was truly a collaborative experience, arguably the most complex for the CADVC to date. With Professor Re as our guide, CADVC staff forged a number of professional relationships that would ultimately steer the project to completion. Off campus, these included the Johns Hopkins University Graduate Program in Museum Studies as well as the School of Architecture & Planning at Morgan State University. At UMBC, the MME Technical Service Center and the Costume Shop in the Theater Department oversaw the fabrication of the structural and material elements that comprise Knoll's "Contemporary American Textiles" pavilion, while the Visual Arts Department supervised the printing of the photographic images related to the "Contemporary American Wallpaper" and "Containers & Packaging" sections.

At the University of Maryland Baltimore County, the Center for Art, Design and Visual Culture, would like to thank Dr. Freeman Hrabowski, President of the University of Maryland, Baltimore County; Dr. Philip Rous, Provost; Dr. Karl Steiner, Vice President for Research; and Dr. Scott Casper, Dean of the College of Arts, Humanities and Social Sciences for their continued support of the programming initiatives of the Center for Art, Design and Visual Culture.

Outside the university, the presentation of "A Designed Life" benefitted enormously from the operational support the CADVC receives from the Maryland State Arts Council and the Baltimore County Commission on Arts and Sciences. Each of these granting organizations continues to play a pivotal role in supporting the organization and presentation of the CADVC's exhibitions and public programs.

In conclusion, the staff at the Center for Art, Design and Visual Culture, Dr. Maurice Berger, Sandra Abbott, Janet Magruder, and Mitchell Noah, deserve special mention for their continued excellence in all phases of their programming responsibilities, especially as related to the organization and presentation of "A Designed Life." Their combined efforts greatly assisted in making the presentation of "A Designed Life" at UMBC an unqualified success.

Symmes Gardner
Executive Director

The "A Designed Life" exhibition project began with a visit to the Archives of American Art to view the Florence Knoll Bassett papers that Knoll assembled herself. Sandwiched within a portfolio of her life's work were sketches and photographs depicting a small modular pavilion titled "Textilien aus U.S.A." These materials were accompanied by a magazine article titled "Knoll's Kaleidoscopic Knock-Down" — which described how Knoll was commissioned to design a traveling exhibition of American textiles for presentation in German museums — and diagrams and drawings in support of exhibit assembly instructions. That the architect who designed the interiors for buildings as expansive as the CBS tower and Connecticut General Life Insurance would accord equal importance to such a small exhibition intrigued me. This initial visit grew into a multiyear project that explored how the Traveling Exhibition Service and the United States Department of State used design as a form of soft power and visual diplomacy in postwar Europe.

Many institutions and people helped make this project possible. The Saxony-Anhalt Arts Foundation and UMBC's Dresher Center for the Humanities awarded me fellowships. The project was awarded support by the Coby Foundation, the National Endowment for the Arts, the Maryland State Arts Council, the Baltimore County Commission on Arts and Sciences, and UMBC through its START and SURE funds. Knoll Inc. provided many of the fabrics used in the recreation of "Textilien aus U.S.A." Carol Burtin Fripp, Charles and Todd Lee, Tina Henle, and Erica Stoller shared the life and work histories of family members. I am grateful that these organizations and individuals recognized the potential of "A Designed Life" and the importance of the discussions that it opens.

The "A Designed Life" exhibition involved collaborations between UMBC, the Johns Hopkins University Graduate Program in Museum Studies, and the School of Architecture & Planning at Morgan State University. At JHU, Program Director Phyllis Hecht facilitated this partnership. Program Coordinator and Senior Lecturer Karen Wizevich developed a front-end evaluation study that was supported by graduate students Sean Blinn and Madeleine Pope. Madeleine Pope also assisted with editing exhibition text panels. JHU faculty member Deborah Howes expertly guided audience development and visitor outreach efforts. Morgan State University School of Architecture & Planning faculty member Adam Bridge led undergraduate students Sheldon Alfred, Ta'Kesihia Barnes, and Andrew Ngure in the development of initial exhibition concepts.

I thank my CADVC colleagues who contributed to this project: Executive Director Symmes Gardner; Research Professor and Chief Curator Maurice Berger; Curator of Collections and Outreach Sandra Abbott; Exhibition Preparators Michael Woodhouse and Mitchell Noah; and Business Manager Janet Magruder.

I also thank the Department of Visual Arts students who were involved in research, design, installation, and educational outreach, including Sadaf Rehman, Samual Buettner, Selene LaMarca, Tyler Spooner, Grant Booher, Brandee Blumenthal, Cassie Le, Nina Enagonio, Adam Stevens, and graduate students Mandy Morrison, Aimi Bouillon, and Rahne Alexander. Visual Arts alumni who contributed to this project include Linehan Artist Scholars Frankie Cerquetti, Melissa Regelin, and Amanda Roth. Costume Shop Manager Erika Krause and theater students Isabelle Tabet and Jayden Smetana, working under the direction of Costume Shop Director Joan Mather and with the support of Theater Department Chair Colette Searls, sewed the fabric panels used in the recreation of the pavilion originally designed by Knoll. MME Technical Service Center staff members Tim Buckheit and John Cataldi fabricated the aluminum structure used to recreate Knoll's pavilion. History graduate student Chelsea Merton researched and wrote the majority of the biographies included in this publication with the support of Department Chair Amy Froide.

This project has benefitted from the analytical rigor of a team of consultants. A debt of gratitude is owed to Greg Castillo (University of California at Berkeley); Stuart W. Leslie and Emily Margolis (Johns Hopkins University); Jan Logemann (Georg-August-Universität Göttingen); and Virginia Gardner Troy (Berry College). I thank former United States Information Agency Director Jack Masey and Beverly Payeff-Masey for their encouragement and willingness to share resources from the Masey Archives. Poet Rosemary Klein served as dramaturge. Smithsonian Institution lighting designer Scott Rosenfeld lent his expertise on 1950s lighting systems. Dan Meyers photographed the exhibition. Editor Charles Gute brought consistency and clarity to a publication written by multiple authors. Architect James Yonkos was indispensable in developing planning models and fabrication drawings.

Institutional and individual lenders were generous with their support and research assistance. Thanks are extended to the Archives of American Art, Smithsonian Institution: Marisa Bourgoin; Bauhaus-Archiv/Museum für Gestaltung: Wencke Clausnitzer; Cooper Hewitt, Smithsonian Design Museum: Susan Brown, Greg Herringshaw; Cranbrook Academy of Art: Corey Gross; Esto Photographics: Caroline Hirsch, Erica Stoller;

Historic New England: Stephanie Kraus; documenta Archiv Kassel: Petra Hinck, Gabriele Wittenbruch; Knoll Inc.: David Bright, Dorothy Consonas, Keita Nishimaru, Lucas Onetti, Maia Weston, Brittany Wright; Library of Congress: Jan Grenci, Sara W. Duke, Simonette dela Torre, Rachel Waldron; Los Angeles County Museum of Art: Nancy Carcione; The George C. Marshall Foundation: Cathy DeSilvey, Jeffrey S. Kozak; The Metropolitan Museum of Art; National Archives and Records Administration; National Museum of American History: Bernard Gallagher, Kay Petterson; New York School of Interior Design: Nora Reilly; Philadelphia Museum of Art: Dilys Blum, Barbara Darlin, Kristina Haugland; Rochester Institute of Technology, Cary Graphic Arts Collection: Steven Galbraith, Kari Horowicz, Amelia Hugill-Fontanel; Smithsonian Institution Archives: Tad Bennicoff, Mary Markey; United States Holocaust Memorial Museum: Megan Lewis; University of Illinois, Chicago Special Collections & University Archives: Kellee E. Warren, Valerie Harris; Estates of Stefan P. and Juliana D. Munsing; Estate of Robert Damora; Peter and Kathy Rose; and Seth Tillett and Nicole Rauscher. Image permissions were secured with the assistance of Artist Rights Society specialists J'Aimee Cronin and Larissa Rubic.

I also thank members of the UMBC community for their continued project support, including Karl V. Steiner, Vice President for Research; Don Engel, Assistant Vice President for Research; Scott E. Casper, Dean of the College of Arts, Humanities, and Social Sciences; Tyson King-Meadows, Associate Dean of the College of Arts, Humanities, and Social Sciences; Matthias K. Gobbert, Department of Mathematics and Statistics; Preminda Jacob, Chair, Department of Visual Arts; Jessica Berman, Director, Dresher Center for the Humanities; Rachel Brubaker, Dresher Center Assistant Director for Grants and Program Development; Timothy Nohe, Director, Center for Innovation, Research, and Creativity in the Arts; Marie Lily, Tom Moore, and Catherine Borg, Office of Institutional Advancement; and Albin O. Kuhn Librarians Drew Alfgren, Jodi Hoover, and the Interlibrary Loan staff.

Many colleagues within the Department of Visual Arts encouraged this project. In particular, I thank Professors Kathryn Bell, Vin Grabill, and James Smalls. Professional staff members who generously helped meet research needs include Photo and Print Lab Manager Chris Peregoy, Program Specialist Melissa Cormier, Business Manager Andrea Lorick, and Administrative Assistant Sharda' Ham-Alston. I thank them as well.

Finally, I thank my family for their love, support, and encouragement. This book is dedicated to Nell Re Yonkos.

Margaret Re

The exhibitions presented within the "A Designed Life"
exhibition were recreated and interpreted using images borrowed
from the following institutions:

Cooper Hewitt,
Smithsonian Design Museum

Cranbrook Art Museum,
Bloomfield Hills, MI

Damora Archive

Esto Photographics Inc.

Historic New England

Knoll Inc.

Landor Design Collection, Archives Center,
National Museum of American History,
Smithsonian Institution

Los Angeles County Museum of Art

The Metropolitan Museum of Art,
New York

The Museum of Modern Art,
New York

New York School of Interior Design,
Archives & Special Collections

Philadelphia Museum of Art

Prints & Photographs Division, Library of Congress

RIT Cary Graphic Arts Collection, Wallace Center,
Rochester Institute of Technology

The George C. Marshall Foundation,
Lexington, VA

University of Illinois, Chicago,
Special Collections & University Archives

United States Information Agency,
National Archives and Records Administration,
College Park, MD

Contemporary American Textiles, Wallpapers, and Containers & Packaging

A Designed Life, 1951–54

Margaret Re

In the early 1950s, in response to mounting political pressures, the Department of State, the federal agency that represents the interests of the United States of America outside of its borders, was charged with creating a national portrait for worldwide distribution through a variety of media. This Cold War cultural diplomacy program was intended to provide a platform that would define and explain America's democratic ideals and economic system to the international community while tacitly encouraging democratic government in a divided Germany and other parts of Europe. This effort simultaneously was intended to counter and dispel charges from the Soviet Union and others that "Americans [were] a materialistic people, totally lacking in culture."[1]

One way that this mandate was accomplished was through a set of Department of State–funded exhibitions organized by the Traveling Exhibition Service (TES), an agency established in 1951 that operated on a self-supporting basis under the auspices of the Smithsonian Institution's National Collection of Fine Arts.[2] The Department of State funded thirteen exhibitions,[3] which presented a curated portrait of the American people, their history, environment, and innovations. These exhibitions were planned to circulate through West German and Austrian schools, museums, trade fairs, and the Amerika Haus program, a US government–funded system of information centers tasked with acting as agents and interpreters of American culture through the facilitation of free discussion and the presentation of public programming intended to increase cultural and political prestige on the part of the United States. In creating these exhibitions, TES contracted museum and design professionals, qualified to act as cultural interpreters because of educational, familial, and professional ties to Germany and other parts of Europe, to develop and fabricate these displays.

This essay recovers, preserves, and makes visible the three TES-organized exhibitions that presented products designed and manufactured in the United States: "Contemporary American Textiles" designed by Florence Knoll, "Contemporary American Wallpapers" designed by Tom Lee, and "Containers & Packaging" designed by Will Burtin. These representations of American design and culture, showcasing well-designed domestic goods made for consumption, sought to convince German and other European citizens that the United States afforded more and better lifestyle choices than those offered by the Soviet Union and its proxies. The exhibitions are described as existing only from 1951 through 1954. In this period, when most German and other European citizens had lost family, personal possessions, heirlooms, and other forms of cultural property and heritage, the Department of State used these exhibitions to symbolize a quality of life presented as characteristic of what could be achieved through the American economic system, and to deliver the underlying message that every individual possessed the means to improve and shape their environment. In short, the Department of State planned for these exhibitions to help link the domestic recovery, cultural reform, and economic regeneration of Germany and Europe with an American narrative. By piecing together primary sources found within archival collections, libraries, and special collections, we can see how the Department of State deliberately employed design, a process that binds people to daily life, to embody and connect consumer choice with political choice.

BURNED FINGERS AND COLD WARS

By the late 1940s, American foreign policy makers were confident that the European middle class would play a determining role in the struggle between Western democracies and the Communist bloc. One of the stated principles used in establishing the TES program was to present American industrial progress as the accomplishment of a democratic government founded on individual freedoms. At a time of European scarcity and want, the TES design-related exhibitions were intended to make visible the implied promises of democratic government to a divided Germany — Europe's prewar economic engine. These promises, which built on aspirations outlined by Franklin Roosevelt in his 1941 "Four Freedoms" address,[4] were iconized in 1943 by Norman Rockwell for the *Saturday Evening Post,* an influential magazine geared to the American middle class, in four covers that actualized these abstract ideas via vignettes of everyday life that showed American affluence, traditions, and customs.[5]

Passage of the first major legislation on US international information activities — the US Information and Educational Exchange Act of 1948 (Public Law 402) — legitimized American government public diplomacy activities on foreign soil. Known as the Smith-Mundt Act, the law authorized "the preparation, and dissemination abroad, of information about the United States, its people and its policies through press, publications, radio, motion pictures, and other information media, and through information centers and instructors abroad."[6] In licensing the Department of State to contract

with almost any person or organization, foreign or domestic, that it envisaged as a crucial participant in the battle against communist ideologies, Smith-Mundt paved the way for funding and establishing TES.[7] At the same time, ironically, Smith-Mundt contained a *de facto* restriction that prevented the Department of State from presenting cultural diplomacy projects domestically, ostensibly to avoid the appearance of propagandizing US public opinion,[8] and thus these exhibitions slipped from the (American) public record.

Still, even though Smith-Mundt authorized the Department of State to fund cultural diplomacy programs as well as underwrite and send art exhibits abroad, direct congressional authorization had to be obtained for the latter as a result of an injunction put in place after the controversial 1946 "Advancing American Art" exhibition[9] that featured works created by a culturally diverse group of emerging American modernists. Developed by the Department of State in response to requests from US embassies and cultural missions for displays of modern American art, "Advancing American Art" presented the concepts of freedom of expression and individualism as fundamental democratic values enjoyed by American artists and therefore all Americans. It did so through a plurality of views as conveyed by a State Department–owned collection of seventy-nine oil paintings and seventy-three watercolors.[10]

The US government sponsored transnational art exchanges as early as 1927, relying on organizations such as the Inter-American Office housed within the National Gallery of Art and other cultural institutions such as New York's Museum of Modern Art (MoMA) to organize and curate these shows. Now, however, the Department of State made the decision to directly curate "Advancing American Art," an exhibition that it intended to travel over a five-year period through Latin American republics, Eastern Europe, and Asia. Partnering with other institutions had proven to be complex and expensive undertakings, and, in the Department of State's opinion, did not always deliver a message that supported its agenda. "Advancing American Art" was an attempt by the Department of State to assert direct control over all the decisions made — political, curatorial, and economic — on behalf of the art exhibits that it afforded, sponsored, and circulated internationally. Freeing itself from the constraints placed on it by other institutions and lenders, the Department of State took responsibility for managing all exhibition-related elements, including message, content, costs, and scheduling.[11]

Opening in October 1946 to rave reviews at New York's Metropolitan Museum of Art and presented as part of an UNESCO event in Paris, "Advancing American Art," which soon thereafter was divided into two parts, with one part sent to Prague and the other to Port-au-Prince, quickly became the center of a political controversy because of the avant-garde paintings contained within it. The exhibition featured works created by Milton Avery, Stuart Davis, Philip Evergood, Ben Shahn, and other painters now associated with Abstract Expressionism and who were then considered by some to be politically dangerous and subversive.[12]

It has been suggested that this controversy could have been avoided had the show's contents been vetted by established curators and museum officials.[13] Instead, a conservative press, members of Congress, and the executive branch itself — fueled by a public-relations campaign that objected to tax dollars being spent to buy art that, unlike Rockwell's paintings, rejected a narrative style, traditional subject matter, and representational ways of depicting form and space — assailed the exhibition as unworthy of public support, declaring it communist-inspired and un-American. The Department of State's newly discovered self-sufficiency may have also threatened cultural institutions, administrators, and other members of the arts sector who saw themselves as arbitrators of taste and custodians responsible for the creation and preservation of a national identity. Such insiders surely took exception to the idea of a state-sanctioned art movement or style, particularly one emblematized by a selection of paintings that were now government property.[14]

As a result of these contentions, the Department of State, which had hoped to reset the world image of the United States "beyond refrigerators and radios,"[15] found itself in the uncomfortable position of defending its decisions to the US House of Representatives Appropriations Committee. Threatened with the revocation of a portion of its budget, the Department of State abandoned what it thought would be an important tool in a war of information that used cultural diplomacy to persuade against communism. The exhibition was closed and returned to the United States; its contents were auctioned off through the War Assets Administration[16] at the order of Secretary of State George C. Marshall, the lead proponent of the 1948 Economic Cooperation Act, which sought to rebuild the economies of Europe and to contain Soviet influence.[17]

Therefore, because of the congressional injunction — and despite the fact that cultural officers stationed abroad were constantly requesting "good, well-rounded exhibition[s] of contemporary or historical American art"[18] — a decision was made within the Department to avoid any association with the organization and curation of art exhibitions. Instead, the Department of State requested that the Commission of Fine Arts — which in response to a 1951 presidential request surveyed the government's activities in the field of fine arts[19] — help it develop a program by which it could send cultural material overseas. This commission recommended that the Department of State contract with federal agencies such as the Library of Congress and the Smithsonian Institution's National Gallery of Art under which the National Collection of Fine Arts operated, so that "the Department would not find itself operating in fields beyond its competence."[20] Ultimately, the TES, whose relationship with the Department of State was modeled after that of the Inter-American Office, was established within the National Collection of Fine Arts.[21] Funding for this newly established semipublic agency was provided by the Department of State under the guise of a grant,[22] with the understanding that these two organizations would work in close cooperation. The Department of State would advise the TES as to which countries to target for American culture outreach, and the TES would organize and coordinate these cultural exchanges on its behalf.

FIGURE 1 Installation view of the exhibition "Good Design" featuring Morton Goldsholl's logo design. The exhibition was on view at the Museum of Modern Art, New York, November 27, 1951, through January 27, 1952. *Digital image © The Museum of Modern Art; Licensed by SCALA/Art Resource, NY.*

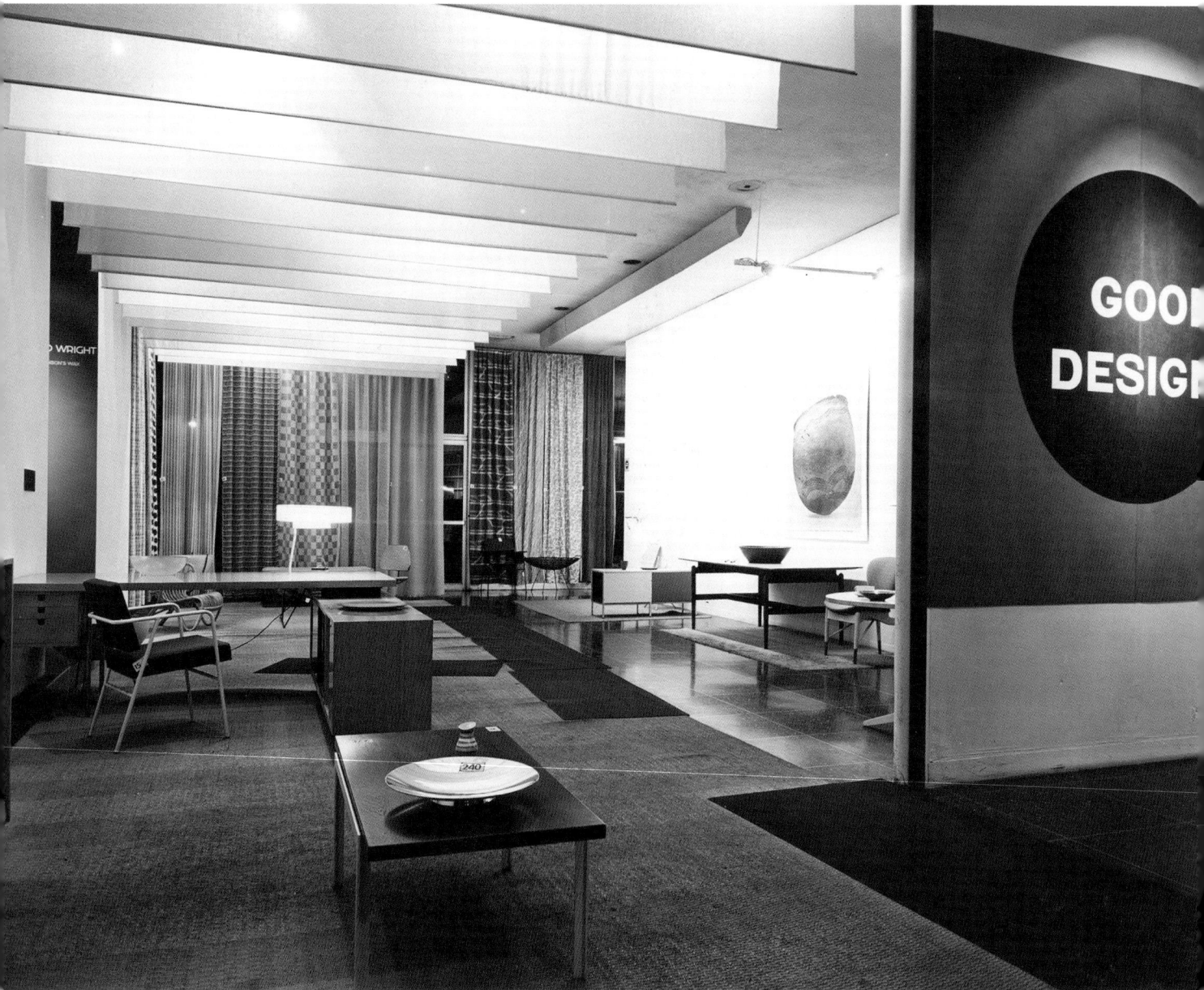

INTERPRETATION AND DESIGN

In mounting these traveling exhibitions, TES chief Annemarie Henle Pope, a German émigré art historian and former assistant director of the American Federation of Fine Arts,[23] accepted the recommendations of Knoll, Burtin, and Lee offered by Edgar Kaufmann Jr.[24] As director of MoMA's Department of Industrial Design and the "Good Design" exhibition program **[FIGURE 1]**, a design competition established by MoMA's and Chicago's Merchandise Mart that attempted to shape national consumer buying habits by

allying art with commerce, Kaufmann had a broad view of the American design scene. Intent on making explicit the relationship between modern design and the concepts of individualism and individual choice, Kaufmann, a Department of State consultant in his own right, advanced the theory that "modern design [was] intended to implement the lives of free individuals" and thus crucial to determining democratic life.[25]

Design professionals Knoll, Lee, and Burtin, purposefully contracted by Pope, had worked with the US government and private industry in prior capacities and knew why and how to build visual identities that emphasized value. Given their family relationships and education, each brought a crucial skill set qualifying them to design these exhibits and create a brand — that of cultural interpreter. They were able to relate American identity to the emerging concepts of modernism that joined art with industry as a means of marketing goods. Aligning identity inextricably with economic outcomes and the newly expanding idea of branding resulted in products, services, and experiences that created in the public mind emotions, perceptions, and expectations that would come to be associated with postwar consumer-driven individualism and planned consumption.

As design professionals with diverse social and cultural backgrounds, Knoll, Lee, and Burtin created seamless communication strategies that reached American and international audiences. Architect Florence Knoll was a partner in Knoll Inc., a company that focuses on modern furniture and interiors, founded by Hans Knoll, the émigré son of an industrialist who manufactured furniture designed by Bauhaus artisans,[26] with whom she began working in 1941. Dissatisfied with the materials available for use on furniture and in the modern interior, she founded Knoll Textiles in 1947. Knoll had close friendships with Cranbrook Academy of Art director Eliel Saarinen; Bauhaus directors Walter Gropius and Mies van der Rohe; and Bauhaus master Marcel Breuer. All were modernist architects whom she studied or worked with after they immigrated to the United States.[27]

Born and raised in Cologne, Germany, Will Burtin was reportedly asked to serve as design director for the Nazi Ministry of Propaganda.[28] In 1939, he fled with his Jewish wife to the United States, where he eventually became art director of *Fortune* magazine. In 1947, Burtin, who had spent the war years assigned to the presentation branch of the Office of Strategic Services, creating Air Force training materials that explained complex subjects to soldiers who were often illiterate or semiliterate,[29] designed a series of spreads for the magazine titled "The American Bazaar: A picture gallery on the chief activity of Americans — selling things to one another." Burtin manipulated type and image in order to create a sense of what the accompanying text described as the art of American salesmanship and its frenzied antics.[30] Deeply influenced by the modernist aesthetic, in 1948 Burtin developed "Integration: The New Discipline in Design," an important exhibit that joined art and science and demonstrated the influence of avant-garde European design.[31]

Heralded as one of New York's best "display men," and famed for witty and imaginative window and store interior displays best represented by the Lever House Christmas windows, Tom Lee, the son of an American diplomat, spent his childhood between Vermont, Costa Rica, Brazil, and Great Britain. During the war, he served with the United States Army Air Force in England, where he created camouflage systems used to hide airfields from enemy bombers, before joining the Office of Strategic Services. Lee contributed to the design of the American Pavilion at the 1958 Brussels World's Fair and the 1959 American National Exhibition in Moscow. He also designed sets and costumes for musical comedies and burlesque shows; trade shows, salons, factories, and packages for the textile, jewelry, beauty, and home appliance industries; and torchlight parades for the Fifth Avenue Association of Retailers. In this way he cultivated a unique brand of American identity for international audiences.[32]

BRANDING AND SELLING AMERIKA

By 1953, the important historical roles that Knoll, Lee, and Burtin's displays had in selling democracy were noted. Industrial designer George Nelson published *Display*, dedicated to presenting examples of trade fairs and product displays whose modern design excelled at selling goods and values. His book singled out Knoll's "Contemporary American Textiles" and included several Burtin-designed exhibits. Acknowledging that the purpose of a traveling display could be to establish identity, attract attention and buyers, indicate real or desired social position, and convey cultural and social information, Nelson emphasized a display's basic purpose as being "to persuade someone to buy something he may or may not need or want,"[33] a core concept of an expanding postwar consumerism that emphasized individual personal choice.

As part of Department of State efforts to shore up support for democracy in postwar West Germany, Knoll, Lee, and Burtin were charged with curating and designing exhibits that showcased American industrial and cultural progress. These were intended to foster an appreciation and understanding of the nature, characteristics, and elements of social, economic, and political processes in the USA.[34] But it was also understood that by aligning physical, economic, and national security with the marketplace, what Knoll, Lee, and Burtin *really* designed and produced were circulating point-of-sale displays that branded, advertised, and sold the frameworks for the idea of "America" to a foreign audience.

The Amerika-Hauser program **[FIGURE 2]**, already usefully providing free-access public squares for the German people, were, in addition to schools, museums, and trade fairs, a primary environment through which the TES-organized exhibitions that Knoll, Burtin, and Lee created were intended for display. In the immediate postwar period, a devastated Germany was a contested space in which the United States

FIGURE 2 Window displays at the new Amerika Haus always attract the attention of passersby. November 24, 1952. *United States Information Agency, National Archives and Records Administration, College Park, MD.*

and the Soviet Union vied to provide systems of governance, culture, and economics. Out of this Cold War tension, the Amerika-Hauser program, whose title served as a brand suggesting domestic comforts, evolved as a means to sell the German public on siding with the United States. To counteract and reshape established beliefs, this network of information centers, some of which were located within structures or on sites significant to the former regime so as to symbolically claim them, employed the openness of the American community library system. Accompanying services and

activities, equally and freely available to patrons regardless of age, gender, class, or ethnicity, provided insight into the American people and their system of government through discussion groups, lectures, film screenings, exhibitions, and other activities.

The Department of State approached the TES exhibitions as display windows: productions that billed wants over needs, with carefully scripted political messages that provocatively staged showcased products. The product packaging included promotional posters hawking populist themes that referenced

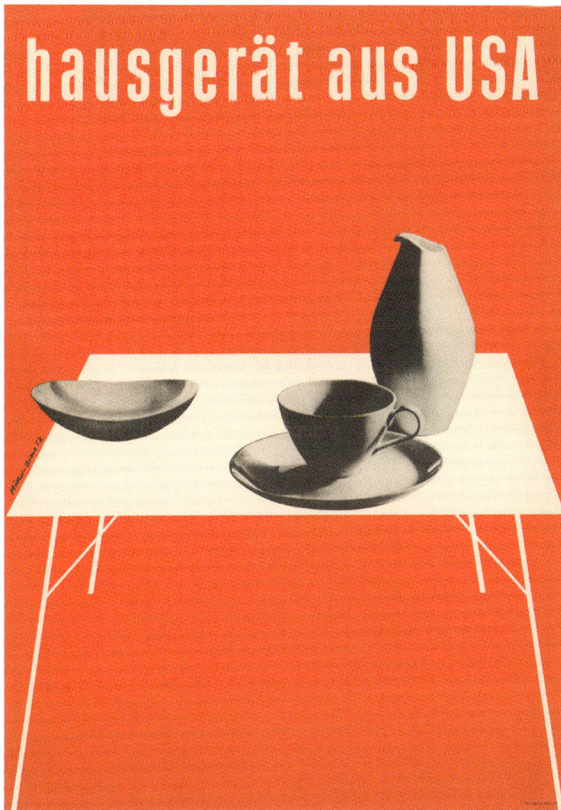

America or the USA in their titles **[FIGURE 3]**. These designs illustrated the concepts the Department of State intended to present as afforded to all American citizens: stylish environments, elegantly functional wares, and individual lifestyles born from personal freedom **[FIGURE 4]**. The Department believed in the abilities of these exhibitions and their products to link the domestic recovery, cultural reform, and economic regeneration of Germany — a potential market for American exports — with an American narrative suggestive of what a new and progressive West German culture might look like.

In this stressed environment, the Department of State identified the desires, needs, and decision-making ability of women as important to the stability of the German family unit and economy. Having singled out women as a constituency available to assume a leadership role in political and economic life, the Department believed it could sell the idea that the American dream of self-determination was also a German dream. This dream — an ideal identified with material goods, lifestyle choices, and home ownership — included the right to secure happiness and the opportunity to pursue a better life through hard work and ambition. With a generation of men lost to war, women, as heads of families, managed scarce resources and regulated income. Women, therefore,

would play an important part in the economic and political regeneration of Germany. It was thought by the Department of State that with advice, assistance, and encouragement, women could be made aware of their significant role in the reconstructed society as citizens "responsible for developing democratic ideas and practices in the local community and national life."[35] Recognized as important to advancing democratic ideals, German women were specifically targeted for inclusion in Amerika-Hauser events.[36] The TES displays provided each viewer, as a probable consumer, opportunities to imagine her own uses for the products on display and, therefore, to visualize her own potential as a citizen in the new democracy "with the right[s] and obligation[s] of a citizen to debate and determine the general welfare."[37] These offerings of household goods contributed information regarding what a new and progressive West German culture might look like. The pluralities of expression represented through these visual displays presented opportunities for self-selection and, thus, self-expression and self-realization, supporting the new concept of individuality that was being sold: the self-defined or "self-made" person.

THE EXHIBITIONS

Each exhibition included the work of design professionals who ignored discipline-specific boundaries as they sought to uphold the tenets of modernism while creating customized designs for specific purposes. As a set, these exhibitions document the overlapping aesthetic found between the decorative arts and the art and architecture of this period. Shipped to Germany between August and late November 1952, they were shown under the imprimatur of the Smithsonian Institution. TES contracts outline that Knoll, Lee, and Burtin were each responsible for object selection, design, and fabrication; assembly instructions; documentary photography; and copy for a catalogue to be produced within Germany. Each was paid $5,000 for their individual exhibition. With the exception of price,[38] the provided checklists followed the *Good Design* catalogue format and listed each displayed product by title, manufacturer, and designer. The hope was to appeal to individuals eager to afford these items as part of rebuilding in a postwar German economy.[39]

Contemporary American Textiles

The initial proposal governing "Contemporary American Textiles" envisioned an exhibition composed of textiles manufactured by individually identified, newly established firms that prioritized design as a form of consumer status, as well as by conventional mass manufacturers whose individual contributions often went uncredited. Knoll intentionally included products made using power looms, screen-printing, and handweaving "that demonstrate the effective use of new and striking fibers, many of them still unavailable in Germany."[40] Doing so met the requirements of modern furniture, which now coupled design with functionality, and modern architecture that responded to technological innovations such as window walls and air conditioning. Emphasizing individuality, variety, and availability as well as social and physical mobility, the Knoll-selected textiles served as a cultural aesthetic closely woven with emerging American Cold War values.

Linking American industrial achievement with the Bauhaus ideal of fitness of purpose in the catalogue introduction, Knoll wrote:

> This exhibition is meant to offer an overview of the best American textile production, starting from the simplest and least expensive fabrics to the highest, most artistic, and most expensive work of handloom weavers. Through the relationships of fabric, color, and space, we have tried to demonstrate how beautiful and attractive each weave can be.[41]

Conceptual drawings, plans, and photographs[42] **[FIGURE 5]** document how the Knoll-designed structure met identifiable purposes. "Contemporary American Textiles" was organized as a self-contained architectural space meant to be viewed and experienced as a whole: a twenty-four-by-sixteen-by-eight-foot aluminum-framed pavilion from which panels composed of individual textiles arranged and sewn into geometric shapes were hung by straps and braced by crosswire supports. Fourteen tapestries were used in creating double-sided wall panels assembled from patterned and woven textiles stitched together into geometric compositions. Rather than a line of objects viewed at eye level, textiles floating within a grid were deployed as scrims to make a room within a room. Sight lines formed by shape and pattern afforded a continuously changing viewpoint that encouraged movement through the exhibit.

"Contemporary American Textiles," as documented by the catalogue checklist, featured more than 150 textiles, many by well-known designers and manufacturers. Knoll included handwoven fabrics produced by the Bauhaus-educated Anni Albers, Cranbrook Academy's Marianne Strengell, and Evelyn Hill, who had studied under Bauhaus master Josef Albers. Architect Philip Johnson, curator of an influential 1932 exhibition that included the work of Walter Gropius and Mies van der Rohe, designed the Arundell Clarke–manufactured *Van Dyke Squares*. Serge Chermayeff, the design director of Chicago's New Bauhaus, contributed geometric prints produced by L. Anton Maix. The products of industrial manufacturers such as the United States Rubber Company, Kalistron Plastics, and Guilford Leather, companies that had modified their production to support the war effort, were also included. Wamsutta Mills, known for high-quality shirtings, sheets, and sailcloth, and for the development of fabrics used in gas masks and uniforms, presented a new woven textile. Wellington Sears presented a manufactured sailcloth. And Knoll, who initiated a textile division within Knoll Associates as a result of her dissatisfaction with the fabric selections available for use on the furniture that she designed, did not hesitate to insert the work of her own firm, which was in the midst of expanding into Europe as Knoll International. "Contemporary American Textiles" showcased fifty textiles manufactured and distributed under the Knoll Textiles brand, including cotton prints designed by the Breuer-recommended Eszter Haraszty.

FIGURE 5 Florence Knoll, color study for "Contemporary American Textiles." *Florence Knoll Bassett Papers, 1932–2000, Archives of American Art, Smithsonian Institution.*

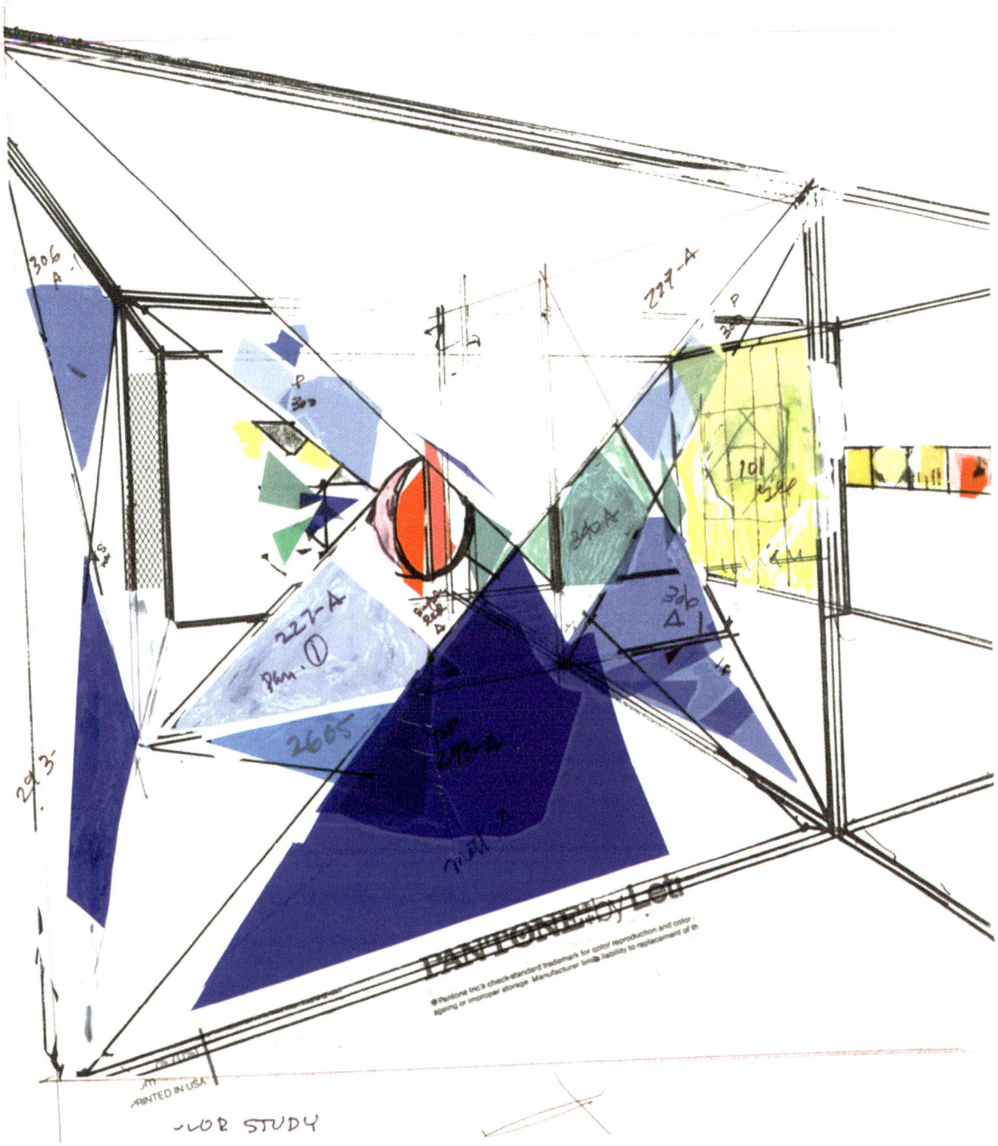

Contemporary American Wallpapers

Reporting on "Contemporary American Wallpapers" for the *New York Times* in 1952, Betty Pepis wrote, "Residents of Western Germany will have an opportunity to examine esthetic qualities of walls in American homes when a just-completed exhibit arrives." She argued that the exhibition showed "that the inhabitants of the United States are not concerned solely with the machine and what it can produce, but also have a strong interest in esthetics."[43] The physical presence of the exhibition can only be extrapolated from written sources; no images or drawings have survived other than a line drawing used on the exhibition catalogue cover. Correspondence exchanged among the State Department, TES, and Lee describe an exhibition that could be arranged

"in rectangles, hexagon[s], or a maze of almost any other shape to suit whatever space is available."[44] It would consist of sixty framed and papered panels "mounted to wooden supports that could be displayed as either freestanding or wall-mounted [...] with the panels separated and the supports stored."[45]

Lee's display appealed by showing "residents of foreign countries" how the "characteristics of the typical American home" could respond to "the real needs of modern life [as well as] the requirements of style and mode"[46] by unifying and harmonizing interiors with furnishings. Wallpapers could expand a room's optical appearance — an important quality given the expense of construction and the importance of space planning. *Interiors* magazine editor Francis N. Schroeder, author of the exhibition catalogue's preface, noted this advantage when he wrote,

> Today, people are building smaller. [But spaces can] be made to look larger. Such planning helps [one] handle pieces of furniture whose size must be in harmony with the smaller rooms. One can create astonishing optical illusions by the use of cleverly selected wallpaper patterns.[47]

Schroeder championed the cost effectiveness of wallpaper, its durability, and the wide variety of industry choices. Period Bauhaus wallpaper advertisements emphasized many of the points that Schroeder made regarding the exhibited coverings, including their ability to unify an environment; their effectiveness as protection against dirt and damage; their ability to conceal surface irregularities; their ease of replacement; and their washability that made them compliant with hygiene standards.[48] All of these traits were meant to appeal to women who were eager to define their living spaces with objects that expressed individuality as well as the family as a unit.

Schroeder, writing in support of Lee's selections, noted that the wallpaper industry had recruited "first class artists," many of whom worked in a variety of design-related disciplines. The catalogue checklist documents that the exhibition included manufacturer Katzenbach and Warren, considered to be "consistently avant-garde in both design and technical innovations," and designers Marion Dorn and Ilonka Karasz. Lee chose Laverne Originals proprietors Estelle and Erwin Laverne, independent designers and producers of textiles, wallpapers, and furniture, who made a concentrated effort to support the fine and applied artists and designers commissioned by them: industrial designers Ray Komai and Ross Littell, and artist Alexander Calder. Also included were artists György and Juliet Kepes, who were affiliated with the New Bauhaus school of design in Chicago; illustrator Saul Steinberg, commissioned by Piazza Prints; and designer and manufacturer Ben Rose, who received a number of Good Design awards in the early 1950s for wallpapers and textiles. Rose's designs were featured in both Knoll and Lee's exhibitions, as were designs by George Nelson, who, through his *Architectural Forum* essays, widened the American reception to Bauhaus ideals.

Containers & Packaging

Will Burtin, like Knoll, addressed the ideal of fitness to purpose with "Containers & Packaging," an exhibit that showcased innovative packaging solutions developed by American manufacturers. "If a good design represents the sum total of the knowledge and capabilities of a designer in the light of the intended purpose, then you can say that package design and manufacture are understood as progress in America."[49] Photographs taken by architectural photographer Ezra Stoller and memos exchanged between TES and the Department of State show that "Containers & Packaging" consisted of three sets of framed horizontal shelves, described as "crate-panel units." Each crate-unit was divided into eighteen equally sized compartments that evoked the shadow box, a format used to commemorate an individual's achievements via a symbolic portrait. The individual domestic and industrial products featured were silhouetted and abstracted through the use of the grid and thus removed from a consideration of cost and context. Viewed collectively, these shadow boxes became a larger entity, a symbolic representation of the American people through the material goods used to create and order daily life.

Braced on its outside edges by a pair of opposing isosceles triangles — suggestive of a Star of David when viewed from certain angles — each unit rested on three points **[FIGURE 6]**. To accommodate the differing dimensions of presentation space, the crate-units could be organized in a variety of configurations. Each crate-unit was themed — "Purchase Appeal & Grabbing Attention," "Technical Resourcefulness," and "Mass Production & Design Issues" — and the products within were categorized by types of "packaging solutions," such as those inspired by the natural packaging of oranges, peas, apples, and walnuts. On display were everyday household products, produced by a range of manufacturers, as well as products with dedicated medical, pharmaceutical, automotive, agricultural, and hygienic uses.

In his foreword to the catalogue, Burtin highlighted the centrality of marketing in US consumer society. He addressed the distance that exists between American cities as well as the importance of packaging in shipping goods to physical markets — packing methods intended to protect, reduce volume and weight, and make products easier to transport. He listed the cost-saving advantages of paper cushioning and separators to transport industrial goods and fruit; soft plastic containers for toiletries, lubricants, and foodstuffs; and cardboard containers that were sturdy enough to contain and protect "grapes and live chickens."[50] Burtin's discussion emphasized the need for packaging that promoted the contents held within as part of a manufacturer's goal of

FIGURE 6 Will Burtin, overview of "Werbepackung in Amerika."
Will Burtin Papers, Cary Graphic Arts Collection, RIT. Photographer:
Ezra Stoller © Esto.

creating market share for itself by attracting customers, especially "housewives."[51] Successful companies, he noted, used "form, size [and] a special color or combination of colors"[52] to establish a signifying brand, build value, and distinguish itself from others. He argued the significance of packaging in America — "a visual phenomenon whose importance up to now has been largely unresearched." He also noted that "few people or organizations [...] have recognized [packaging's] cultural value,"[53] implicitly including his and the other TES exhibitions among the few.

The checklist shows that Burtin relied on the commodities of several design firms, including the Design Laboratory, a division of the Container Corporation of America, a

Chicago-based company led by industrialist Walter Paepcke that manufactured cardboard packaging and paper-based shipping products. Other design professionals affiliated with the exhibition included Good Design symbol designer Morton Goldsholl, industrial designer Harry H. Farrell, graphic designer Paul Rand, and package designer Alma Shon.

In addition to detailing product, designer, and manufacturer, Burtin specified manufacturer location, thus tying the American landscape and its natural resources to its industry. The majority of the companies, including the Ford Motor Company, General Motors, Eastman Kodak, and Pyramid Rubber, were located around the Great Lakes in what was the American industrial heartland. Other organizations concerned with transporting fragile and perishable goods from coast to coast, such as the California Fruit Grower's Company, were located in the Inland Empire. Their needs were met by firms like Landor Associates, headed by German émigré Walter Landor, who designed packaging for the emerging postwar frozen food industry and whose architect father was associated with the Bauhaus. Like Knoll, Burtin included his own work in the exhibit — in all three categories.

TENSION AND RECEPTION

Uncovered correspondence between the Department of State and TES provides a sense of the tensions that played out not only among these institutions but among program managers, TES director Annemarie Pope, Richard Brecker, the head of the Washington-based Department of State exhibition section, and Herwin Schaefer, the Frankfurt-based Department of State officer directly responsible for circulating the exhibitions within Germany.

While Pope considered "Contemporary American Textiles" "as simple and uncluttered as a painting by Mondrian,"[54] Brecker judged the exhibition "impractical" because its "inflexible box-like structure limits its adaptability," making it unable to be shown within any of the Amerika-Häuser.[55] Pope, aware of Brecker's judgment, concurred that its structure was "most impractical," noting, "As it is, the cage that was evolved after long trial and error cannot be used in any type of room."[56] This scarcely bothered her, however, as she considered the Amerika-Häuser to be the least important of the Department of State–specified venues, and thought that the exhibit structure, with its abstract display of textiles, might itself create a great deal of excitement and positive press. She had her eye on a greater mission, believing that the effectiveness of the TES program would only be accomplished by addressing all manner of arenas: "schools, universities, America Houses, museums, and fairs — big fairs with unlimited space such as the Berlin Trade Fair, Berlin Cultural Fair, the Constructa."[57] The fairs that Pope referenced were among the first representations of the Marshall Plan. By 1950, the idea "that an American cultural program was vitally necessary" was being advanced to rebut the German opinion that American culture consisted of "lady wrestlers, bloody strikes, and boogie-woogie fiends."[58] Additionally, establishing and participating in fairs allowed the United States to counter Soviet-sponsored cultural activities such as its 1950 World Youth Festival. American ideas and values needed to penetrate and be accepted within the sphere of the German family, both collectively and individually.[59]

While other cities devastated by war such as Cologne, Munich, and Berlin were rebuilt in the immediate aftermath

of the war, Pope's reference to the Constructa — held in 1951 in Hannover, the city regarded as the postwar model of progressive reconstruction planning — is particularly telling in light of the West German response to the TES exhibitions under discussion. Visitors to this fair, in which the US government presented a fully equipped model kitchen, furnished apartment, and "movie picture theater,"[60] were invited to learn about the latest in regional and town planning. Displays provided examples of what controlled growth, building standardization, and the latest construction techniques could offer a populace longing to rebuild. While the fair presented a city standardized in its construction, it also stressed "useful, pleasant houses,"[61] each of which was meant to be individually furnished — thus reinforcing the idea of home and giving value to household management and thereby legitimizing and encouraging the female voice in national discussion.[62]

Pope, who earned a PhD with a study of German baroque sculpture before immigrating to the United States, had an exclusive education that included postgraduate work in museum studies with Harvard's Paul Sachs during the depths of the Depression. In all likelihood, in coordinating the development of the TES exhibitions she relied on her experience as assistant director of the American Federation of Arts, where she was responsible for circulating exhibitions between member institutions.[63] This background did not allow her to understand that these exhibitions of well-designed goods were meant by the Department of State to extend beyond the purposes of connoisseurship. That the Department of State planned for these displays to be viewed outside of museums and galleries, and that these presentations might be presented in "less exclusive" environments to general audiences, was of little consideration to her. What pragmatism she exhibited was limited by an agenda that prioritized and valued an aesthetic experience intended for an affluent, cultured, and educated audience above all else. The TES may have organized these exhibitions on behalf of the Department of State, but Pope's remarks reflected no interest in reaching the Department of State's identified audience, expressly described by Brecker as "the masses in Germany."

This perspective was echoed in a trade publication review of "Contemporary American Textiles" held at the Ruhr Amerika-Haus Essen.[64] Noting that the context provided by General Consul LaVerne Baldwin, who presented the exhibition, was focused not on sales but toward evoking a sense of mutual understanding between the German and American people, the review suggested a response more singular than mutual on the part of both countries. The reviewer's reaction to the featured designs — "stylized fish designs, barbed-wire designs, star-like forms," clearly marked horizontal stripes in various colors, including real awning designs as well as a "forest of glasses" and "walnuts"— was a marked "So what?" The reviewer emphatically opines that these designs "absolutely *might have* been produced in West Germany."[65] This discussion of shared form extended to color, with the critic noting that "the present tastes of West Germans and Americans diverge." She states that "in the USA they love very garish color tones, placed closely to each other, which sometimes hurt our eyes,"[66] suggesting with this visceral reaction that the attempt at mutuality was unfamiliar and unwelcome. She further comments that the exhibition would have benefitted from larger fabric samples "in order to achieve a correct understanding of their effect"[67] and from furniture and windows dressed by some of the displayed textiles, modeling the potential for these materials to be coordinated with each other within an architectural space and upon three-dimensional forms. The reviewer's sentiments, taken altogether, suggest a baldly American exhibit so abstract that it fails to engage the West German imagination.

"Contemporary American Wallpapers," on the other hand, was deemed by Pope to be appropriately flexible, with the TES director asserting it to be "one of the best installations I have ever seen, especially for traveling purposes."[68] Still, it didn't satisfy its intended cultural purposes any better than "Contemporary American Textiles." Upon its October 1952 arrival in Germany, Schaefer, a former assistant curator within MoMA's Department of Architecture and Industrial Design, edited Lee's exhibit down from sixty to forty panels because, in his judgment, "a number of the designs were not acceptable for German consumption." This appraisal was supported by the reaction of a German press that in its reviews humorously and benevolently complimented the American wallpaper industry on its "experimental courage."[69]

Although scheduled to open in Germany at the Kassel Wallpaper Museum, "Contemporary American Wallpapers" never appeared there. Instead, it opened at Kassel's Museum of Natural Wonders, which houses curiosities and oddities. A wallpaper composed of realistic pocket watches presented alongside early colored German wallpapers and four large pictures of nineteenth-century American life greeted visitors as they entered the exhibition. Several nails placed next to the opening paper, on which visitors were invited to hang their own watches, reflected the exhibition's avant-garde nature. The displayed papers, intended for residential and commercial use, included motifs inspired by chicken wire, burlap, brick walls, marbled paper, foliage, and empty frames. A local newspaper review suggested that the exhibition was not wholly received as the Department of State had planned, noting that "many preconceived notions"[70] had to be

"dispelled" in a "calm and sober" manner by Schaefer in his opening remarks. Schaefer's words not only calmed, they elicited "a more unprejudiced" response from the West German audience, whom he urged to see that in addition to the unorthodox representations, there were more traditional patterns incorporating imaginative, singular designs; gradual, minute color transitions; and graphics that piqued curiosity. The review concluded that the Schaefer-supplied context opened the audience to "lively discussions about the possible usages of patterns."[71]

The Department of State carefully documented attendance at Amerika Haus events and other sponsored activities, the intention being to measure a message's political and cultural impact whenever possible. Pope wrote that Brecker requested "Contemporary American Textiles" to be featured in 1953 at the Munich Amerika Haus[72] and in Essen; and for the Berlin Festival, even if it arrived late.[73] Based on the date of Pope's memo it can be surmised that the Berlin Festival referenced by Pope was the 1952 Berlin Cultural Festival, a program that was part of an American foreign policy undertaking whose goal was to counter the European opinion that America was an aesthetic desert.

By 1954, the Amerika Haus program had circulated "Contemporary American Wallpapers" through its centers in Munich, Berlin, Mannheim, and Essen, and the exhibit had been presented at the Darmstadt Wallpaper Fair, in the Ulm town hall, and at Hagen's Karl Ernst Osthaus-Museum. It was also showcased at a large Düsseldorf wallpaper store, where it was estimated that 525,000 visitors viewed it. That this presentation coincided with the DRUPA printing fair was considered especially advantageous, as "almost everybody who is connected with printing […] visited the DRUPA and also came to this exhibition."[74] Later records for this same year tell that the Hof Amerika Haus deemed "Contemporary American Wallpapers — already poorly received at Hannover's For Every Woman Fair and rejected by the Bremen Amerika Haus — as "too advanced for […] visitors." The Bonn Amerika Haus planned to offer this exhibit primarily to "art schools and museums specializing in modern crafts and industrial design."[75]

While no documentation of a German response has been found to date, other than the repeated theft of packages that contained products that could be eaten or used,[76] the Department of State felt that, like the wallpaper exhibit, "Containers & Packaging," with its wide array of household goods, could "be of real use to German Museums"[77] interested in American design and manufacturing. It may be that the Department of State hoped that the latter show, while smaller in scale, would be received with an enthusiasm similar

FIGURE 7 Display of American presidents at Amerika Haus Augsburg library, Germany, c. 1950. *Prints & Photographs Division, Library of Congress.*

to that enjoyed by MoMA's "Design for Use, USA," the Kaufmann-curated 1951 exhibition of American household goods presented at Stuttgart's Landesgewerbemuseum, which attracted sixty thousand visitors over a five-week period.[78] In its effort to equate the selection of democratic government with lifestyle choice, **[FIGURE 7]** the Department of State was interested in presenting these exhibitions in a wide range of venues. Still, placing an exhibition within a recognized cultural institution made it less likely to be dismissed outright as propaganda. Additionally, these displays, with their direct reference to shopping and selection, suggested that people's needs, wants, and desires — and

therefore lives — were basically similar regardless of social or geographic distance. The anticipated result was a heightened sense of mutuality. Overall, the aims of the Department of State were too political to be practical. Both the Department and the newly founded TES lacked experience in organizing, programming, and curating exhibitions. The former was left to stumble through this process because of the restrictions placed upon it by congressional injunction in the aftermath of "Advancing American Art." Yet TES, as the outside organization responsible for directly contracting with the professionals who curated and designed these exhibitions, was too aesthetically oriented to guide the Department of

State in a manner that would allowed it to achieve its desired messaging — the end goal being the creation of a portrait of the American people.

Both Brecker and Schaefer were placed in the role of mediators, with Brecker responsible for coordinating the overall program with TES and Schaefer responsible for circulating the exhibitions within Germany. Correspondence between Brecker and Schaefer document the tensions that each felt with their respective roles in crafting and implementing a public diplomacy agenda that was dependent upon materials produced by outside organizations. As Brecker wrote to Schaefer, working with TES, although required, was a burden because "almost as much time and work is […] expected of us as would be if we contracted [the designers] directly," and the arrangement did not guarantee that the exhibitions' design and message would be on target. Speaking of the Knoll-designed exhibition, Brecker lamented that "a great deal of our own staff [resources] went to the mere problem of trying to get it completed in time for the Berlin Festival." Writing that he did not advocate a "sledge-hammer approach" because propaganda could be "more effective when subtle," Brecker reiterated the importance of using the exhibitions as tools for introducing the American people and culture to German citizens and other Europeans; shaping mass attitudes; and cultivating a readiness and desire to cooperate with the United States. Schaefer, who is on record as being responsible for extensively reshaping the literal and figurative context in which these exhibitions were seen, echoed this sentiment from within Germany.[79]

LOST AND FORGOTTEN

What ultimately happened to the exhibitions designed by Knoll, Lee, and Burtin is unknown. Nevertheless, there are possibilities that may singularly or collectively provide a sense of legacy.

The exhibitions were ultimately made unusable because contents went missing or were damaged. TES and Department of State records document that packages from Burtin's exhibition were stolen. When the Department expressed dissatisfaction with Knoll's exhibition because its size and structure prevented it from being used in the Amerika Haus system, TES countered that it had been asked to provide exhibitions for all levels of cultural institutions, including trade fairs and festivals through which thousands of people would walk. The exhibitions, which contained no original material, may have been forgotten, ignored, or donated to academic or cultural institutions as a means of earning good will and establishing authority as the Department of State lessened its partnership with TES,

in part because of inefficiencies in cost, time, and management. Both Burtin and Lee's exhibitions may have been offered to a cultural institution geared toward the study of industrial design. The Department of State, which wanted to better assure itself that it met its messaging goals and the demands of its target audiences, recognized that larger presentations — involving durable goods showcased by models who could demonstrate the use of these products in idealized environments — would be necessary in order to establish a more representational and thus more convincing national portrait. Such efforts seemed unlikely given the increasingly discussed inefficiencies of the TES partnership. Additionally, the association with TES may have been curtailed as the Department of State began to pursue larger-scale and more ambitious public and cultural initiatives in alliance with the United States Information Agency, established in 1953, and the Office of International Trade Fairs, established in 1955.

What we do know is that in terms of transmitting American values and lifestyles, these three exhibitions did not wholly represent the Department of State's intended vision. In their day, however, and historically, they well capture the impress of modernity upon postwar America. The strained cultural disconnects between the traditional and modern as well as the artistic and functional would, however, be more fully expressed within the decade — at the 1959 American National Exhibition, elevated to the historical record by Nixon and Khrushchev's so-called "kitchen debate," at which the US exhibition presented the American way of life in two separate areas: a house of culture that contained a diorama of American life; and a house of items that held consumer goods.

NOTES

1   U.S. Commission of Fine Arts, *Art and Government: Report to the President by the Commission of Fine Arts on Activities of the Federal Government in the Field of Fine Art* (Washington, DC: Government Printing Office, 1953), 52.

2   Betty Miles, "Mrs. Pope Puts Smithsonian Shows 'On the Road,'" *The Evening Star* (Washington, DC), May 6, 1953, B-2.

3   "Man and his Environment," "Mississippi Panorama," "The City of New York," "The World of Paul Revere," "How Movies are Made," "200 Years of American Glass," "American Ceramics," "Color," "American Containers & Packaging," "Influences on American Architecture," "American Wallpaper," "American Fabrics," and "Fashion and Color Photography." Smithsonian Institution Archives, Record Unit 316, Smithsonian Institution, Traveling Exhibition Service, Records, "Report on the Status of the Twelve Exhibitions Prepared by the Traveling Exhibition Service of the Smithsonian Institution for the Department of State," Box 17, Folder 10. The report discusses thirteen exhibitions, of which twelve were still in development; "Fashion and Color Photography" had already been released to the Department of State for shipment to HICOG in Bonn, where it was scheduled for presentation as part of Photokina in 1952, held in Cologne.

Correspondence exchanged between and within the TES and Department of State documents that the Knoll-designed exhibition was variously referred to as "New Textile Materials," "American Fabrics," "Contemporary American Fabrics," and "Contemporary American Textiles." A decision was made to use "Contemporary American Textiles" for the purposes of "A Designed Life" because this title was listed on the final invoice submitted by

Knoll to the Smithsonian Institution. Similarly, internal documents sometimes referred to "Contemporary American Wallpapers" as simply "American Wallpaper."

4   In his 1941 State of the Union address, Roosevelt spoke of four freedoms— "speech and expression," "worship," "freedom from want," and "freedom from fear" — and claimed them as American values. "President Roosevelt's Address to Congress on January 6," *Bulletin of International News* 18, no. 1 (1941): 13–15.

5   James J. Kimble, "The Illustrated Four Freedoms: FDR, Rockwell and the Margins of the Rhetorical Presidency," *Presidential Studies Quarterly* (March 2015): 60.

6   United States Information and Educational Exchange Act of 1948 (Smith-Mundt Act), Sect. 501. Accessed January 18, 2017, https://www.state.gov/documents/organization/177574.pdf

7   U.S. Commission of Fine Arts, 21.

8   While sources such as Laura A. Belmonte's *Selling the American Way: U.S. Propaganda and the Cold War* (Philadelphia: University of Pennsylvania Press, 2008), 32, suggest that Smith-Mundt prevented materials created for overseas dissemination from being presented in the United States, Weston R. Sager, in "Apple Pie Propaganda? The Smith-Mundt Act Before and After the Domestic Dissemination Ban," *Northwestern University Law Review* (Winter 2015): 519–520, argues that this restriction was a *de facto* ban.

9   U.S. Commission of Fine Arts, 52.

10   Dennis Harper, "Advancing American Art: 'LeRoy Davidson's Blind Date with Destiny,'" in *Art Interrupted: Advancing American Art and the Politics of Cultural Diplomacy*, ed. Dennis Harper, et al. (Athens: Georgia Museum of Art, 2012), 13–15, 16.

11   Harper, "Advancing American Art," 11.

12   Mark Andrew White, "One World: Advancing American Art, Modernism, and International Diplomacy," in *Art Interrupted: Advancing American Art and the Politics of Cultural Diplomacy*, 32.

13   Aline B. Louchheim, "Government and Art: A Symposium," *New York Times*, December 3, 1950, 9.

14   Jane De Hart Matthews, "Art and Politics in Cold War America," *The American Historical Review* 81, no. 4 (October 1976): 762–87, 786.

15   Michael L. Krenn, *Fall-Out Shelters for the Human Spirit: American Art and the Cold War* (Chapel Hill: The University of North Carolina Press, 2005) 34.

16   Krenn, *Fall-Out Shelters*, 44; Harper, "Advancing American Art," 33, 34.

17   Harper, 51.

18   U.S. Commission of Fine Arts, 21.

19   U.S. Commission of Fine Arts, III.

20   U.S. Commission of Fine Arts, 53–54.

21   The Smithsonian Institution's National Collection of Fine Art is now the Smithsonian American Art Museum.

22   The Alice Pike Barney Fund.

23   Annemarie Henle Pope, oral history interview with Buck Pennington, April 21, 1981, Archives of American Art, Smithsonian Institution.

24   Memo from Annemarie Pope to Thomas M. Beggs, "Official Business Trip to New York, November 3-8," November 26, 1952, Smithsonian Institution Archives, Record Unit 316, Box 15, Folder: Mrs. Pope.

25   Edgar Kaufmann Jr., *What is Modern Design?* (New York: Museum of Modern Art, 1950), 8.

26   Jan Logemann, "Hans Knoll," in *Immigrant Entrepreneurship: German-American Business Biographies, 1720 to the Present*, vol. 5, R. Daniel Wadhwani, ed. (Washington, DC: German Historical Institute, 2014), http://www.immigrantentrepreneurship.org/entry.php?rec=63

27   Bobbye Tigerman, "I Am Not a Decorator: Florence Knoll, the Knoll Planning Unit and the Making of the Modern Office," *Journal of Design History* 20, no. 1 (2007): 61–74.

28   R. Roger Remington and Robert S. P. Fripp, *Design and Science: The Life and Work of Will Burtin* (Burlington: Lund Humphries, 2007), 21.

29   Margaret Re, "Will Burtin," in *Transatlantic Perspectives*, May 13, 2014, http://www.transatlanticperspectives.org/entry.php?rec=161

30   Margaret Re, "Will Burtin."

31   Margaret Re, "Will Burtin."

32   Todd Lee, telephone conversation with the author, October 17, 2016.

33   George Nelson, *Display* (New York: Whitney Publications, 1953), 7.

34   Lizabeth Cohen, in *A Consumer Republic* (New York: Alfred A. Knopf, 2003), discusses the changes that took place in postwar America as the promises of mass consumption were aligned with American values, attitudes, and politics. Cohen argues that in the immediate aftermath

of the war, the acquisition of material goods was promoted as a means to ensure stable economic growth (prosperity) and social and political participation (democracy).

35   Office of Public Affairs, Assistance in German Women's Organizations, April 11, 1951; HICOG Cultural & Exchange Program, Folder: AGS Budget 1952, FY 1952 DM, Box 3 MLR 5324, General Records of the Department of State, Record Group 59, National Archives and Records Administration College Park, College Park, MD.

36   Ursula Koelsch, "The Amerika-Haus in Germany: The Impact of the Cold War on the Development of U.S. Information Centers during the American occupation of Germany, 9145–1949," Master's thesis, University of Maryland, College Park, 1991, 136.

37   Erica Carter, *How German is She? Postwar West German Reconstruction and the Consuming Woman* (Ann Arbor: University of Michigan Press, 1997), 31.

38   Correspondence between Pope and each designer, supported by the introductory text provided by Knoll and Schroeder for their respective catalogues, references "the least expensive fabrics [...] and expensive work" and "a wallpaper of medium range," suggesting that item costs were originally included. Because the catalogues were produced in Germany by the Department of State, it may be that costs were deleted because the majority of the showcased products were not readily available for sale in Germany, which was in the midst of economic and currency reform.

39   The catalogue for *Textilien aus USA* (Smithsonian Institution, 1952) can be found in the library of New York's Museum of Modern Art. *Tapeten aus USA* (Eine Ausstellung der Amerikahäuser in Deutschland, 1956), with a forward by Francis de N. Schroeder, can be accessed through the Richardson Memorial Library at the St. Louis Art Museum. *Werbepackung in Amerika* (Eine Ausstellung der Amerika-Häuser in Deutschland, n.d.) is stored in Folder 1: United States Information Agency, 1950–59, Will Burtin Papers, RIT Libraries: Graphic Design Archives, Rochester Institute of Technology.

40   Letter from Thomas M. Beggs to Dr. Wetmore, "Smithsonian Traveling Exhibition Service," April 3, 1952. Smithsonian Institution, Traveling Exhibition Service, Records.

41   Florence Knoll, *Textilien aus USA*, trans. William Gilcher (New York, 1952), 5.

42   Florence Knoll Bassett papers, 1932–2000, Archives of American Art, Smithsonian Institution; Knoll Corporate Archives; "Knoll's Kaleidoscopic Knock-Down," *Interiors* (December 1952): 112–15, 175.

43   Betty Pepis, "Germans to View U.S. Wallpapers," *New York Times*, August 18, 1952, 14.

44   Pepis, "Germans to View," 14.

45   Unsigned letter with handwritten note dated July 9, 1952, Record Unit 316, Box 2, Folder 2: American Wallpaper, 1952, Smithsonian Institution, Traveling Exhibition Service, Records.

46   Francis de N. Schroeder, *Tapeten aus USA*, trans. William Gilcher (Solingen: Deutsches Klingenmuseum, 1956), 2.

47   Schroeder, *Tapeten aus USA*, 3.

48   Schroeder, 2. See also, Burckhard Kieselbach, ed., *Bauhaustapete: Reklame & Erfolg einer Marke = Advertising & Success of a Brandname*, trans. Claudia Spinner (Cologne: DuMont, 1996), 94.

49   Will Burtin, *Werbepackung in Amerika*, trans. William Gilcher (Eine Ausstellung der Amerika-Häuser in Deutschland, n.d.), 3. Folder 1: United States Information Agency, 1950–59, Will Burtin Papers, RIT Libraries: Graphic Design Archives, Rochester Institute of Technology.

50   Burtin, *Werbepackung*, 2.

51   Burtin, 1.

52   Burtin, 3.

53   Burtin, 3.

54   Letter from Annemarie H. Pope to Mr. Thomas M. Beggs, "Official Business Trip to New York, New York, July 9th to 12th, 1952," August 6, 1952. Smithsonian Institution Archives, Record Unit 316, Smithsonian Institution, Traveling Exhibition Service, Records.

55   Letter from Richard L. Brecker, Special Program Branch, Information Center Services to Herwin Schaefer, Chief, Exhibits Staff, Frankfort, Entry 5323, Exhibits Folder, Box 8, Subjects Files 1949–52, Record Group 59: National Archives at College Park, MD.

56   Letter from Annemarie Pope to unknown person at "Smithsonian Traveling Exhibition Service," July 29, 1952. Record Unit 316, Box 15, Folder: Pope Correspondence, Smithsonian Institution, Traveling Exhibition Service, Records.

57   Letter from Annemarie Pope to unknown person.

58   Krenn, *Fall-Out Shelters*, 64–65.

59   Krenn, 68.

60   *Current Informational Report American Section at the 'Constructa' Exhibition in*

Hannover. American Federation of Art, Box 72, Folder: Exhibition Files State Department Exhibitions Correspondence, 1949–51, Archives of American Art, Smithsonian Institution

61   Jeffery M. Diefendort, *In the Wake of War: The Reconstruction of German Cities After World War II* (New York: Oxford University Press, 1993), 149.

62   Victoria de Grazia, "Chapter 9, A Model Mrs. Consumer," in *Irresistible Empire: America's Advance Through Twentieth-Century Europe* (Cambridge: Belknap Press, 2005).

63   Pope, oral history, Archives of American Art.

64   "Deko-Proben aus USA," trans. William Gilcher, *Heimtex 8*, no. 5 (1953), 15. I am grateful to Professor Jutta Beder for providing me with this reference, published in her work *Zwischen Blümchen und Picasso: Textiledesign der fünfziger Jahre in Westdeutschland* (Münster: Beder, 2002).

65   *Hiemtex* (italics mine).

66   *Heimtex.*

67   *Heimtex.*

68   Letter from Mrs. John A. Pope, Chief, Traveling Exhibition Service, to Mr. Tom Lee, dated August 29, 1952. Record Unit 316, Box 2, Folder 2: American Wallpaper 1952, Smithsonian Institution, Traveling Exhibition Service, Records.

69   Memo from Bonn Om July 17, 1954, Exhibition Progress Report. Record Unit 316, Box 2, Folder 2: American Wallpaper 1952, Smithsonian Institution Traveling Exhibition Service, Records.

70   Friedrich Herbordt, "Maschendraht als Tapetenmuster," Trans. Blair Connelly, *Kasseler Lokalausgabe,* May 7, 1953.

71   Herbordt, "Maschendraht als Tapetenmuster."

72   Alexander Krause, *Arcisstraße Nr. 12* (Munich: Allitera Verlag, 2010), 80.

73   Memo from Annemarie H. Pope to Mr. Thomas M. Beggs, "Appointment with Mr. Brecker," August 18, 1952. Record Unit 316, Box 15, Smithsonian Institution, Traveling Exhibition Service, Records.

74   "Desp. No. 117, From: HICOG, USIS, Bonn, 11/9/54." Record Unit 316, Box 2, Folder 2: American Wallpaper 1952, Smithsonian Institution, Traveling Exhibition Service, Records.

75   Memo from Bonn Om July 16, 1954, Exhibition Progress Report. Record Unit 316, Box 2, Folder 2: American Wallpaper 1952, Smithsonian Institution, Traveling Exhibition Service, Records.

76   Annemarie H. Pope to Mr. Richard L. Brecker, "Items missing from 'Containers and Packaging,'" February 12, 1954, Exhibition Group 316, Box 1, Folder 8: American Containers and Packaging, Smithsonian Institution, Traveling Exhibition Service, Records.

77   Pope to Beggs, "Final Payment for exhibition, 'Containers and Packaging,'" December 22, 1952, Record Group 316, Box 1, Folder 8: American Containers and Packaging, Smithsonian Institution, Traveling Exhibition Service, Records.

78   Gay McDonald, "The 'Advance' of American Postwar Design in Europe: MoMA and the Design for Use, USA Exhibition 1951–1953," *Design Issues* 24, no. 2 (Spring, 2008), 15.

79   Letter from Richard L. Brecker, Special Programs Branch, Information Center Service to Herwin Schaefer, Chief Exhibits Staff, Office of Public Affairs, Information Division, HICOG, Frankfort, Germany, n.d. Exhibits Folder, Box 8, Entry 5323, RG 59, General Records of the Department of State, National Archives at College Park, MD.

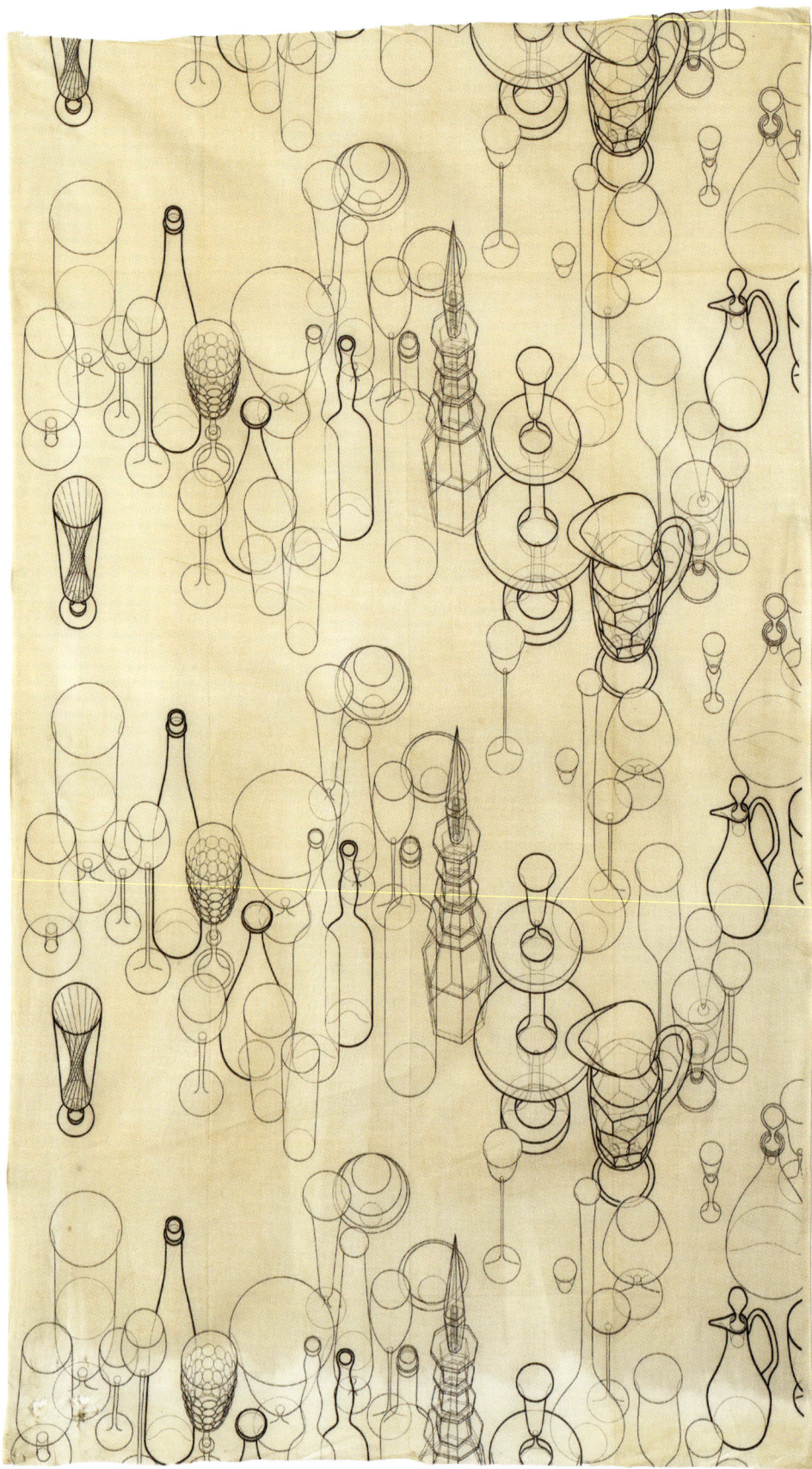

Contemporary American Textiles, 1951–54

Virginia Gardner Troy

"Contemporary American Textiles" was the first postwar US Department of State–sponsored exhibition of exclusively American-produced textiles organized for European audiences. Textiles were among the most visible and industrially innovative products produced in the United States at the time; as elements for interior design and as materials for modern life — from automobile upholstery to fiberglass curtains — textiles impacted many aspects of postwar life. This versatility was promoted to convey US industrial progress and design creativity to European countries receiving American recovery aid. "Contemporary American Textiles" was a self-contained portable exhibition of 156 textiles that traveled in Germany and France from 1952 to 1954. The textiles were selected by Florence Knoll, director of interior design services for Knoll Associates since 1943; she also designed the innovative installation, and designed and wrote the accompanying catalogue. Knoll was assisted in the project by Knoll textile designer Eszter Haraszty,[1] and Susanne Wasson-Tucker, who from 1944 to 1945 served as acting curator in the Museum of Modern Art's Department of Industrial Design before joining Knoll Associates as an interior architect.[2] Knoll was recommended for the exhibition position by Edgar J. Kaufmann Jr., director of the Department of Industrial Design at the Museum of Modern Art (MoMA) in New York, and the son of the president of Kaufmann's Department Store.[3] Kaufmann knew Knoll from her work on the Executive Committee for the 1949 "Exhibition for Modern Living" at the Detroit Institute of Arts; he included her work in MoMA's 1946 exhibition "Useful Objects for the Home," which he curated, as well as the 1951 and 1952 "Good Design" exhibitions at MoMA and the Chicago Merchandise Mart, and he enlisted her design expertise to select textiles for the 1953 "Good Design" exhibition.[4] Their collaboration is significant as evidence of the strong interrelationship between museums, design corporations, department stores, and government diplomatic programs in postwar America.[5] This reciprocal interrelationship presented an ideal example of American resourcefulness to serve as a model for postwar European recovery and modernization efforts.

FIGURE 8   Don Wight, *Garden of Glass*, Quaintance Fabrics, New York, c. 1950. Cotton print, 78 ½ x 44 ½ in. *Digital image © The Museum of Modern Art; Licensed by SCALA/Art Resource, NY.*

"Contemporary American Textiles" paralleled a concurrent and much larger Department of State–sponsored exhibition abroad. "Design for Use, USA" was organized by MoMA, curated by Kaufmann, and included an exhibit installation design by Alexander Girard. It comprised more than five hundred examples of contemporary American-designed household goods, including 101 textiles, and traveled to audiences in Germany and France from 1951 to 1953. The goals of the exhibition were to showcase recent American manufacturing developments; spur European rebuilding efforts and trade through example; and recognize American designers as "design originators" — so described by Kaufmann, who possessed an authentic American "style leadership" that no longer looked to Europe for inspiration.[6] Many of the "design originators" he spoke of were also among those featured in the "Contemporary American Textiles" exhibition, and represented a new type of textile designer: trained in the applied arts and architecture, they used their design, production, and marketing skills to create smartly designed interiors and furnishings for modern homes and offices.

The idea of presenting a wide variety of textile examples, chosen by discerning design professionals, was a strategy intended to cultivate awareness of high standards in the design and consumption of everyday goods, and to democratize consumer buying choices through the presentation of numerous options.[7] The objective was to provide recovering populations with opportunities to make choices based on aesthetic, practical, and economic values through the display and accessibility of goods that met and guided those needs. "Things needed that are well selected," Kaufmann explained, "can be a source of lasting enjoyment."[8] Kaufmann, Knoll, and others believed that American textiles could satisfy the objectives of providing consumers with the ability to make choices based on price, practicality, and artistic taste because textiles touched on all of these elements.

Interestingly, many of the textiles and designers in the "Contemporary American Textiles" and "Design for Use, USA" exhibitions were also included in the "Good Design" exhibitions directed by Edgar J. Kaufmann Jr., that were held at MoMA and the Merchandise Mart in Chicago from 1950 to 1955.[9] The guiding principles uniting all three exhibitions were to reinforce name and object recognition, to elevate certain products as being among the consistently selected elite, and to provide exemplars of good design. The exhibitions might also create a desire for the lifestyle associated with the objects — modernity, convenience, high style — that tastemakers deemed to be progressive.[10]

As explained by the editors of *American Fabrics* magazine at the time, the fast pace of American industrialized society meant that design ideas flowed to the mass market with increasing speed, particularly regarding textiles, and this reciprocal connection between art and mass production led to higher levels of style and greater accessibility to well-designed everyday objects.[11] Furthermore, there was a supportive infrastructure of museums, journals, corporations, and department stores that were linked through their endorsement of well-designed textiles, whether produced by machine or hand. These connections led to the rise of interdisciplinary textile designers trained in multiple mediums and practices, who envisioned and understood how textiles — fiber, weave, pattern, and texture — would function in modern environments. For example, before being named head of the inaugural textile department at Herman Miller Company in 1952, Alexander Girard was trained as an architect, became a distinguished exhibition designer, and designed textiles for Knoll Associates from 1947, the year the textile division was formed, to 1949.[12] Promotional materials written by Girard described his textile work for Herman Miller as

> [...] completely original. His focus is not on the work of others, but rather on new potentials hidden or unused in both old or more recent manufacturing methods and processes. His aim has been to extract the maximum inherent quality out of each specific method and to let it show to its best advantage.[13]

Textiles provided designers with nearly limitless possibilities for combining and arranging patterns, textures, and structures in new ways; in turn, textiles provided consumers with myriad possibilities for use in homes and offices. This flexibility and creativity introduced a set of conditions unique to postwar America. According to designer Alvin Lustig, such "courageous experimental thinking and planning" in the field of textile design "attests to the vital creative development that is still possible in this country," heralding an "unprecedented period in the development of design in America."[14] That courageous and experimental thinking not only captured the postwar spirit of the time but also, according to Kaufmann, reflected American democratic values. "Modern design should fulfill the practical needs of modern life," Kaufmann wrote in his 1950 book *What is Modern Design?* "It can do more than reveal the character of an age, it can be beautiful."[15] Most importantly, he continued, "modern design is part of a democratic life [...] intended to implement the lives of free individuals."[16]

In her catalogue essay, Knoll stressed that textiles from the United States were exceedingly diverse: they embodied both woven and printed processes, were both hand- and machine-made, and in all examples, from the simplest to the most complex, from least expensive to most expensive, viewers would find evidence of creativity and originality in the way designers worked with the principles of color, pattern, and texture.[17] Types of fabric ranged from cloth made from plastic or glass fiber to durable blue jean denim. She also included canvas and sailcloth in the exhibition, intending to show that such industrial and non-textile materials could be adapted and repurposed for everyday use. Indeed, for her Knoll Planning Unit interior design projects, Knoll was one of the first postwar designers to repurpose industrial and suiting material for home and office use.[18] Similarly, textiles in the "Design for Use, USA" exhibition ranged from silk to nylon to screen-printed linen. According to the MoMA press release, "American synthetics are well represented in this show since they are so highly developed here. Thus, a number of rubber and plastic films by the yard, woven plastics, and woven fibers are included in the upholstery section."[19]

The exhibitions also emphasized the abundance of examples available to US consumers. This was in contrast to developments taking place in Germany, which was struggling to regain its once-strong position in textile production. The textile industry in postwar Germany needed to rebuild and modernize, a process that was complicated by the division of the country into zones. For example, in 1945 most of the yarn and weaving plants were in the West, spinning plants were in the East, textile stockpiles were diminishing, the

previously robust clothing industry in Berlin was wiped out, and, until 1948, few textiles went to the civilian population.[20] Establishment of the Marshall Plan in 1948 increased Western Zone access to imports and provided funds and expertise for technical assistance, eventually leading to the growth of fashion and design centers there.[21] But the slow growth of research and development in the East, as well as inaccessibility to new materials and processes, meant that the United States held the lead in postwar textile and design innovation.

TEXTILES AND DESIGNERS

Two significant commonalities become apparent upon examination of the textiles and designers featured in all three exhibitions: the prominence and interdisciplinarity of the designers, who today represent the iconic face of mid-century modernism; and the visual neutrality of the designs. Individuals featured repeatedly included recent émigrés such as Anni Albers, Marianne Strengell, and Juliet and György Kepes; and American-born designers Dorothy Liebes, Paul Rand, Alexander Girard, Emily Belding, Ray Eames, Don Wight **[FIGURE 8]**, and the duo from Design Unit, Benjamin Baldwin and William Machado. Additional designers included Evelyn Anselevicius, Eszter Haraszty **[PLATES 1 AND 7]**, Serge Chermayeff, Philip Johnson **[PLATE 2]**, Estelle Laverne, Stig Lindberg, Ross Littell **[PLATE 3]**, Noémi Raymond **[PLATE 6]**, Bernard Rudofsky, Angelo Testa **[PLATE 4]**, and D. D. Tillett **[PLATE 5]**.

Albers, Strengell, and Liebes can be considered the most progressive and innovative weaver-designers of the period. Described by others as "leaders," each demonstrated remarkable skill at uniting hand and machine production, at creating utilitarian goods that were also structurally sound and visually beautiful, and at experimenting with new materials.[22] Girard, Baldwin and Machado, and Ray Eames brought a sense of whimsy and play to printed designs that incorporated irregular and seemingly spontaneously created patterns. In most cases, the designs or weaves were distinctively neutral, meaning that printed patterns were composed of nonrepresentational geometric or biomorphic forms, and weaves were not pictorial but relied on the inherent vertical and horizontal structure of the weaving process to form the pattern.

Maintaining design neutrality meant that images depicting individualized objects or symbols, or using applied patterns such as embroidery or appliqué, were rejected in favor of grids, diamonds, circles, squares, or blobs that emphasized overall pattern sequences varying according to drape and pleat. Girard stressed this approach: "Fabric design is not easel painting or illustrating, it is fabric design; realism

FIGURE 9   Benjamin Baldwin and William Machado, *Carnival*, Design Unit, New York, c. 1950. Cotton print. *Clement Kois for Patrick Parrish Gallery, NY; Licensed by SCALA/Art Resource, NY.*

in printed fabrics should be avoided."[23] Many modern textile designers rejected ornamentation, in part because neutral designs could echo industrialized processes through repeated forms, and neutrality could be used to exploit new synthetic fibers through the use of metallic or reflective materials for surface effects. How materials were formed and shaped helped determine the pattern — not idiosyncratic ornamentation. Kaufmann in particular linked modernism's lack of ornament to democracy and good design. He wrote:

> Modern design has had a century to evolve a practice and theory suited to the industrializing, democratizing world that has been taking shape. Influenced by science, modern design has held that each problem indicates its own solution, the full investigation of the needs will reveal the necessary form. [...] Influenced by democracy, modern design has given precedence to mass production as a means of spreading the good things of life. In good modern design, the peculiarities of materials and fabrication, the expression of masterly forming are as influential and recognized as ever.[24]

This theory guided Kaufmann throughout his curatorial career, and is reflected in the objects he selected to represent "Good Design." Good design, he wrote, is simply "the best its designers produce; it should be simple, its structure evident in its appearance, avoiding extraneous enrichment" or irrelevant decoration.[25] Similarly, Florence Knoll emphasized the fact that she practiced interior design, not interior decoration, for her office-planning projects at Knoll. For these room designs she utilized unified color palettes and uncluttered, geometric object placements that allowed functional flexibility and neutrality through lack of dramatic focal points.[26] In describing the "Contemporary American Textiles"

exhibition, she emphasized how each designer skillfully merged materials and processes to create practical, beautiful, and well-designed fabrics. She wrote that each fabric "has its own value and is designed and fabricated for a specific purpose. The designers were aware of this part of their task and therefore strove to bring together beauty and utility."[27]

Unlike Art Nouveau textiles that incorporated undulating whiplash lines and embroidery, or Art Deco textiles composed of aerodynamic forms, bold color contrasts, or scenes from modern life, the postwar textiles showcased in these exhibitions were meant to serve as unifying elements of an overall design plan. Postwar modern suburban architecture demanded new applications for textiles; walls of glass, open floor plans, and streamlined furniture called for textiles such as open weaves to let in light, sailcloth stretched across room partitions to form flexible walls, and textured synthetic blends for durability. Lustig described modern textiles as integral parts of architecture, functioning "as planes of color or texture rather than as panels to hang on either side of a hole in the wall."[28]

Anni Albers believed that modern design — the way we form objects according to function and appearance — should be "anonymous and timeless" rather than flashy. She advocated working with materials for solutions to design challenges:

> If we, as designers, cooperate with material, treat it democratically, you might say, we will reach a less subjective solution [to] this problem of form and therefore a more inclusive and permanent one. The less we, as designers, exhibit in our work our personal traits, our likes and dislikes, our peculiarities and idiosyncrasies, in short, our individuality, the more balanced the form we arrive at will be. [...] A useful object should perform its duty without much ado. The tablecloth that calls 'Here I am, look at me,' is invading the privacy of the consumer. [...] The unknown designer or designers of our sheets or of our light bulbs performed their task well. Their products are complete in their unpretentious form.[29]

Printed textiles were used as primary sources of pattern and color depending on the surface size and style of drape. Baldwin and Machado's *Carnival* fabric **[FIGURE 9]** evokes a festival atmosphere with colors and shapes resembling balloons and flags but without actually depicting them. Instead, the pattern focus is neutralized through abstraction without becoming banal or tedious. Not all printed textiles were nonrepresentational; Don Wight's *Garden of Glass*,

FIGURE 10 Ray Komai, *Masks,* Laverne Originals, New York, c. 1948–49. Screen print on paper (facsimile), 46 × 53 in. *Digital image © 2018 Museum Associates/LACMA. Licensed by SCALA/Art Resource, NY.*

[FIGURE 8] used in all three exhibitions, was one of the only patterns portraying recognizable objects: a range of generic bottles and glasses. When pleated or folded the pattern becomes distorted to an abstract arrangement of black lines on a white ground. When hung or stretched, the sheer cotton batiste allows light to flicker through it, thereby creating additional patterns and minimizing the pictorial aspect. Similarly, Ray Komai's *Masks* [FIGURE 10] depicts a charming assortment of doodle-like faces on irregular green blobs, at once abstract and recognizable depending on the pleating format.

DISPLAY

MoMA's "Design for Use, USA" was intended as a transatlantic extension of the parallel "Good Design" exhibitions, but with exclusively US products. According to the press release, this was "the first exhibition of home furnishings prepared by MoMA to be limited to American products only."[30] The "Design for Use, USA" and the "Good Design" exhibitions utilized an innovative approach to display that merged home, museum, and department-store display techniques.[31] Viewers encountered objects arranged as simulated rooms, or on display shelves for individual objects, or as consumer goods on tables available for closer inspection, indicating that some objects and furniture were intended to be handled by viewers, even sat on, crossing the line between museum and department-store behavior.[32] Installation photographs from the inaugural "Design for Use, USA" exhibition in Stuttgart show textiles draped vertically from poles as if curtains, or stretched as if shades; according to the MoMA press release, fabrics were "grouped according to types of fabrics, which are caught at the top and bottom for neatness of display."[33] Like an advertising brochure, the exhibition catalogue included manufacturer info and pricing, allowing viewers to consider cost differentials. All of this provided viewers with the ability to make informed choices while envisioning these textiles and objects functioning in their individual lives.

FIGURE 11   Florence Knoll, "paste-up" for a Cowles publication. *Courtesy Knoll Inc.*

"Contemporary American Textiles" was a starkly different type of exhibition than "Design for Use, USA," in large part due to its comparatively small scale. For the former, examples were arranged in three ways on scaffolding made of metal rods: stretched triangular pieces that formed walls of cloth alternating with empty spaces to create triangular "windows"; vertically stretched lengths of printed and solid fabric placed side by side to form fabric walls; and swatches of fabric resting on an outwardly extended shelf. Together, the arrangement created the effect of a visual and textural collage, illuminated by a built-in lighting system. Viewers, surrounded by various patterns, weaves, textures, and colors, were directed through the space by floor arrows. Clearly one could reach out and touch any example — a tactile aspect of an overall sensory effect. Installation photographs indicate that numbers were attached to each example, ostensibly corresponding to catalogue entries; otherwise viewers had no way of knowing what they were looking at. Lack of a price list meant that viewers were unable to gauge cost differentials. All of this detracted from the viewers' ability to make discerning choices, instead relying on visual and textural dynamism to achieve audience excitement and engagement.

Knoll's "Contemporary American Textiles" exhibition resembled her mock-up room plans for Knoll Planning Unit interiors. For these, Knoll carefully arranged patches of fabrics and finishes, wood chips, and furniture silhouettes, to create room plans so that customers could envision a physical, textural, and tonal environment **[FIGURE 11]**. Dubbed "paste-ups" by Knoll, this technique is now used by most interior designers today for presentation purposes.[34] Knoll's "Contemporary American Textiles" exhibition installation

turned the paste-up technique into three-dimensional rooms that viewers walked within. This method provided a flexible, portable, self-contained display showcasing the variety and quantity of American textiles. The exhibition display also resembled a number of Knoll textile showrooms that similarly displayed a wide variety of textile samples and swatches in collage-like, wall-mounted displays in addition to walls of draped fabric, as seen in a 1948 photograph of the Knoll showroom at 601 Madison Avenue.[35] Both were feasts for the eyes; the difference was that in the latter case customers had the aid of showroom consultants and sales representatives in order to make practical choices.

The collage/paste-up display method for "Contemporary American Textiles" was most likely not as effective in capturing audience curiosity as the display techniques of the MoMA-organized exhibitions because viewers may have felt overwhelmed by the variety and quantity of examples, the lack of wall text, the lack of a price list, and an inability to connect to the examples as consumers without an intermediary to aid with decisions. However, the exhibition presented a dazzling assortment of textiles to Europeans looking to modernize and renovate. The exhibition also served as an introduction to the Knoll International corporate look; the company had recently opened European subsidiary showrooms in Paris (1951) and Stuttgart (1952).[36] Knoll International's advancement into European markets was boosted by contracts with the Federal Buildings Office of the Department of State to refit and modernize embassy buildings.[37] The showroom interiors echoed some of the design features employed for the "Contemporary American Textiles" exhibition, including fabric-covered partitions and model rooms. In 1954, Knoll furniture and textiles were featured in a dynamic display of model rooms at the luxury Parisian department store Le Printemps, providing customers with greater access to the brand and its range of products; before long, the Knoll look in France became synonymous with modern chic.[38]

CONCLUSION

The exhibitions shared similar goals and content. Both sought to showcase examples of American collaboration, creativity, variety, and democratic values, and to create new trade opportunities. Both featured textiles characterized by neutrality, sleekness, and practicality — the output of a new generation of postwar professionals. "Contemporary American Textiles" was not intended to be a permanent exhibition, but was created to be dismantled and moved to a variety of locations. This flexibility perhaps contributed to the fact it did not receive a lot of press, and that, importantly, the display and the examples were not preserved or returned to the United States. Knoll nevertheless recognized the significance of the project by including it with her life's work that she donated to the Smithsonian Institution Archives of American Art. MoMA's "Design for Use, USA" was a larger exhibition viewed by larger audiences, bolstered by the museum's international reputation and by its supporting exhibitions in New York and Chicago. In addition, many of the objects subsequently became part of the twentieth-century design collection catalogue and ongoing installations at the museum, contributing to the exhibition's legacy.[39] Today we can appreciate how these exhibitions helped to catapult American textiles and designers to international renown.

NOTES

1   A memo documents that Pope met with Haraszty on May 1, 1952: Annemarie Pope to Thomas M. Beggs, "Meeting on May 1," May 8, 1952, Record Unit 000316 16/17, Box 5.

2   A memo documents that Traveling Exhibition Service (TES) chief Annemarie Pope met with Wasson-Tucker at Knoll Associates on November 8, 1951: Annemarie Pope to Thomas M. Beggs, "Official Business Trip," November 26, 1951, Record Unit 316 15/17, Box 5, Folder Detail: Mrs. Pope; see also Juliet Kinchin, "Women, MoMA, and Midcentury Design," in *Modern Women: Women Artists at the Museum of Modern Art,* Cornelia Butler and Alexandra Schwartz, eds. (New York: The Museum of Modern Art, 2010), 286–87; MoMA press release 441113-39, 1944. [Thanks to Margaret Re for her research related to this and the previous citation.]

3   Memo from Annemarie Pope to Thomas M. Beggs, "Official Business Trip to New York November 3–8," November 26, 1952, Smithsonian Institution Archives, Record Unit 316, Box 5, Folder: Mrs. Pope.

4   Alexander Girard, *Exhibition for Modern Living* (Detroit: Detroit Institute of the Arts, 1949), 3; Arthur J. Pulos, *The American Design Adventure 1940–1975* (Cambridge, MA: MIT, 1988), 117.

5   See Terence Riley and Edward Eigen, "Between the Museum and the Marketplace: Selling Good Design," *MoMA Journal* (1994), 151–73; Mary Anne Staniszewski, *The Power of Display: A History of Exhibition Installations at the Museum of Modern Art* (Cambridge, MA: MIT Press, 1998); Greg Castillo, *Cold War on the Home Front: The Soft Power of Midcentury Design* (Minneapolis, MN: University of Minnesota Press, 2010).

6   Gay McDonald, "The 'Advance' of American Postwar Design in Europe: MoMA and the Design for Use, USA Exhibition 1951–1953," *Design Issues* 24, no. 2 (2008), 15–27; MoMA press release #510104-1, January 8, 1951, 3.

7   MoMA press release #510104-1, January 8, 1951, 3.

8   Edgar Kaufmann Jr., "Hand-made and Machine-made Art," in *Everyday Art Quarterly 1* (1946), 4.

9   *Good Design: November 22, 1950 to January 28, 1951: An Exhibition of Home Furnishings* (New York: MoMA, 1951), 5–10.

10 Cammie McAtee and Fredie Floré, "Knolling Paris," in *The Politics of Furniture: Identity, Diplomacy, and Persuasion in Post-War Interiors* (London: Routledge, 2017) 98–118.

11 *American Fabrics 37* (1956), 44–46.

12 Earl Martin, ed., *Knoll Textiles, 1945–2010* (New Haven: Yale University Press, 2011), 332–33.

13 Alexander Girard, promotional material for the Herman Miller Fabric Collection, Herman Miller Archives, G.1.1, 1957, 3.

14 Alvin Lustig, "Modern Printed Fabrics," in *American Fabrics 20* (1951), 59–72.

15 Edgar Kaufmann Jr., *What Is Modern Design?* (New York: Museum of Modern Art, 1950), 6–7.

16 Kaufmann, *What Is Modern Design?,* 8.

17 Florence Knoll, *Textilien aus USA,* trans. William Gilcher (New York, 1952), 4–5.

18 Martin, *Knoll Textiles,* 102.

19 MoMA press release 510104-1, January 8, 1951, 1.

20 Marjorie Yahraes, "Textile and Clothing Industry," in *Information Bulletin* (Frankfurt: US Army Office of US High Commissioner for Germany, 1949), 21–26.

21 Yahraes, "Textile and Clothing Industry," 25–26.

22 Ed Rossbach, "Fiber in the Forties," in *American Craft 42,* no. 5 (1982), 15–19.

23 Alexander Girard, in *American Fabrics,* no. 38 (1956), 35.

24 Edgar J. Kaufmann, "Modern Design Does Not Need Ornament," in *College Art Journal 6,* no. 2 (1946), 140–42.

25 Kaufmann, *What Is Modern Design?,* 9.

26 Bobbye Tigerman, "'I Am Not a Decorator': Florence Knoll, the Knoll Planning Unit and the Making of the Modern Office," in *Journal of Design History 20* (2007), 67–76.

27 Knoll, *Textilien aus USA,* 5.

28 Lustig, "Modern Printed Fabrics," 66.

29 Anni Albers, "Design: Anonymous and Timeless," 1947, in *On Designing* (Middletown, CT: Wesleyan University Press, 1987), 2–9.

30 MoMA Press Release #510104-1, January 8, 1951, 1.

31 See Riley and Eigen; Staniszewski; Castillo, 38–40.

32 Yahraes, "Textile and Clothing Industry."

33 MoMA press release #510104-1, January 8, 1951, 3.

34 Martin, *Knoll Textiles,* 181.

35 Martin, 206.

36 Castillo, 62–65; McAtee and Floré, 101.

37 https://www.knoll.com/knollnewsdetail/knoll-showrooms

38 McAtee and Floré, 104.

39 Arthur Drexler and Greta Daniel, *Introduction to Twentieth Century Design for the Collection of the Museum of Modern Art* (New York: MoMA, 1959).

Domestic Design as a Cold War Weapon

American Home Exhibitions, 1949-59

Greg Castillo

Objects of domestic design, in ways less obvious than political posters and other graphic propaganda, also played a crucial role in advancing postwar ideologies and polemics.[1] Central to the Cold War division of Europe was US insistence, over the objections of other European nations, of German inclusion in the European Recovery Plan (ERP), better known as the Marshall Plan. By 1949 it had become clear to administrators in Washington that operating the program "without a strong information arm was as futile as trying to conduct a major business without sales, advertising, and customer-relations departments."[2] Among the resulting torrent of posters and publications, exhibits, film documentaries, and radio shows, domestic design spectacles served a special purpose in Marshall Plan propaganda. Model home interiors and furnishings provided an ideal medium for affect-laden statements about social and economic reconstruction, transnational trade, and postwar gender roles. These stage-managed "dream homes" lent physical and emotional immediacy to what might otherwise remain abstract ideological concepts. A model home invited its viewers to imagine the texture of a daily life in the future tense, and to project themselves into regimes of consumption that might still be "under construction." By obscuring the mechanics of state-sponsored pedagogy, the cozy intimacy of a simulated domestic setting concealed propagandistic intent. Regimes of postwar household consumption — capitalist and socialist alike — were not simply the byproducts of a given approach to economic and social reconstruction, but also the subjects of carefully wrought indoctrination campaigns.[3]

Marshall Plan administrators faced a two-front battle in Western Europe. On one hand, intellectuals and public-opinion leaders often regarded America as the purveyor of "a primitive, vulgar, trashy *Massenkultur* [mass culture], which was in effect an *Unkultur* [nonculture], whose importation into postwar Europe had to be resisted," as historian Volker Berghahn has described.[4] On the other, Western Europe's communist labor unions and party propagandists leveraged these stereotypes to portray the United States as a military empire

FIGURE 12   Kurt Krapeik, *Wir Bauen ein neue Europa*, Austria, c. 1950. "We're Building a New Europe," the title of this European Recovery Program (ERP) poster, associates the continent's reconstruction with doves of peace building a nest of elements collected from across all of the Marshall Plan nations: a trade strategy fundamental to US postwar economic intervention and celebrated in American household exhibitions like "We're Building a Better Life." *Courtesy George C. Marshall Foundation.*

ruled by parvenus. Dispelling "the old stereotype of the Yank as a cross between a cinematic gangster and an uncultivated bumpkin" was crucial to America's postwar "fight to wage the peace," according to Paul G. Hoffman, the former Studebaker corporation executive who coordinated Marshall Plan administration through the Economic Cooperation Administration (ECA).[5] Allegations of a US consumer "nonculture" were more than just insulting. In denigrating American materialism, they also subverted the Marshall Plan blueprint for postwar recovery. European reconstruction was to be built upon a New Deal variant of "Fordism," the formula used by Henry Ford to mollify assembly-line workers as efficiency engineers rationalized factory tasks to yield higher productivity. In Marshall Plan Europe, the benefits of low-cost mass production were to be shared with workers through affordable mass consumption. American planners advocated the elimination of the tariff barriers between Marshall Plan member nations in order to create a larger pool of potential European consumers, encouraging industrial investment in higher-volume production and, theoretically, lower-priced goods. **[FIGURE 12]** The system could only work with organized labor as a compliant partner — a role that communist-affiliated labor unions, particularly those in France and Italy, were determined to undermine.[6] "Today's contest between freedom and despotism is a contest between the American assembly line and the Communist Party line," declared Hoffman.[7] Marshall Plan efforts to unleash European consumer desire redefined Franklin D. Roosevelt's "Four Freedoms," transforming "freedom from want" into the freedom *to* want.

SELLING AMERICAN AFFLUENCE

The US launched its campaign to promote the benefits of an "American Way of Life" in Marshall Plan Europe under the problematic rubric of "propaganda." For most Americans, the word was synonymous with "deceit and trickery, with totalitarian rather than democratic methods," as ECA director Hoffman was painfully aware. He defended propaganda by referring back to the term's original meaning: the propagation of a belief system. Hoffman defined information as a form of communication intended merely to enlighten. In contrast, propaganda connoted "the communication of facts (or nonfacts) and opinions in an effort to influence." When he assumed his post with the Marshall Plan, Hoffman had felt that only a small-scale "information effort" would be needed: "a man or two in each of the ECA missions overseas to get out press releases, contact local editors, and report back home." He soon was persuaded otherwise, warning that in Italy, France, and Western Germany, "sleight-of-hand practitioners of Communist propaganda" backed by lavish Soviet funding had created an apparatus that was "incredibly adroit, incessant, and tailored to the prejudices and emotions of people in all walks of life." It demanded a counter-initiative led by "men who can use all the tools of propaganda with

imagination, boldness, and skill, tempered by [...] a sensitive awareness of the forces of world ferment." Combating anti-Americanism required "a creative approach to the propaganda task" and "a continuing program of research and testing, just as [in] our military forces." The effort would advance a "free-world doctrine" based upon religious freedom, political civil liberties, "socially conscious capitalism," and the expansion of economic opportunities while insuring citizens against "life's common hazards."[8] As defined by Hoffman, the Marshall Plan synthesis of industrial capitalism with New Deal social welfare policies provided ECA propagandists with a visionary inventory of the Cold War assets in America's soft power arsenal.[9]

Germany's western zone of allied occupation, united as a postwar nation only in 1949, was a relative latecomer to the Marshall Plan alliance. By then, propaganda efforts defending American culture and values against communist denigration were well underway. A classified US intelligence report of 1947 examined Soviet propaganda ridiculing the American way of life, and recommended a counter-propaganda offensive based on the themes "American living standards" and "try it our way." In the spring of 1948, US military administrators in Frankfurt launched their first attempt to link American consumer ideals with anti-communist propaganda. Peter G. Harnden, the director of exhibitions programs at the Office of Military Government, United States (OMGUS), an organization charged with administration in the US zone of occupied Germany, was charged with producing the first official display of American housing developments to be seen in postwar Germany. Hampered by limited resources, Harnden relied upon photographs solicited from architecture schools at Harvard, Columbia, and MIT to illustrate prefabricated construction, advanced household technology, and trends in suburban planning. He contracted the OMGUS Exhibitions Workshop, led by Joost Schmidt, a former master instructor of graphic design at the Bauhaus, to produce the show's eight scale models and 150 display panels depicting residences ranging from single-family houses and apartments to "homes of the American wealthy." "How America Lives" (*So wohnt Amerika*) opened in Frankfurt in August 1949. Visitor attendance was modest, to put it nicely. Despite stellar production talent, the show was a critical flop. Photographs and scale models of houses neither captivated the general public nor dissuaded elites of the idea that cultural barbarism had found its home in America. The head of Frankfurt's US Information Center, Donald W. Muntz, recognized the error and prescribed its solution:

> If real honest-to-god electric stoves, refrigerators, and deep-freeze units had been on hand, the general attendance figures would have been astronomic. I can well imagine that the problems in bringing these gadgets together would be manifold, but an effort here would have paid off.[10]

The "particular failure," as Muntz called it, of "How America Lives" would not be repeated in Harnden's subsequent household exhibitions.

In the battle to win European hearts and minds, the notion of conscripting American household "gadgets" (and housewives who used them) found scholarly support in 1949. A contemporary book review judged the "demonstration effect" theorized by James S. Duesenberry in *Income, Saving, and the Theory of Consumer Behavior* to be "one of the most significant contributions of the postwar period to our understanding of economic behavior."[11] Duesenberry broke from the economic orthodoxies of his time, which modeled consumption as a set of individual choices based on factors like relative price and real income. According to Duesenberry, rational decision-making was less important than learned habit in establishing consumer preference. Consumers made choices by observing other people's possessions, not just in terms of status symbols, as proposed in Thorsten Veblen's notion of

"conspicuous consumption," but as perceived material necessities. Utility, in other words, was a subjective construct, and purchasing habits intended to satisfy a simple need would change with exposure to more affluent versions of need. "Mere knowledge of the existence of superior goods is not a very effective habit breaker," Duesenberry wrote. "Frequent contact with them may be."[12] His theory of a "demonstration effect" posited that individuals became dissatisfied with current consumption standards through first-hand exposure to superior products being used by others. While State Department exhibition documents make no mention of Duesenberry, given his theory's enthusiastic reception it is not surprising that the tactic of exposing Europeans to "real, honest-to-god electric stoves, refrigerators, and deep-freeze units" — gleaming kitchen appliances that exemplified American middle-class affluence — would become crucial in Cold War household propaganda.

Within five years of Nazi Germany's unconditional surrender, the United States had unleashed the largest international propaganda effort ever mounted in a time of peace. Marshall Plan administrators orchestrated a forceful response to continental *Konsumterror*, or "consumption terror," as sociologists Theodor Adorno and Helmut Schelsky dubbed the fear that a culture of mass consumption would undermine the integrity of home and family. Marshall Plan propaganda attempted to induce "a radical shift in the priorities of individuals, towards new ideals of personal progress which could be defined in the language of income and consumption," as historian David Ellwood observes.[13] *Productivity, Key to Plenty*, a Marshall Plan film dubbed into a number of languages, took continental audiences on a tour of an American suburban home. As the camera lingered on its appliances, a voice-over soundtrack asked: "What housewife has not dreamed of a kitchen like this? [...] One can remain attached to moral values which give a precise meaning to existence without neglecting the material factors which contribute to the good things in life."[14] In the interest of liberating repressed consumer desire, US exhibition planners set their sights on European domestic environments. Model homes concocted by Marshall Plan advisors were deployed as incubators of a model citizen soon to be available for emulation in Europe: the modern mass consumer *à la Americaine*. The intention of "Trojan house" exhibitions was not to market a specific type of housing or the product lines displayed within, but rather to sell the idea that escalating private affluence was a fundamental measure of good postwar governance — a criterion that Eastern Europe's Stalinist satellite nations, devoted to constructing state-owned heavy industries through heroic worker sacrifice, could not possibly meet.

FIGURE 13   German visitors waiting to tour the 1950 "Amerika zu Hause" (America at Home) exhibition: a fully furnished prefabricated suburban home shipped from Minneapolis to West Berlin courtesy of the Marshall Plan. *Credit: US National Archives, Text Division, RG59 862A.191, Box 5225.*

WEAPONIZING THE SUBURBAN HOME

"America at Home" (*Amerika zu Hause*), the first successful Marshall Plan promotion of US consumer domesticity, took place at West Berlin's first annual German Industrial Exhibition (*Deutsche Industrie-Ausstellung*) in October 1950, just as a national election was in progress across the border in East Germany. Within the newly inaugurated George Marshall-Haus, a permanent fairground pavilion built with US funds, an installation produced by Harnden extolled the collective effort made by American labor unions and industrial managers to increase productivity. The exhibition's coda, a single-family American suburban home, sat just outside the Marshall-Haus against a lush backdrop of poplars. Shipped from Minneapolis to Berlin as a knock-down kit of precut lumber, the six-room home (with carport) lent physical substance to the American promise that workers would be rewarded for engaging in collective bargaining with employers rather than conspiring against them. German carpenters, working in round-the-clock shifts, had assembled the home from crates in just five days, a feat said to again demonstrate how productivity advances and harmonious labor relations could benefit Europeans.[15] An internal memorandum shifted to a more militant rhetorical tone, calling "America at Home" a "patriotic reaffirmation of our way of life" and part of "a struggle as vital to the peace and prosperity of the world as any military campaign in history."[16] The jingoism was a sign of the times. Exhibition planning had begun in July 1950, just weeks after North Korea's Soviet-backed government launched a surprise invasion of South Korea. John McCloy, the US high commissioner for Germany, regarded "America at Home" as "the chance to put [a] living monument to American life in Berlin."[17] And as monuments go, this one was a bargain: $24,000 exclusive of assembly labor, but including shipping costs for the entire prefabricated kit and a full complement of interior furnishings.[18]

Predictions of astronomical attendance for an exhibition featuring "real, honest-to-god" American appliances proved right on the mark. From the moment "America at Home" swung open its front door it was mobbed. Visitors arrived in such numbers that police had to be posted at the front and back doors, and foot traffic was limited to groups of ten to avoid damage to the timber floor structure **[FIGURE 13]**. Young female American studies majors from West Berlin's new Free University worked the floor as tour guides, answering questions about "such household miracles as the electric washing machine, illuminated electric range, vacuum cleaner, Mixmaster, Toastmaster, etc."[19] Among "the many miracles which left the average German gasping," according to an American newspaper report, was "a model American kitchen with gleaming electrical appliances which are already the talk of Berlin."[20] Given the relative impoverishment of the audience, imported electrical appliances were bound to create a sensation. In 1950, about one-sixth of West Germany's industrial labor force remained unemployed, and an equal proportion of the population was crowded into housing at three or more inhabitants per room. The average working class family of four spent nearly half its disposable income on food.[21] Five years after the war's end, the glint of American kitchen appliances represented unbridled wealth for West Germans, not middlebrow aspirations.

Marshall Plan administrators deemed "America at Home" a success. Attendance over the course of the two-week exhibition far exceeded expectations. As calculated by the discounted admissions purchased with an East German identity card, of the 750,000 visitors to the Marshall-Haus, 400,000 had crossed Berlin's internal border to get there.[22] Spatial and structural limitations of the exhibit's wood-frame house had resulted in visitor numbers that had fallen short of demand, however.[23] Braving long waits, only 43,000 Germans, 15,000 of whom came from the East, were able to tour the model home. US officials called "America at Home" "a gratifying demonstration of what can be accomplished in selling the American democratic way of life from the Berlin 'showcase' behind the iron curtain in an incredibly short space of time."[24] A final public-relations coup dreamed up by the US high commissioner called for the model home to be raffled off as a prize on the last day of the German Industrial Fair. Media coverage on RIAS (Radio in the American Sector) and in local newspapers, according to a classified telegram, was expected to generate a "first-class nonpolitical news story at the time of Soviet controlled [East German] elections. Should [an] east sector resident win, we would very much welcome it because publicity of favorable or unfavorable action by East [German] authorities would be extremely valuable propaganda for [the] US."[25] Back in Washington, the acting US secretary of state had his doubts. The Department of State ultimately abandoned the raffle plan, fearing the "possibility [of the] house falling into undesirable hands."[26] With the American suburban home inducted into the nation's propaganda arsenal, just as with any other piece of cold-war weaponry, it had to be secured against unauthorized use.

FIGURE 14   As spectators peer in through a living room window, a young, affluent, two-parent/two-child model family enjoys their modernist home environment at the Marshall Plan's "We're Building a Better Life" exhibit. *Credit: US National Archives, Still Pictures Division, RG286 MP GEN 1903.*

ATLANTICISM BY DESIGN

"We're Building a Better Life," a model home spectacle mounted in 1952 by the Mutual Security Agency (MSA), a Marshall Plan successor agency, envisioned the modernist domesticity of a transatlantic middle class. Its new postwar people, as depicted on the exhibition floor, would be affluent, cosmopolitan in taste, politically democratic, and culturally hegemonic. Their universal household — the native habitat of a "John Smith or Hans Schmidt," as stated by Michael Harris, the German division chief of the MSA — embodied Marshall Plan aspirations of mass-consumer affluence and barrier-free trade.[27] The International Style, a label devised by New York's Museum of Modern Art for a synthetic modernism derived from European sources, would stage a triumphant return to continental homes, courtesy of the US Department of State, as an expression of Atlanticism: the Cold War term for an impending unification of America and Western Europe, as envisioned by the former and revealed to the latter.

MSA exhibition planners proposed a shift in strategy for the US contribution to West Berlin's 1952 German Industrial Exhibition. Rather than creating separate installations related to industry and consumer goods — as had been done in 1950, with "America at Home" representing the latter — they would dedicate the entire US display to private consumption. Its impact upon East Germans was a primary consideration, as a State Department memorandum makes clear:

> The Berlin Industrial Fair in 1950 was most
> impressive because it showed large machines
> being produced by the West at a time when
> Eastern factories were suffering from dismantling
> by the Soviets and when raw materials in the East
> were in extreme shortage. Since that time, however,
> the Eastern emphasis on heavy machinery and
> production goods has brought about a changed
> situation. It is particularly appropriate at this time,
> therefore, to show West Berliners, and more
> especially East Zone and [Soviet] Sector visitors,
> the progress made in the West in developing
> consumer goods designed to raise the standard
> of living of the average family.[28]

The name chosen for the MSA exhibition, "We're Building a Better Life" (*Wir bauen ein besseres Leben*), reflected cold-war rivalry as well. It echoed the East German Party mantra "Produce More — Live Better" (*Höhere Arbeitsproduktivität – Besser Leben*), a slogan used to motivate "worker activists" to boost productivity through imported Soviet labor techniques. East-bloc leaders pledged that voluntary overproduction and piecework wages would yield collective abundance. At the 1952 Berlin Industrial Fair, MSA officials would strive to refute that economic formula.

Exhibition plans were finalized in May, at a moment of heightened border tensions. To exert some measure of control over its porous boundary with the West, East Berlin blocked some two hundred streets that had linked the city's two halves.[29] MSA officers were nevertheless confident that they would draw crowds of East German visitors to their exhibit. It would feature a house within a house — a full-scale "ideal dwelling" built within West Berlin's Marshall Haus pavilion. With respect to previous US exhibits, "We're Building a Better Life" represented a breakthrough in what Barbara Kirshenblatt-Gimblett has called the "political economy of showing."[30] As in a nineteenth-century ethnographic exhibit stocked with exotic subjects, the MSA model home would be populated by model inhabitants: a "man-wife-child family team actually going through [the] physical actions of living in [the] dwelling, making proper use of [the] objects in it," as outlined in a Department of State telegram.[31] Unlike the sense of audience superiority conveyed by imperialist displays featuring "primitive" peoples, however, popular responses to the "Better Life" home and lifestyle display were bound to be fraught with contradictions. While encouraged to identify with the showcased residents, postwar Germans would be reminded nevertheless of their economic inferiority. The exhibition's propaganda gamble was that observation of a fictive German family in their dream home would induce Duesenberry's "demonstration effect," creating the desire for a higher standard of living rather than inciting alienation. To enhance audience identification with their "Better Life" fantasy, MSA exhibition planners departed from Marshall Plan precedent. Their exhibition would assemble its visionary home from local materials: "wherever possible, equipment [is] to be European rather than American." The result was to be an American way of life reformulated for export and "developed in terms of arguments for a high-production, high-wage, low-unit-cost, low-profit-margin, high-consumption system. Emphasis [is] to be placed upon [the] fortunate outcome of American economic philosophy when combined with European skills and resources."[32] The exhibition narrative claimed that prosperity, rather than cultural difference, distinguished the American domestic ideal from its old-world counterpart: a disparity that could be eradicated through hard work and sound economic policy.

Peter Harnden's exhibition design team chose many of the interior appointments of the "Better Life" home from the catalogue of Knoll International. It was an inspired choice, given that Knoll's mid-century modernism was not only a symbol of transatlantic unity but also its economic product.

FIGURE 15 An exhibition narrator in a crow's nest above the roofless model home created for "We're Building a Better Life" explains the affluent household furnishings and amenities used by the installation's resident model family. *Credit: US National Archives, Still Pictures Division, RG286 MP GEN 1841.*

As a corporate entity, Knoll International was born from a proposition made by US Department of State officials to the German expatriate Hans Knoll, a charismatic entrepreneur known to them through federal office building renovation work.[33] With his file of business contacts across Europe, Knoll was the perfect partner for a strategic investment scheme initiated by the Department. Its goal was to create a prototype for the kind of private enterprise needed to plug what US economic planners called the European "dollar gap." The Marshall Plan was based not on cash grants, but dollar-denominated loans to foreign countries. Loans were to be repaid in local currency into accounts controlled by the Department, creating US stockpiles of European "counterpart funds." American officials intended to leverage their supply of local currencies to influence continental monetary policy. The optimum outcome, according to ECA chief Paul Hoffman, would be "a single large market within which quantitative restrictions on the movements of goods, monetary barriers to the flow of payments, and eventually all tariff barriers are eventually swept away."[34] Putting theory into practice was another matter. The crawling pace of Marshall Plan market integration frustrated American advisors. Exports to the

United States declined, threatening to worsen the "dollar gap" — that is, the deficit created when Western European imports of the dollar-denominated goods needed for postwar reconstruction outstripped foreign export income. According to a Marshall Plan midterm review, the monetary imbalance looked set to hit a disastrous three-billion-dollar mark by 1952.[35]

Investigating Western European export opportunities and American market preferences, Marshall Plan economists devised a number of intervention strategies. A large order for furnishings to be used in a Department of State expansion program for postwar diplomatic facilities provided the start-up capital, paid in Marshall Plan counterpart funds.[36] Hans and Florence Knoll scoured Europe for suitable subcontractors for overseas manufacturing operations. "We drove from Stuttgart to Paris, from Paris to Milan, from Milan to Stuttgart," Florence Knoll recalled. "We started producing our designs for Europe, and once this job was done, the companies were there."[37] Wooden furniture was manufactured in Germany and France, textiles in France, and metalwork in Italy — where, after a decade-long disappearance from the market, the chromed steel furnishings designed by Bauhaus masters Marcel Breuer and Mies van der Rohe went back into production under an exclusive Knoll contract.[38] The result, Knoll International, was a model enterprise embodying the transnational flows of goods and capital promoted by the US Department of State as a sure path to Western European economic recovery.

The "Better Life" exhibition reunited a tried-and-true cast. The initial MSA choice for the show's curator was Edgar Kaufmann Jr., whose work for MoMA demonstrated an increasingly international approach to home design.[39] "Good Design II," which opened at the Chicago Trade Fair in January 1951, featured products from Denmark, Finland, France, England, Italy, Germany, and the United States.[40] When Kaufmann turned down the commission, the job of curating "We're Building a Better Life" fell to Peter Harnden, who, in his new post as chief of the MSA presentations branch, assembled an international team to mount the exhibition. He contracted a German architect, Fritz Bornemann, to draft plans for the model home installation. In Bonn, US public affairs officer Herwin Schaeffer was enlisted to secure the show's West German household durables, many available through the Stuttgart office of Knoll International. Freelance consultants were hired to track down additional domestic goods in France and Italy. To deliver the required objects to the exhibition site at short notice, US Department of Commerce officials considered asking the Air Force to mount a new Berlin airlift: one dedicated to the emergency transport of chic furnishings rather than food and coal supplies.[41]

The main attraction at "We're Building a Better Life," which opened in September 1952, was a single-family dwelling — two bedrooms, a living-dining room, bath, kitchen, laundry/home workshop, nursery, and garden — realized down to the kitchen gadgets and garden tools, but built without a roof. All six thousand products in and around the house were modern in design and manufactured in a Marshall Plan member nation. A billboard beside the home's front door announced: "The objects in this house are industrial products from many countries in the Atlantic community. Thanks to technology, rising productivity, economic cooperation, and free enterprise, these objects are available to our Western civilization." A model family inhabited the model home. Two couples and eight pairs of children, all professional actors or models, **[FIGURE 14]** worked the floor in alternating shifts, demonstrating the tasks and leisure rituals of "an average skilled worker and his family" living in a consumer wonderland. Perched overhead in a crow's nest, a narrator dressed in white coveralls explained the features of this exotic household environment **([FIGURE 15]**. Visitors became voyeurs, staring through windows or crowding overhead catwalks to observe the ways in which modern domestic objects constructed postwar subjects.

The exhibit concluded at a gallery of furnishings introduced with a nearly life-size photograph of a male blue-collar laborer, captioned: "This man is a worker and at the same time a consumer." Given the era's gender conventions, which saw home design as a female pursuit, the panel alerted visitors to an exhibition discourse of importance to men as well women. For the East Germans in the audience, it was also a reminder of the lack of material rewards for workers under their nation's Stalinist labor economy. In this final "Better Life" installation, all furnishings seen within the model home could be examined as closely as a shopper might. A tag attached to each item indicated country of origin, retail price, and the number of hours of labor — as measured by a skilled worker's wage — needed to purchase the product. This seemingly guileless calculation of purchasing power assaulted a tenet of communist faith. Marx had used the concept of "labor value" to define capitalist manufacturing and distribution as exploitive. Profit, he had claimed, was the unpaid labor value that industrialists appropriated from workers when products were sold at retail prices. A century later, MSA exhibit planners radically redefined labor value as the amount of work needed to *purchase* an item, rather than produce it. This changed emphasis transformed what had been an indictment of exploitation into a measure of the capitalist reward system.

Marshall Plan and MSA administrators claimed that America's blueprint for postwar capitalism, unlike its nineteenth-century predecessor, would ensure mass prosperity and alter class identities. As a primer in "the modern approach to interior decoration," the "Better Life" exhibition showed how "rationally designed products from different countries in the Atlantic community can be combined harmoniously," according to MSA publicity materials.[42] Another press release explained, "Just as these items from the various countries combine to form a homogenous whole, so the nations themselves can combine to form a homogenous community."[43] The underlying message was summarized in the West German daily *Der Tag:*

> The new style, realism plus simplicity, finds its strongest expression in the US Marshall-Haus. [...] There are different versions of one style and one way of life typical for a "Western bourgeois" household. Nothing is foreign to us, whether it comes from Berlin or Los Angeles, from Stockholm, Sicily, or New York.[44]

"To some visitors, this home of a future 'average consumer' would appear perhaps to be 'American,' but that is incorrect," a design journal reported, reiterating the talking points of an opening-day address by Michael Harris, chief of the German branch of the MSA. "John Smith or Hans Schmidt would be perfectly capable of affording such a house when certain conditions were met: we must make the Atlantic community of nations a reality, eliminate tariff barriers, and raise productivity, thereby allowing us to lower prices and raise wages."[45] According to MSA officials, the "Better Life" International Style was not simply an aesthetic, but also a mode of production and consumption that would cultivate a transnational middle class.

"We're Building A Better Life" was a hit among German audiences. Over a half million spectators, over forty percent of them from the East, waited in line to view the MSA's topless house. In a review of the "Better Life" exhibition titled "The Domestic Culture of the Western People," architect Alfons Leitl asserted that "whoever might not have known it learns emphatically through this exhibition [that] in all countries of the Western world one deals with the same questions, with the same design themes."[46] *Der Tag* told its readers: "Take your time to inspect this exhibit. You will see there what it means to live a decent life."[47] The adjective "decent" (rather than "pampered," for example) described a lifestyle that most postwar Americans would have found enviable. In this textbook example of the "demonstration effect," the act of witnessing a model family's casual use of imported luxury goods had turned those goods into objects of necessity.

THE TROJAN HOUSE, RENOUNCED AND REPRISED

President Dwight D. Eisenhower, the former five-star general who served as supreme commander of the Allied Expeditionary Forces in Europe during World War II, established the United States Information Agency (USIA) in 1953 as a new federal agency devoted to international public diplomacy and ideological warfare. He could not have chosen a less opportune moment. A Republican-controlled Congress had promoted Joseph McCarthy, a senator from Wisconsin, to the position of chairman of the Committee on Government Operations, a platform from which he mounted a national campaign of anti-communist hysteria. McCarthy denounced the US Department of State for harboring "socialists, misfits, and perverts." His aides, Roy Cohn and G. David Schine, toured public libraries operated by the Department in Europe on a "clean-up expedition" and claimed to have discovered thirty thousand subversive books on the shelves, many by communist authors. Literary suspects included Albert Einstein, Ernest Hemingway, Helen Keller, Henry David Thoreau, and Frank Lloyd Wright.[48] McCarthyism's transatlantic adventure degraded a strategic American soft power asset: the perception that intellectual freedom was a cornerstone of US democracy. In testimony before the House of Representatives, Eisenhower found himself forced to defend programs that represented the US abroad through "ice boxes, radios, cars, how much [Americans] have to eat, what they wear, when they get to go to sports spectacles, and what they have available in the way of art galleries and things like that."[49] His position put him at odds with his own party's House and Senate majority, which put its stock exclusively in the hard power of military force. Congress responded to Eisenhower's creation of the USIA by slashing its budget by a third, the first of repeated Republican attempts to sabotage the agency and its mission through chronic underfunding. As the United States reduced its investment in the Cold War "battle for hearts and minds," the USSR poured in resources, using exhibits at international trade fairs to portray communism as technologically and economically advanced.[50]

To insure the nation's soft-power capabilities, Eisenhower created a second agency to mount international exhibitions. The Office of International Trade Fairs (OITF) was placed within the Department of Commerce, dissociating its operations from the beleaguered USIA. By depicting its activities merely as a support service for US manufacturers seeking international markets rather than a conduit for overseas public diplomacy, the OITF camouflaged its mission under the conservative banner of free enterprise. Responding to the Soviet use of exhibitions "as a means of disseminating propaganda and impressing the audience with the wonders

FIGURE 16 An "island" of contemporary furnishings, as installed
by Peter Harnden within the US Pavilion at the 1958 Brussels World's Fair
US Pavilion. *Courtesy of the Ghent University Department of Architecture;
photo: Lucien Willems.*

of life in the Soviet Union," OITF officials envisioned a new kind of display that would be perceived by foreign audiences as something more like a "cultural exhibit" than a "pure trade-fair project."[51] The OITF hired Peter Harnden to direct its European Trade Fair Program headquartered in Paris. By artfully editing a grab bag of donated displays into a series of thematically coherent installations, Harnden produced a new generation of US exhibitions on a shoestring budget. In Washington, OITF officials would choose a trade-fair theme relevant to a specific international venue, and tied to a particular facet of American life. US business sponsors supplied product displays and demonstration personnel. Harnden would review the stockpile of available displays, select those that seemed appropriate, and integrate them into a cohesive

exhibit. OITF methods for producing low-cost overseas propaganda, quickly adopted by the cash-strapped USIA, turned the exhibition designer into a bricoleur, and Harnden was soon a master. This novel genre of installation art also came with unintended consequences. Since exhibitions representing the United States had to be assembled from the "found" material of corporate donations, an unofficial federal endorsement was suddenly available to any business willing to pay for the privilege.

An air of crisis also surrounded discussions of how to represent America at the 1958 Brussels World's Fair. Despite estimates that the USSR would allocate fifty million dollars to build and operate its pavilion, a congressional subcommittee reduced Eisenhower's requested fifteen-million-dollar budget by twenty percent. The *Washington Post* reported the conflict under the headline: "We're Set to be Shamed at Brussels."[52] At the USIA, meanwhile, administrators urged a new approach to overseas diplomacy that entrusted visitors to formulate their own positive views of the United States, as opposed to bombarding them with "heavy, belabored" propaganda.[53] Commissioned to devise installations for the Brussels pavilion, Harnden, assisted by Bernard Rudofsky, a frequent guest curator at MoMA, made the fateful decision to dispense with the usual model kitchens, which he believed had lost impact both through overexposure at trade fairs and because Western Europe's rising economic tide had brought local household technology onto the market. Instead, they opted for a fashion show and a gallery of household objects organized with playful panache. Howard Cullman, the exhibition's US commissioner general, appointed a committee from Boston's Institute of Contemporary Art (ICA) to assemble household goods for display at Brussels. Composed of volunteers from the fields of industrial design, crafts, and interior decoration, the committee identified seven categories of products "peculiar to the American mode of living": mobility, portability, flexibility, disposability, outdoor living, toys, and the decentralized kitchen.[54] Joseph Carreiro, the committee director, stated in a press release:

> We have made no effort to provide a complete story, or to convince or persuade anyone that our approach to living is the right one. We have tried through fragments, relationships, contrasts, and the value revealed by the object, to point up our [national] diversity and uniqueness.[55]

After the trial run of a downsized collection at the ICA, Harnden and Rudofsky installed approximately six hundred objects along the mezzanine of architect Edward Durrell Stone's Brussels pavilion. Their "Islands for Living" display, used as a staging area for fashion shows, included objects like an Eames leather and rosewood recliner, a George Nelson desk, an antique Shaker chair, and a mix of other domestic artifacts ranging from artful to oddball[56] **[FIGURE 16]**. While favorably received by European visitors, US critics pointed to the Soviet pavilion's installations of industrial prowess and, in comparison, judged the lighthearted "Islands for Living" display utterly pointless.[57]

The impossible task of satisfying cultural conservatives in the US and cosmopolitan audiences abroad would dog USIA exhibitions for the next twenty years. The agency's design talents continued to develop Harnden's Brussels experiment, which used objects of American material culture for their emotive appeal, rather than to boast about national affluence

or might. At Expo 67 in Montreal, the twenty-story-tall US Pavilion, a geodesic dome engineered by Buckminster Fuller in collaboration with Shoji Sadao, contained a stacked exhibition space exploring the theme "Creative America." Curated by USIA design director Jack Masey and graphic designer Ivan Chermayeff, the installation charted an epic developmental narrative in reverse chronological order. Ascending a 250-foot-long escalator, visitors arrived at the upper platform's high-tech spectacle, featuring full-scale spacecraft on a simulated lunar surface. Moving down one level, a display of Pop art confirmed Manhattan's preeminence as the imperial capital of Western contemporary art. Descending further, visitors absorbed an exhibit on Hollywood film culture followed by installations of folkloric and Native American craft. In contrast to the Soviet pavilion, which exuded an "oppressive impressiveness" through its inclusion of "every piece of hardware but the kitchen sink," according to a Canadian journalist, the kaleidoscopic sensorium assembled by Masey and Chermayeff radiated playfulness. Its portrait of a sanguine superpower was intended to be "easily understandable by the emotions and the senses alone," in Chermayeff's words.[58] "Creative America" was celebrated by foreign journalists but reviled by their conservative American counterparts, a fate consistent with Harnden's pioneering venture in emotive propaganda a decade earlier in Brussels.[59]

In 1958, Harold "Chad" McClellan, a former administrator of the OITF as an assistant secretary of commerce, and USIA veteran Jack Masey selected George Nelson, one of the nation's acknowledged masters of mid-century modernism, to coordinate the design of the 1959 American National Exhibition in Moscow. The target audience for the Moscow show would be "university youths, people in cultural work and teaching, middle-level bureaucrats and skilled workers," considered by the USIA "potentially [the] most influential citizens of the Soviet Union."[60] Displays highlighting "the unimpeded flow of diverse goods and ideas" would, it was hoped, increase "pressures tending in the long run toward a reorientation of the Soviet system in the direction of greater freedom." To avoid the Brussels experience of snatching defeat from the jaws of victory, organizers of the American National Exhibition in Moscow reverted to tried-and-true ideological narratives and relied far more heavily upon corporate donations to circumvent fiscal constraints imposed by a Congress incapable of properly managing the nation's soft-power assets.

Nelson's brainstorming group included Masey, the husband-and-wife design team of Charles and Ray Eames, and Hollywood director Billy Wilder. During a marathon four-day meeting, they developed the spatial and narrative sequence for the Moscow exhibition. Functioning as "a kind of 'information machine,'" a geodesic dome designed by Buckminster Fuller would open the visitor's tour. Inside, an audiovisual spectacle produced by the Eames team would depict a typical week in the life of an American suburb. Emerging from the dome's hypnotic dazzle, visitors would enter a glass-walled warehouse of goods. It was to be, according to Nelson, "a bazaar stuffed full of things, [the] idea being that consumer products represented one of the areas in which we are most effective." Nelson's "bazaar" took shape as a two-story grid that transformed the modular storage systems Nelson and other modernists had invented for domestic use into a habitable environment accessed by stairways and mezzanine catwalks.[61] Visitors literally could wander the shelves, examining merchandise donated by hundreds of corporate sponsors, or look down from the elevated catwalks at demonstrations of American name-brand products. Given a relatively modest budget, Nelson stocked the pavilion with corporate trade-fair attractions. At the General Foods/General Mills kitchen, hostesses conjured thousands of recipes from 110 different packaged ingredients.[62] The source for the processed foods featured in this magic act was showcased in a supermarket display. The RCA "Miracle Kitchen of the Future," previously displayed in 1958 at a trade fair in Milan, entertained visitors with futuristic home technology. Additional exhibits included a home workshop stocked with power tools for the do-it-yourselfer, and a Singer sewing machine demonstration, both seen at previous European trade fairs.[63] From labor-saving appliances to prepared food wizardry, a patchwork of corporate trade-fair displays would pit American consumer technology against Soviet achievements in heavy industry and military hardware.

In assembling the exhibition's model apartment — the narrative point of convergence for all goods and services on display — Nelson and interior designer Lucia DeRespinis kept a far tighter reign. Nelson envisioned its five-room residence as that of an affluent family, with "children at play and the parents enjoying hi-fi, television, and reading." The domestic stage set came with a model resident: the Russian-speaking wife of a US journalist.[64] Many of the furnishings on display were Herman Miller products — no surprise, given Nelson's rise to glory as the firm's impresario — but the apartment interior also showcased the work of a virtual honor roll of American designers, including Florence Knoll, Paul McCobb, and Edward Wormley.[65] Finding even one item from this sterling collection of mid-century modernism in a typical US home, much less the whole collection, would have been highly unlikely. "We are assuming that the couple has pretty sophisticated taste and a pretty good income," Nelson

remarked, estimating the model family's annual income at about $12,000 — in 1959, over twice the national average.[66]

A second American model home in Moscow conveyed a more representative middle-of-the-middle-class life on the nation's suburban frontier: a display almost certainly included to rectify its omission at the Brussels fair. Herbert Sadkin of All-State Properties, a Long Island developer of bedroom communities for Manhattan's commuters, answered a USIA call for donations before Nelson and Masey were able to secure a home with more sophisticated design credentials.[67] The All-State prefab reflected "less advanced taste," according to Nelson, but was meant to display more affordable furnishings.[68] Pale blue wall-to-wall carpeting and contemporary oil-finished walnut furniture, a closet filled with colorful towels and linens, and the consumer electronics said to be "indigenous to almost every modern American home" provided a visual sampler of middle-class affluence.[69]

Differences in press coverage launched the two model residences into divergent historical trajectories. The Soviet news agency TASS ridiculed the American exhibition's "allegedly typical" model homes and the notion that "the Pennsylvania miner or Indiana metal worker always comes home to an apartment with deep-fitted carpets, and that the textile workers of New England all have huge television sets, expensive radios, record players and tape recorders, all in fine cabinets."[70] In fact, it was Nelson's cosmopolitan apartment, not Sadkin's suburban prefab, that grossly misrepresented an average white, middle-class lifestyle. The former went all but unmentioned in Soviet press coverage, while the latter was the subject of furious denunciation. Criticism of Nelson's luxurious apartment would have generated implicit comparisons with cramped and poorly equipped Soviet residential units churned out by Khrushchev's mass-housing program. With its thin wood-framed walls, the American suburban prefab struck many Russians as flimsy and temporary. It was not only easier to depict as a Potemkin village cottage, but also more alien to locals than Nelson's city apartment, with its Russian-speaking hostess who conversed with guests while doing household chores. Whatever the logic behind the vitriol directed by Soviet news sources at the All-State home, it captured the attention of American journalists, politicians, and entrepreneurs, who proceeded to script its place in Cold War history.

Soviet premier Nikita Khrushchev seemed testy on his opening-day tour of the exhibition, hosted by US Vice President Richard Nixon. What turned out to be the opening round of an extended sparring match began during their visit to an RCA-sponsored television display. In front of live video cameras, Khrushchev made a rash wager: "In another seven

FIGURE 17 The historic "kitchen debate." Center front, from left-to-right: Soviet Premier Nikita Khrushchev; US Vice President Richard Nixon; Communist Party Central Committee Second Secretary Leonid Brezhnev. American consumer bounty is represented by a box in the foreground containing a selection of ten individually wrapped servings of breakfast cereal; on the right, a sunshine-yellow GE washer-dryer incites a tense Cold War argument about the transience of so-called "consumer durables." *Glasshouse Images/Alamy.*

years we will be on the same level as America. When we catch up with you, while passing you by, we will wave back to you."[71] US Department of State personnel watched transfixed as the level of tension rose. *New York Times* reporter James Reston wondered, "Why [doesn't] somebody pull the plug on the whole thing?"[72] According to Tom Wicker, another *Times* correspondent, Khrushchev was then led to the site of a premeditated ambush. William Safire, a Nixon admirer who would later work on his presidential campaign, steered the two dignitaries toward the All-State home's General Electric–sponsored kitchen. Peter Blake, the curator of an architecture display at the Moscow exhibition, recalls that

press photographers had received the tip to stake out the suburban house for a photo opportunity. Given that Safire was a publicist for RCA/Westinghouse, a General Electric competitor that provided the exhibition's "Kitchen of the Future," political allegiance apparently trumped corporate loyalty.[73]

Posed beside a GE washer/dryer, Khrushchev and Nixon faced off **[FIGURE 17]**. Their famous "kitchen debate" began as Nixon, gesturing toward a gleaming row of appliances, explained to Khrushchev that labor-saving devices, made affordable when manufactured in massive cost-saving runs, eased the burden of housework for American women. Khrushchev objected to Nixon's characterization of "the capitalist attitude toward women," and maintained that the US had no exclusive franchise on advanced domestic technology — making the preposterous claim that "All of our houses have this kind of equipment." When Nixon praised the virtues of US twenty-year home mortgages, Khrushchev countered that the wood-framed prefab was so cheaply built that it would only last twenty years, forcing the owner to purchase a new home just as the final mortgage installment was paid. Nixon responded that the house would last longer than that, but that its kitchen equipment certainly would be obsolete in twenty years, and went on to extol planned obsolescence in a consumer economy "designed to take advantage of new inventions and new techniques."[74] The kitchen debate pitted Soviet socialism against American capitalism, assessing the two world orders in terms of their ability to "deliver the goods" to citizens. Kitchen amenities suddenly were not just domestic conveniences but also ideological conveyances: vehicles for a dispute about citizen enfranchisement, housework and gender equity, and the economics of consumption and planned obsolescence.

From mass-media accounts, Americans learned that the battle of the superpowers was not simply about military capability but was also being fought along a domestic front. The message was telegraphed in a *Washington Post* headline: "U.S. Typical Home Enters Cold War."[75] In fact, this bulletin from the Cold War's home front arrived ten years late. Although journalists and historians credit the kitchen debate with turning the American postwar home and its contents into anti-communist icons, the 1959 Moscow exhibition was the campaign's parting volley rather than its opening shot. Ten years earlier, the US Department of State made divided Germany the proving grounds for Cold War home propaganda. Its trial and error trajectory led from the ineffective "How America Lives" exhibition of 1949 to the multiple domestic environments displayed at the 1959 American National Exhibition in Moscow, proclaimed by officials in Washington to be "probably the most productive single psychological effort ever launched by the US in any communist country."[76] Home environments deployed in this cold-war *Kulturkampf* must not be mistaken for actual residences, however. These "exhibitionist houses," as architectural theorist Beatriz Colomina calls them, instead were domestic simulacra. While they survive today only in images and texts, "exhibition experiments gain their force precisely by physically disappearing while inhabiting the spaces of publication, of memory, of fantasy," as she observes.[77] In fact, the domestic culture proselytized as a touchstone of US democracy in the 1950s no longer exists — or, more accurately, has undergone a mutation so radical that its current

manifestation bears only a passing resemblance to its mid-century progenitor

The dream home displayed in 1950 at West Berlin's "How America Lives" exhibition was typical of the nation's new suburban residences, which were, on average, 983 square feet (91.3 square meters) in size — or about the area of the three-car garage appended to twenty percent of new homes built in 2005 in the United States (in the Western states, the proportion increases to thirty-one percent). In 2006, America's average new home had a living area of 2,459 square feet (228.4 square meters): an increase of 150 percent in fifty years. Over the same period, the size of the average US household decreased by twenty-three percent, meaning that, over the same period, the living area per family member increased in the average new home by a factor of three: from 290 square feet (27 square meters) in 1950, to 893 square feet (83 square meters) in 2003.[78] Residences of more than five thousand square feet (465.5 square meters) are now so commonplace in the United States that they have garnered a host of derisive nicknames, including "McMansions" and "Garage Mahals."[79] In comparison with the average household in the European Union, its US counterpart resides in a home eighty percent larger.[80] Because extra residential space rarely consists of empty, unheated rooms, dramatically increased resource consumption has accompanied American home expansion. Enlarged homes use more energy and establish a platform for profligate consumer habits that nurture environmental degradation. Recent studies reveal that far more polluting greenhouse gases are generated by ongoing household consumption of goods and services than by the home's direct impact on energy, water, and land use.[81] As a result, more natural resources have been used by US citizens since 1950 than by everyone else everywhere else in the world who ever lived before them.[82] In short, the American formula for citizen enfranchisement through ever-increasing low-cost mass consumption, slated for global emulation by the Marshall Plan, is now costing us the world. Democratic affluence has succumbed to an unsustainable inflation of consumer desire — one of the conditions that hastened the collapse of Soviet-bloc socialism. Rather than a propagandistic narrative of American triumph, the history of the Cold War dream home should be read as a cautionary tale.

NOTES

1   Fredie Floré and Cammie McAtee, "Introduction: The Politics of Furniture," in Fredie Floré and Cammie McAtee, eds., *The Politics of Furniture: Identity, Diplomacy and Persuasion in Post-War Interiors* (London: Routledge, 2017), 4.

2   Averell W. Harriman, quoted in Benn Steil, *The Marshall Plan: Dawn of the Cold War* (New York: Simon & Schuster, 2018), 315.

3   On the changing scholarly topos of consumption, see Susan Strasser, "Making Consumption Conspicuous: Transgressive Topics Go Mainstream," *Technology and Culture* 43, no. 4 (October 2002), 755–70.

4   Volker Berghahn, *America and the Intellectual Cold Wars* (Princeton: Princeton University Press, 2001), xvii.

5   Paul G. Hoffman, *Peace Can Be Won* (Garden City, NY: Doubleday, 1951), 105.

6   The origins and ideological underpinnings of a Fordist consumer economy are traced in Susan Strasser, *Satisfaction Guaranteed: The Making of the American Mass Market* (New York: Pantheon, 1989).

7   Hoffman, *Peace Can Be Won*, 87.

8   Hoffman, 134–36, 141–43, 147–49.

9   On the Marshall Plan as a "New Deal synthesis," see Michael J. Hogan, *The Marshall Plan: America, Britain, and the Reconstruction of Western Europe, 1947–1952* (New York: Cambridge University Press, 1987), 22, 427. A critique of his analysis can be found in Charles S. Maier, "American Visions and British Interests: Hogan's Marshall Plan," *Reviews in American History* 18, no. 1 (March 1990): 102–111.

10   Donald W. Muntz to Patricia van Delden, "Special Report re America House Publicity Efforts on Behalf of the *So Wohnt Amerika* Exhibition," August 24, 1949, RG260, 390/42/21/3 Box 323, OMGUS Information Control, Records of Information Centers and Exhibits Branch, 1945–49, US National Archives, College Park, MD.

11   Kenneth J. Arrow, review of *Income, Saving, and the Theory of Consumer Behavior* by James S. Duesenberry, *The American Economic Review* 40, no. 5 (December 1950): 906

12   James S. Duesenberry, *Income, Saving, and the Theory of Consumer Behavior* (Cambridge MA: Harvard University Press, 1949), 27.

13   David W. Ellwood, *Rebuilding Europe: Western Europe, America, and Postwar Reconstruction* (London and New York: Longman, 1992), 161–62.

14   Brian Angus McKenzie, *Remaking France: Americanization, Public Policy, and the Marshall Plan* (Oxford and New York: Berghahn Books, 2005), 165–66.

15   Telegram, Dean Acheson to Paul Shinkman, August 18, 1950, RG59 862A.191 (Internal Affairs of State Relating to Exhibitions and Fairs in Germany) Box 5225, US National Archives, College Park, MD.

16   Memorandum, Bruce Buttles to John McCloy, RG59 862A.191 (Internal Affairs of State Relating to Exhibitions and Fairs in Germany) Box 5225, US National Archives, College Park, MD.

17   Telegram, John McCoy to US Secretary of State, September 22, 1950, RG59 862A.191 (Internal Affairs of State Relating to Exhibitions and Fairs in Germany) Box 5225, US National Archives, College Park, MD.

18   *Amerika zu Hause* (Berlin: Deutsche Industrie Ausstellung, 1950), unpaginated.

19   Memorandum, Paul A. Shinkman to Henry J. Kellermann, November 3, 1950, RG59 862A.191 (Internal Affairs of State Relating to Exhibitions and Fairs in Germany) Box 5225, US National Archives, College Park, MD.

20   "Model US Home at West Berlin Fair No. One Attraction for Awed Germans," undated newspaper clipping; RG59 862A.191 (Internal Affairs of State Relating to Exhibitions and Fairs in Germany) Box 5225, US National Archives, College Park, MD.

21   H. B. McCoy to John McCloy, August 16, 1950, RG59 862A.191 (Internal Affairs of State Relating to Exhibitions and Fairs in Germany) Box 5225, US National Archives, College Park, MD; Ellwood, *Rebuilding Europe*, 137; Jennifer A. Loehlin, *From Rugs to Riches: Housework, Consumption and Modernity in Germany* (Oxford: Berg, 1999), 52; Michael Wildt, "Changes in Consumption as Social Practice in West Germany During the 1950s," in Strasser, McGovern and Judt, eds., *Getting and Spending: European and American Consumer Societies in the Twentieth Century* (Cambridge, England: Cambridge University Press, 1998) 305.

22   Telegram, Page to US Secretary of State, October 17, 1950, RG59 862A.191 (Internal Affairs of State Relating to Exhibitions and Fairs in Germany) Box 5225, US National Archives, College Park, MD.

23   Paul Shinkman, "Trade Fair Participation," *New York Times*, June 20, 1955.

24   Paul Shinkman to Secretary of State, October 15, 1950, RG59 862A.191 (Internal Affairs of State Relating to Exhibitions and Fairs in Germany) Box 5225, US National Archives, College Park, MD.

25   Telegram, John McCoy to US Secretary of State, September 22, 1950, RG59 862A.191 (Internal Affairs of State Relating to Exhibitions and Fairs in Germany) Box 5225, US National Archives, College Park, MD.

26   Webb, Frankfurt Office of the US High Commander for Germany (HICOG) to HICOG Berlin, September 12, 1950, RG59 862A.191 (Internal Affairs of State Relating to Exhibitions and Fairs in Germany) Box 5225, US National Archives, College Park, MD.

27   Heinrich König, "Ausstellung: 'Wir bauen ein besseres Leben," *Architektur und Wohnform* 61, no. 2 (November 1952): 87.

28   Berlin Industrial Fair 1952," HICOG Berlin to US Department of State, November 5, 1952, RG59 862A.191 (Internal Affairs of State Relating to Exhibitions and Fairs in Germany) Box 5225, US National Archives, College Park, MD.

29   Paul Maddrell, *Spying on Science: Western Intelligence in Divided Berlin* (Oxford and New York: Oxford University Press, 2006), 125.

30   Barbara Kirshenblatt-Gimblett, *Destination Culture: Tourism, Museums and Heritage* (Berkeley and Los Angeles: University of California Press, 1998), 1.

31   HICOG Bonn to US Department of State Bureau of German Affairs, May 31, 1952, RG59 862A.191 (Internal Affairs of State Relating to Exhibitions and Fairs in Germany) Box 5225, US National Archives, College Park, MD.

32   HICOG Bonn, May 31, 1952.

33   Details of the initial contact by American officials in Europe with Hans Knoll, who died in a 1955 auto accident during a business trip to Cuba, remain hazy. Florence Knoll later recalled that she "had never been quite sure how they got the [State Department] contract, but that this was just the kind of thing Hans was good at." Eric Larrabee and Massimo Vignelli, *Knoll Design* (New York: Harry Abrams, 1981), 176.

34   Carlo Spagnolo, "The Bretton Woods system and the birth of the European Payments Union (1945–1958). Afterthoughts on recent US-Europe clashes on the post-Cold War order," paper presented at the conference "Governing European Monetary Union: Political, Economic, Legal, Historical Perspectives," Florence, October 3–4, 2003, 2. The vision of a "United States of Europe," beginning with the economic unification of Western Europe, was heavily promoted by Henry R. Luce, the editor-in-chief of the influential business magazine *Fortune*, in the immediate postwar years as well; see, for example, the editorial "European Unity: Dream and Hard Reality," *Fortune* 35, no. 3 (March 1947): 2–3.

35   Michael J. Hogan, *The Marshall Plan: America, Britain, and the Reconstruction of Western Europe, 1947–1952* (Cambridge and New York: Cambridge University Press, 1987), 208–10.

36   "After the war," Florence Knoll later recalled, "we were asked to design government projects and produce furniture and fabric in Europe with counterpart dollars": Florence Knoll Bassett, "The Conversation," *Metropolis* 20 (July 2001): 94. The project to build new US consular offices and housing in cities across West Germany, commissioned by Leland W. King of the State Department's Office of Foreign Buildings Operations with architectural design coordinated by Skidmore Owings and Merrill, made extensive use of Knoll pieces. Jane C. Loeffler, *The Architecture of Diplomacy: Building America's Embassies* (New York: Princeton Architectural Press, 1998), 98.

37   L. P. Schreiber, "American Showroom in Germany," *Design* (London) no. 49 (January 1953): 12.

38   Author's interview with Florence Knoll Bassett, Miami, March 2001. Knoll, who had studied under Mies at the Illinois Institute of Technology, convinced him to allow Knoll International to put his leather and steel furniture back into production by guaranteeing that it would never be manufactured in colors or materials unforeseen by Mies himself.

39   While documentation of Kaufmann's role in the 1952 show is sketchy, memoranda of two MSA meetings, of July 21 and 23, 1952, note a contract with the Museum of Modern Art without noting a specific curator. RG59/150/71/35/04, Entry 5323, Box 8 (Records of the International Information Administration, Subject Files, European Field Program 1949–1952, US National Archives, College Park, MD. An August 1952 memo from Elmer Lower of the HICOG Office of Public Affairs, concerning an international "Design for Use" show planned by Stuttgart's Landesgewerbeamt, states: "It is my suggestion that [...] the [US State] Department consult people in the design field, such as Mr. Edgar Kaufmann from the Museum of Modern Art, so that a representative group of high quality materials is sent." Elmer Lower to Richard Brecker, RG59 862A.191, Internal Affairs of State Relating to Exhibitions and Fairs in Germany, Box 5227, US National Archives, College Park, MD. MoMA's archives mention the museum's involvement in "US Selections for Berlin Trade Fair," a traveling European design show. See Gay McDonald, "Selling the American Dream: MoMA, Industrial Design and Post-War France," *Journal of Design History* 17, no. 4 (2004): 398.

40   Betty Pepsis, "For the Home: 'Good Design' is International," *New York Times*, January 16, 1951.

41   John McCloy to US Secretary of State, June 30, 1952, RG59 862A.191
     (Internal Affairs of State Relating to Exhibitions and Fairs in Germany)
     Box 5225, US National Archives, College Park, MD.

42   "Productivity and Integration Make for Higher Standard of Living,"
     March 1953, RG 286/Ger 2219-2226, Visual Collection, US National Archive,
     College Park, MD.

43   "We Build a Better Life," undated typescript, RG59/150/71/35/04, Entry 5323,
     Box 8 (Records of the International Information Administration, Subject Files,
     European Field Program 1949–52), US National Archives, College Park, MD.

44   Article in *Der Tag*, September 22, 1952, translated and quoted in Lyon to
     Secretary of State, September 22, 1952, RG59 862A.191 (Internal Affairs of
     State Relating to Exhibitions and Fairs in Germany) Box 5225, US National
     Archives, College Park, MD.

45   Heinrich König, "Ausstellung: 'Wir bauen ein besseres Leben," *Architektur
     und Wohnform* 61, no. 2 (November 1952): 87.

46   Alfons Leitl, "Die Wohnkultur der Westlichen Völker," *Baukunst und
     Werkform* 5, no. 12 (December 1952): 40.

47   Article in *Der Tag*, September 22, 1952, translated and quoted in Lyon to
     Secretary of State, September 22, 1952, RG59 862A.191 (Internal Affairs of
     State Relating to Exhibitions and Fairs in Germany) Box 5225, US National
     Archives, College Park, MD.

48   Louise S. Robbins, "The Overseas Libraries Controversy and the Freedom
     to Read: U.S. Librarians and Publishers Confront Joseph McCarthy," *Libraries
     & Culture* 36, no. 1 (Winter 2001): 28

49   Kenneth Osgood, *Total Cold War: Eisenhower's Secret Propaganda Battle
     at Home and Abroad* (Lawrence: University of Kansas Press, 2006), 218.

50   Walter Hixson, *Parting the Curtain: Propaganda, Culture, and the Cold War*
     (New York: St. Martin's Press, 1997), 122.

51   Osgood, *Total Cold War*, 220.

52   Warren Unna, "We're Set to be Shamed at Brussels," *Washington Post*,
     January 26, 1958.

53   Hixson, *Parting the Curtain*, 141.

54   "Boston to Get World's Fair Preview," *Boston Globe*, November 24, 1957;
     Cynthia Kellogg, "An American Brussels Fair Designer Gives French Home
     Modern Look," *New York Times*, December 4, 1957.

55   "American Design Preview: Brussels World's Fair," undated press release,
     Institute of Contemporary Art archives, Boston.

56   Marjorie J. Harlepp, "U.S. Revises Home Show at Fair Site," *New York Times*,
     June 6, 1958.

57   Robert Haddow, *Pavilions of Plenty: Exhibiting American Culture Abroad
     in the 1950s* (Washington, DC: Smithsonian Institution Press, 1997), 148–58.

58   Asa McKercher, "The Art of Soft Power at Expo 67: *Creative America*
     and Cultural Diplomacy in the US Pavilion." *Journal of Curatorial Studies* 5,
     no. 3 (2016): 377, 382; Jack Masey and Conway Lloyd Morgan, *Cold War
     Confrontations: US Exhibitions and Their Role in the Cultural Cold War*
     (Baden, Switzerland: Lars Müller Publications, 2008), 340.

59   Masey and Morgan, 344–46.

60   Hixson, *Parting the Curtain*, 166.

61   Nelson's Storagewall, America's first wall system for home storage, was
     featured in a 1945 spread by *Life* magazine, catapulting Nelson from a career
     in architecture to national fame as a designer of modern home furnishings.
     By 1948, Nelson was experimenting with a modular storage system using
     aluminum tubes in standardized sizes to construct a free-standing grid that
     supported shelves and cabinets in a variety of configurations, as determined
     by user need. A decade later, his modular home storage systems were
     available in major department stores. Cynthia Kellogg, "The Evolution of
     Storage: From Clothes Closet to Built-In Walls," *New York Times*, July 1, 1958;
     Stanley Abercrombie, *George Nelson: The Design of Modern Design*
     (Cambridge, MA: MIT Press, 1995), 69–72.

62   Haddow, *Pavilions of Plenty*, 212.

63   Alexander R. Hammer, "Suburban Do-It-Yourselfer Shows the World How,"
     New York Times, May 12, 1956.

64   "Housewife Did Lots of Washing, More Talking at Moscow Fair,"
     Washington Post, December 17, 1959.

65   Abercrombie, *George Nelson*, 333, fn. 18.

66   Rita Rief, "US Exhibit For Moscow Taxing Staff," *New York Times*, March 23,
     1959. The US Department of Commerce estimated the average American
     family income in 1959 to be $5400: "Current Population Reports,
     Consumer Income," *Series P-60*, no. 35 (January 5, 1961): 1.

67   Cristina Carbone, "Setting the Stage for the Kitchen Debate: Architecture
     at the American National Exhibition in Moscow of 1959," paper presented
     at the "Cold War in the Kitchen" conference, Munich, 2005.

68   Rief, "US Exhibit For Moscow Taxing Staff," 24.

69   "Russians to See Ranch-Style Home that is Typically American Throughout,"
     New York Times, April 8, 1959.

70   "Reds Belittle Exhibit of a Typical US Home," *Washington Post*, April 10, 1959.

71   Hixon, *Parting the Curtain*, 179.

72   James Reston, "A Debate of Politicians," *New York Times*, July 25, 1959.

73   Haddow, *Pavilions of Plenty*, 216.

74   Comments by Nixon and Khrushchev have been pieced together from
     various sources. As Hans N. Tuch has noted, "To the best of this writer's
     knowledge there is no verbatim record of this 'kitchen debate,' only
     what the newsmen pieced together either directly or from the interpreters."
     Hans N. Tuch, *Communicating with the World: U.S. Public Diplomacy Overseas*
     (New York: St. Martin's Press, 1990), 63.

75   Malvina Lindsay, "U.S. Typical Home Enters Cold War," *Washington Post
     and Times Herald* (April 20, 1959).

76   1960 USIA Annual Report, quoted in Hixson, *Parting the Curtain*, 210.

77   Beatriz Colomina, "The Exhibitionist House," in *At the End of the Century:
     One Hundred Years of Architecture*, Richard Koshalek and Elizabeth A. T.
     Smith, eds. (New York: Harry Abrams, 1998), 139.

78   Alex Wilson and Jessica Boehland, "Small is Beautiful: U.S. House Size,
     Resource Use, and the Environment," *Journal of Industrial Ecology* 9, no. 1-2
     (Winter-Spring 2005): 278.

79   Lynette Evans, "Increasing portion size not just an eating problem,"
     San Francisco Chronicle, August 13, 2005; Fred A. Bernstein, "Are McMansions
     Going out of Style?" *New York Times*, October 2, 2005; Robert J. Samuelson,
     "Homes as Hummers," *Washington Post*, July 13, 2005; Kathleen Lynn,
     "Experts predict greener new homes," *The Record*, August 12, 2007; Margot
     Adler, "Behind the Ever-Expanding American Dream Home," US Census
     Bureau, "Households by Type and Size: 1900-2002," no. HS 12, Statistical
     Abstracts of the United States, 2002; http://www.npr.org/templates/story/
     stosry/php:storyId=5525283, accessed August 17, 2007.

80   Fredrich Bergström and Robert Gidehag, *EU versus USA* (Stockholm:
     Timbro, 2004), 24.

81   Australian Conservation Foundation, "Consuming Australia: Main Findings,"
     http://www.acfonline.org.au, accessed August 20, 2007.

82   "Affluenza," http://www.pbs.org/kcts/affluenza/diag/what.html, accessed
     August 17, 2007.

European Émigrés and American Commercial Design

Transatlantic Transfers in Mid-Century Marketing

Jan Logemann

Will Burtin, Walter Landor, Marianne Strengell — many of the individuals connected to the exhibitions discussed in this catalogue were European immigrants and émigrés.[1] A number of them had come to the United States to pursue careers in commercial design, and several had fled political and racial persecution on the continent during the 1930s and 1940s. Indeed, the mid-century American world of goods highlighted by these exhibitions drew heavily on transatlantic exchanges. This essay will highlight the broader impact of European émigré designers on mid-century American marketing. These émigrés helped promote the professionalization of commercial design in the United States and contributed to the emergence of a modernist design aesthetic that characterized postwar consumer goods. They were also at the forefront of "consumer engineering" in American marketing, heralding an increased reliance on consumer psychology combined with a new emphasis on graphic and industrial design.

After World War II, European émigrés frequently took on the role of transatlantic mediators in marketing. They translated aspects of American consumer modernity "back" to their European homelands and assured European elites that commercial marketing was nothing foreign, but instead connected back to interwar European traditions of design and notions of "good form." Postwar European marketing experts began to pay close attention to the styling of goods, package designs, and commercial imagery that émigré designers presented in exhibitions such as the ones organized by Burtin. Thus, many of the same immigrants who had been involved with shaping American mass consumption since the 1930s became active protagonists in a process long discussed as an "Americanization" of Western European mass consumption, but which turns out to have been much more reciprocal and complex than commonly assumed.

Mid-century "consumer engineering" placed a new emphasis on professional, systematic marketing. In 1932, the advertising professionals Roy Sheldon and Egmont Arens had suggested that "consumer engineering" would be crucial for companies to respond to the

FIGURE 18 Felix Müller and Karl Oskar Blase, "Industrial and Fine-Art Printing in the USA," 1954. Poster for an exhibition at Amerika Haus Berlin 1954. Color screen print, 36 ¾ × 27 ¼ in. *Prints & Photographs Division, Library of Congress, LC-DIG-ds-07680.*

challenges of crisis and competition.[2] Writing at the height of the Great Depression, the authors defined "consumer engineering" as "shaping a product to fit more exactly consumers' needs or tastes. [... In] its widest sense it includes any plan to stimulate the consumption of goods," including the introduction of modern design and styling.[3] New experts in "humaneering," they demanded, needed to tackle the "deeper and subtler problems [... of] the sociologist and the psychologist."[4] Consumer engineering called for the systematic inclusion of psychological consumer research and modern design in the industrial process. This, in turn, opened the door to both academics and artists to play a much greater role within professional marketing — and many Americans, including Sheldon and Arens, looked to European art and psychology for inspiration. European designers who crossed the Atlantic in the interwar years would benefit from this new trend, as did numerous social-science émigrés such as Paul Lazarsfeld, George Katona, and Alfred Politz. They helped establish new market research methods and approaches to consumer study in the United States. Viennese immigrant Ernest Dichter opened an Institute for Motivation Research that employed in-depth interviews and Freudian psychology to probe the unconscious motives of consumers.[5]

Design, too, became an increasingly important factor in marketing. Informal "fashion intermediaries" such as retail buyers had long provided industry with a sense of changing consumer tastes and up-to-date styles.[6] By the interwar decades, product design and styling became more systematically integrated into the production process. In retailing, department store displays and new shopping environments required professional design expertise. At the same time, modern art increasingly found its way into commercial graphic design for advertising, product packaging, and corporate public relations. Looking beyond individual products, mid-century designers ultimately helped develop the concepts of brand image and corporate identity. Even more, they offered a vision of consumer modernity that promised to fulfill the physiological and psychological needs and aspirations of consumers.

Over the course of the mid-century, a new profession of commercial designers emerged in the United States, replete with professional organizations and new educational programs. Design and consumer research were integrated into the marketing process through specialized corporate departments, advertising agencies, and independent studios. French-born industrial designer Raymond Loewy, whose firm was represented in the Burtin exhibit, exemplified a new generation of nationally known industrial design consultants that rose to prominence during the 1930s.[7] Loewy and his colleagues saw themselves as consumer engineers who could bring creative impulses and aesthetic expertise to consumer marketing. For his designs, Loewy claimed to draw on the latest insights of academic sociology and psychology, but especially on his experiences with manufacturers. A design consultant "in all fields of manufacturing — from lipstick to locomotives," Loewy promised the attendees of a 1944 marketing conference that design innovations could achieve "extraordinary things" for the postwar economy in the United States and overseas.[8] Significantly, the fact that he was born and educated in Europe added special cachet to Loewy's claim to aesthetic expertise at a time when European modernism commanded significant attention in the United States.

ÉMIGRÉS AND
THE PROFESSIONALIZATION
OF "AMERICAN" DESIGN

Indeed, numerous European immigrants and émigrés helped to shape the nascent American design profession. Partially, this reflected a fascination with modernism in graphic and industrial design among American trade publications such as *Advertising Arts*. In 1935, architect Ely Kahn praised European design education and observed a pervasive notion that "an object to be interesting [had to] be made in Paris, Berlin, or some exotic corner in Europe." While American design had made great strides especially with consumer durables, he noted: "I venture the [...] premise that many of the designs made in America for goods also made here were executed by Europeans, or Americans trained in Europe."[9] Even after World War II, historian Jeffrey Meikle notes, many US design- ers felt like "second-grade citizens" in their own country, because the postwar American debate about "good design" was often cast in European terms and because émigrés such as Walter Gropius or Ludwig Mies van der Rohe seemingly dominated public design in the United States.[10]

European-born immigrants such as Raymond Loewy and György Kepes contributed to a transfer of design forms and methods of education from interwar Europe to mid-century America. Most prominently, émigrés from the Bauhaus (along with radical modernists allied with CIAM, the Congress International d'Architecture Moderne) provided a major transatlantic influence.[11] Their emigration during the 1930s helped to establish the modernist ideals of "good form" in the United States.[12] Among the first Bauhaus members to cross the Atlantic were Joseph and Anni Albers and the graphic artist Xanti Schawinsky, who each took up teaching positions at Black Mountain College in North Carolina. Other former Bauhaus members followed into American exile. In August of 1937, Marcel Breuer and Herbert Bayer crossed the Atlantic to meet up with Gropius, who had recently accepted a posi- tion at Harvard's School of Design. While Bayer became a freelance design consultant in New York, Breuer followed Gropius to Boston and the two launched a private architec- ture firm together. The Bauhaus group appealed to US institu- tions for their reputation as part of the radical European design avant-garde.[13]

"European" modernism, however, crossed the Atlantic in many different forms, and European immigrants could be found at nearly all major centers of design education in the United States during the 1930s. It was not just Bauhaus masters Gropius at Harvard, Laszlo Moholy-Nagy in Chicago, or Josef Albers at Black Mountain College who left their mark on the American profession. Alexander Dorner, for example,

had studied in Berlin and was director of the State Museum in Hannover before he headed the Rhode Island School of Design from 1937 to 1941. Peter Müller-Munk took over the design program established by Donald Dohner at Pittsburgh's Carnegie Institute. He, too, had been born and raised in Berlin in the early decades of the twentieth century. One of the most successful kitchenware designers of his time, he had studied with Bruno Paul in Berlin and later became president of the US Society of Industrial Designers. They all were part of a broader modernist design reform movement that was swept from interwar Europe to the United States, and their students would include some of the most prominent designers of postwar America.[14]

Immigrant designers could be found in various fields. Some, like Walter Baermann or railroad designer Otto Kuhler, came out of engineering or technical drafting with an affinity for designing for the "machine age."[15] Many female immi- grants were able to carve out professional spaces for them- selves in interior design as well as in textiles and household wares.[16] Bauhaus designer Anni Albers's work in textiles at Black Mountain College influenced a new generation of American artists. Her weaving workshop, along with the workshops taught by Finnish immigrants Loja Saarinen and Marianne Strengell at Cranbrook (prominently on display in Knoll's exhibit) and by German émigré Marli Ehrman at the Chicago Institute of Design, helped bring constructivist ideas in textile design across the Atlantic. Noted for her work in ceramics, Eva Zeisel (née Stricker) had been educated in Hungary and came to the United States via Vienna with her husband, market researcher Hans Zeisel.[17] In graphic design, European-born artists such as Herbert Bayer, György Kepes, Herbert Matter **[FIGURE 19]**, and Leo Lionni helped shape the visual appearance of American advertising and corporate design.

By 1950, works by European-born designers and their American students were featured prominently in the Museum of Modern Art's nationally recognized "Good Design" exhibi- tions. Their aesthetic language had become part of the American mainstream. Some of the émigrés embraced design as a form of consumer engineering. Others remained more critical of new forms of "styling" to create consumer demand, emphasizing the role of designers as artists rather than as marketing specialists. Still, both as protagonists and as critics of consumer engineering, European émigrés were crucial in shaping commercial design in the United States.

FIGURE 19 Herbert Matter, Knoll Inc. advertisement featuring
Stig Lindberg's *Apples*, Astrid Sampe's *Stripes*, and Noémi Raymond's
Chinese Coins, 1948. *Courtesy Knoll Inc.*

ÉMIGRÉ CAREERS IN MID-CENTURY DESIGN

The careers of Lazlo Moholy-Nagy, Herbert Bayer, Walter Landor, and Hans Knoll exemplify the breadth and diversity of European influences on American design. They highlight different roles played by émigrés in shaping mid-century consumer goods.

Laszlo Moholy-Nagy:
Design Education at the American Bauhaus

The establishment of the "American" or "New" Bauhaus in Chicago in 1937 marked perhaps the most comprehensive effort to introduce European modernism to American commercial design education. The program's director, László Moholy-Nagy, had been one of the most radical design theorists in interwar Europe.[18] After World War I he had fled Hungary for Berlin, then imbued with ideas of artistic constructivism. In 1920 he met Walter Gropius and settled at the Weimar Bauhaus, where his ideological radicalism quickly translated into an experimental approach to photography and painting. Moholy-Nagy became one of the leading Bauhaus theorists, and his artwork reflected the functionalist philosophy of the school during the 1920s. He stood for a comprehensive artistic and social approach, a "totality of vision" that did not mesh easily with commercial demands. Like many of his Bauhaus colleagues, however, Moholy-Nagy also did industrial design and advertising work during the early 1930s.[19]

Moholy-Nagy was invited to create a new design school by the Association for Arts and Industries in Chicago. These area business interests had looked specifically for a Bauhaus émigré in hopes of bring a cutting-edge design program to the Midwest. Once Moholy-Nagy arrived in the United States, he quickly set out to recruit faculty from among both American and émigré modernists such as György Kepes. Sibyl Moholy-Nagy, who later became connected to TES director and fellow German émigré Annemarie Henle Pope, encouraged her husband early on to focus on design for commercial purposes.[20] In spite of this, the "American Bauhaus" and its successor organizations remained small, financially struggling, and continuously on the verge of closure between 1938 and 1946. The Bauhaus vision of comprehensive design education frequently clashed with the practical needs of Chicago corporations. Moholy-Nagy was at odds with American business culture, vehemently attacking such conceits as "streamlining" and other overly commercialized design trends.[21]

Still, the American Bauhaus garnered a great deal of attention among American designers, and its records show much successful interaction between European émigrés and corporate America. No one touted the school's business potential more vigorously than Walter Paepcke, president of the Container Corporation of America (CCA). Paepcke was a second-generation German-American dedicated to promoting modern art in industry.[22] As Moholy-Nagy's school was struggling, Paepcke helped to keep it afloat through generous donations and active fundraising efforts among his colleagues. Indeed, the American Bauhaus built a sizeable support network during the 1940s. Renamed the Institute of Design in 1942, the school's board of directors included such influential businessmen as William Patterson of United Airlines, John Kraft of Kraft Foods, Herbert Johnson of S.C. Johnson & Son, Don Mitchell of Sylvania Electric, and Edgar Kaufmann of Kaufmann Department stores in Pittsburgh.[23]

The school collaborated on design projects with area companies and offered night classes to their employees. Moholy-Nagy presented his school's design work nationally at advertising companies such as J. Walter Thompson. The most lasting impact of the New Bauhaus on American commercial design, however, was its influence on professional design education. Shortly before his death in 1946, Moholy-Nagy participated in the Museum of Modern Art's conference "Industrial Design: A New Profession." He, Bernard Rudofsky, and other émigrés critiqued what they perceived as "American" trends toward "artificial obsolescence" and advertised "novelty." Many of the assembled designers (including European immigrants such as Loewy) vehemently disagreed with their views, but when it came to design education even the most ardent "consumer engineers" deferred to Moholy-Nagy.[24] Joseph Hudnut introduced him as "the most able and vigorous and successful pioneer in educational discipline based upon objective analysis of the modern scene. We imitate him at Harvard and he is imitated over the world."[25] Moholy-Nagy's emphasis on practical teaching of fundamentals and abstract concepts of space, color, and material resonated with the assembled leaders of mid-century American design. Many students of the school and its teachers became successful designers and are represented in the exhibitions discussed here, including Angelo Testa and Ben Rose in textiles, James Prestini in wallpapers, and advertising artist Saul Bass.

Herbert Bayer:
A "New Type" of Artist

Few émigrés illustrate the close mid-century ties between art and commerce better than graphic designer Herbert Bayer. He, too, came from the Bauhaus, where he had been in charge of the advertising workshop from 1925 to 1928.[26] Bayer's work and teaching at the Bauhaus were geared toward the psychological effects and commercial potentials of graphic design. His photomontage and collage work won acclaim at the first exhibition of European advertising art in New York in 1927.[27] Bayer's embrace of new technologies in advertising quickly translated into commercial work. He left the Bauhaus to work as an art director for Condé Nast's *Vogue* and for the advertising agency Dorland in Berlin. He headed the American-owned agency's graphic design subsidiary "Studio Dorland" for much of the 1930s. Here, Bayer put his interest in modern art to commercial application in campaigns for new consumer products such as Telefunken records, Boehringer cold medication, and Venus underwear.[28]

Building on Bauhaus ties and on his connections to Dorland and *Vogue*, Bayer left Germany for the United States in 1938.[29] Upon coming to America, he helped prepare the Bauhaus exhibition at MoMA and soon made a good living as an independent design consultant in New York City.[30] One of his first professional contacts was Robert Lincoln Leslie of the Brooklyn-based graphic arts agency The Composing Room, who had helped several émigrés get their start in commercial New York.[31] Bayer created posters for New York Subways Advertising Inc. and did freelance work for Wanamaker's department stores and for magazines including *LIFE* and *Fortune*.[32] When Peter Piening left *LIFE* magazine to become art director at *Fortune* in 1941, Bayer got Walter Gropius to write Henry Luce on his behalf. Bayer, Gropius wrote, would be a "most ingenious and versatile art director" with innovative ideas for the magazine.[33]

Yet Bauhaus modernism still pushed the boundaries of accepted commercial design, as Bayer found out working for J. Walter Thompson in 1944. He experienced the leading Madison Avenue ad agency to be rather conservative and quickly ran afoul of his co-workers in the creative department. "Bayer's type of art was new to this country and was entirely different to anything existing here," one of his JWT colleagues recalled in a 1950s interview, and "his form of art was not accepted" within the creative department. "I will say that Bayer's form of art is generally accepted now," he was quick to add. "[Bayer] was years in advance of our thinking at that period of time."[34] Several other former JWT co-workers mirrored the sentiment that during the mid-1940s Bayer had

been "too advanced" for the agency and that the quality and commercial potential of his artistic style had not been adequately recognized.

Bayer brought to American graphic art the same attention to consumer psychology and its commercial ramifications that had infused his work since the 1920s. In workshops for the American Advertising Guild he taught the use of montages and jarring pictorial contrasts in magazine ads. Bayer tried to "influence his students to aim for the emotions of people," Percy Seitlin wrote in the trade journal *A-D*, insisting that they must understand the psychological interplay between stimulus and response in order to create attention. Bayer's techniques, Seitlin concluded, "were progressive and modern because they try to utilize a body of knowledge about psychology as it relates to design. They are not art for art's sake."[35]

After World War II, Bayer attained national renown as a modernist art director and as a "new type of artist" who continuously straddled the line between art and commerce. His most recognized contributions to American advertising included ads for the Container Corporation of America's (CCA) "Great Ideas of Western Man" campaign initiated by Dutch-born graphic designer Leo Lionni at N. W. Ayer.[36] CCA had already built up a strong design department during the 1930s, recruiting modern artists such as A. M. Cassandre from France and Toni Zepf from Germany. Chairman Walter Paepcke was instrumental in organizing a 1945 Art Institute of Chicago exhibition on "Modern Art in Advertising" that featured Bayer prominently alongside Cassandre, Jean Carlu, and other luminaries of interwar European poster design.[37] Bayer and Paepcke connected over a shared interest in art in industry, and the designer followed Paepcke's invitation to come to Aspen, Colorado, where Bayer became regional director of the International Design Conference. He devoted a significant share of its postwar activities to promoting transatlantic exchanges at the intersection of modern art and corporate capitalism.[38]

FIGURE 20   Walter Landor, advertisement for Bel-Air frozen vegetables. *Whitney Frozen Food Co., Sacramento, CA. Landor Design Collection, Archives Center, National Museum of American History, Smithsonian Institution.*

Walter Landor:
The Designer as Brand Engineer

German émigré Walter Landor's legacy presents a very different case, highlighting the growing use of consumer research in mid-century design. Based in San Francisco, Landor's design consultancy resembled the East Coast studios of Raymond Loewy and other design stars. Initially his client base was regionally focused and limited to the food and beverage industry. His firm had a dozen packages for frozen fish, fruits and vegetables, and other products included in Burtin's "Containers & Packaging" exhibit **[FIGURE 20]**. Over the course of the 1950s, Landor Associates had broadened its business portfolio, developed its own approach to research-driven design, and ultimately emerged as one of the leading American firms in brand and corporate identity design.[39]

Also rooted in interwar European modernism, Walter Landor became part of a sizeable group of European-born designers and architects who had settled in California since the 1920s, including Kem Weber, Richard Neutra, and Victor Gruen.[40] Born as Walter Landauer into a Jewish-German family in Munich in 1913, Landor early on developed an affinity toward modern art. "I grew up in my father's office. He was one of the Bauhaus architects," Landor misleadingly claimed in a 1992 interview, suggesting that as a teenage boy he was "influenced already [...] by the Werkbund movement, which believed that design was an important part of the everyday environment."[41] Instead of the Bauhaus, however, it was the British design world in which Landor received his first significant professional experiences. During the early 1930s he received his initial training in both advertising design and market research at the London-based advertising agency W. S. Crawford. Later he joined Milner Gray and Sasha Black's "Industrial Design Partnership" during the 1930s.[42] The firm pioneered modernist designs, pursued early "corporate identi-fication schemes," and engaged in research for design.[43]

When his firm was commissioned to plan a pavilion at the New York World's Fair, Landor crossed the Atlantic in 1939. He quickly became acquainted with leading American designers, many of whom had their own pavilion projects at the fair. He met with Viennese émigré and "father of the mall" Victor Gruen, Walter Teague, Gilbert Rhode, and, of course, Raymond Loewy. Introduced by émigré socialite Anita Warburg, Landor was able to study industrial design at Henry Dreyfuss's studios.[44] With Europe embroiled in war, Landor decided to settle in San Francisco, and initially found employment teaching industrial design at the California College of Arts and Crafts before opening Landor Associates as an independent design office in 1941. San Francisco's dearth of industrial production led him to focus on packaging and labeling for food and beverages with early clients such as the food distributer S&W. In campaigns for Sick's Beer of Seattle and other firms he began to use design as a form of strategic marketing.[45]

By the 1950s, Landor Associates was one of the leading design studios on the West Coast. The firm's offices at Pier 5, adjacent to the San Francisco harbor, now employed dozens of designers, and its client portfolio had expanded to other regions and branches of industry. Eventually, the firm gained national recognition, employing "about three hundred artists at any given time around the world," according to Landor.[46] The firm's success was built heavily on the use of consumer research. Initially, this entailed unsystematic consumer surveys at supermarkets conducted by the designers themselves, who interviewed patrons about product design preferences.[47] Soon, however, the firm had its own research department, which conducted surveys and consumer panels and commissioned outside studies from the Institute for Motivational Research headed by émigré consumption expert Ernest Dichter.[48]

Landor Associates referred to their integration of consumer research into the various steps of the design process as "consumer response design." In their own work, the design studio used motivation research tools to elicit and record consumer responses, including consumer observations of supermarket behavior, panel tests, and in-depth individual interviews.[49] Experimental research analyzed a given prod-uct's visual properties, and eye cameras were used to deter-mine the direction of the shopper's gaze and to measure how quickly a product could be recognized and categorized by

consumers. The firm's research facilities even included a small mock supermarket in which researchers could study consumers under "laboratory conditions."[50]

To the consumer engineer Landor, self-service stores were "machines for selling" whose design depended on consumer psychology and effective merchandising, "aiding and abetting the package."[51] A 1957 *Good Packaging* feature on Landor's retail design noted: "A rare product succeeds today without being dressed right; dressed to make the right kind of consumer impression." Successfully researched package design, Landor explained, achieved "impulse purchase appeal," inspiring confidence and conveying a "feeling" of the product, a "package personality" that carried well in visual advertising and was "styled for instant recognition."[52] While he saw himself within the tradition of European design modernism, Landor, much like Raymond Loewy, counted among those immigrants who most directly promoted marketing-oriented design in the United States and ultimately back in Europe.

Hans and Florence Knoll:
Design as Transatlantic Business

In 1961, the German journal *Deutsche Bauzeitung* observed: "A European style emigrated, conquered America and then returned to a burned-out Europe, to succeed most rapidly in the very country where once [...] it had generated so much enmity as to be condemned and exiled." The article was devoted to the tenth anniversary of the design furniture firm Knoll International on the German market. "The return to Germany of the ideas and forms [...] of the Twenties and Thirties, came about after the Second World War. [...] Since the beginning of the Forties, Knoll International in America has continued to a great degree to advance the work of European Avant-garde architects in liberating design from the false and the showy."[53] Founded in 1939 by immigrant entrepreneur Hans Knoll, the design firm came to define "modern" furniture for corporations and high-end consumers on both sides of the Atlantic.[54] His wife and business partner Florence, furthermore, was among the most prominent postwar interior designers. She curated the textile exhibit "Contemporary American Textiles," intended to circulate through American cultural centers, schools, trade fairs, and museums around Europe.

From its inception, Knoll Associates thrived on a business model that brought modern design to commercial furniture. Walter Knoll, the founder's father, owned a furniture firm in interwar Germany, which drew on design innovations by Werkbund and Bauhaus artists.[55] Hans Knoll, born in 1914, learned the furniture trade in the family business and spent time abroad working for Plan Ltd. in Great Britain.[56] The firm

FIGURE 21   Portrait of Florence Knoll, photographer unknown.
Courtesy Knoll Inc.

specialized in metal-tube designs and was headed by
Serge Chermayeff, a Russian émigré who later moved to the
United States and succeeded Moholy-Nagy as director of the
Institute of Design.[57] Intent on leaving Nazi Germany and his
father's firm, Hans Knoll decided in 1938 to form his own
business in the United States.[58] While setting up his Chicago
school, Moholy-Nagy received a letter from his wife, Sibyl,
who was then still in England. She told her husband of Hans
Knoll, a young man dealing in patent furniture, who was bringing "quite new and interesting ideas" with him.[59] Indeed, the
transatlantic transfer of design was part of a conscious business plan for Knoll, who wanted to bring "modern
furniture" to the United States. "It was my whole idea," he
later claimed, "to develop new products working with well-
known designers and to encourage their particular talents."[60]

Upon arrival in New York City he incorporated Hans G. Knoll
Furniture Inc. in 1939.[61] The company struggled in its early
years, lacking designers who could create furniture. An early
associate was Danish-born architect Jens Risom, who
designed the first line of furniture for the company.[62]

The company's eventual impact on transatlantic design
and marketing history was largely due to two factors closely
connected to Hans's wife, Florence Knoll: its vast network of
modernist designers; and its new and systematic approach to
interior design. Celebrated as the "First Lady of the modern
office," Florence Knoll **[FIGURE 21]** stands out as one of the few
prominent women among the mid-century consumer engineers, and it was she, more so than Hans, who was well
connected within leading design circles in the United States.[63]
She had been trained as an architect at the Cranbrook

FIGURE 22 View of Florence Knoll-designed interior featuring Barcelona chairs and ottoman by Ludwig Mies van der Rohe, 1951. *Photograph Robert Damora © Damora Archive, all rights reserved.*

Academy under the tutelage of Finnish-born architect Eliel Saarinen as part of a new generation of leading designers including Eero Saarinen, Charles and Ray Eames, Harry Bertoia, and Ralph Rapson. She later studied in London and worked as an apprentice to Marcel Breuer and Walter Gropius in Boston. In 1941 she finished her education at the Illinois Institute of Technology under the supervision of Ludwig Mies van der Rohe. Her connections to European émigrés were a crucial asset to the young company, which by the early 1950s opened showrooms across the United States.

Knoll Associates built up a substantial network of modernist designers, many of them immigrants, such as Italian-born designer Harry Bertoia, whose lattice steel-wire Diamond chairs were among the most notable pieces of the Knoll collection.[64] Milan-trained Franco Albini contributed glass-topped desks and wire-and-glass shelving. Pierre Jeanneret, the Swiss-born cousin of Le Corbusier, had his Scissor chair sold through Knoll.[65] Knoll reproduced numerous Bauhaus designs under licensing agreements, including Breuer's Wassily chair and Mies van der Rohe's Barcelona chair[66] **[FIGURE 22]**. Eero Saarinen, too, contributed several designs to their collection, including the Womb chair in 1946 and his iconic molded Tulip chair in 1956.[67] In addition to designers from Cranbrook and the Pratt Institute, the network also included artists from countries such as Argentina and Japan. Still, most Knoll contributors were influenced by a functionalist modernism that had been particularly prevalent in interwar Europe.

In creating the modernist "Knoll look," connections to European émigrés were central to the firm's strategy. For its graphic work, Knoll Associates turned to Swiss-born Herbert Matter, a friend of Hans Knoll's, who had created advertising art in Paris with A. M. Cassandre and Le Corbusier. Matter designed the company's trademark "K" logo and several prominent advertising campaigns. Textiles were another crucial element of the "Knoll look," which included designs by Bauhaus designer Anni Albers and Cranbrook's Loja Saarinen. Hungarian-born designer Eszter Haraszty was the company's color specialist and headed the textile division from 1949 to 1955. Haraszty, who was trained in Budapest and also worked as a consultant to émigré architect Victor Gruen, was responsible for the vivid color schemes that characterized Knoll's signature look.

Soon after the war, Knoll Associates "returned" to Europe with branch offices in several countries. More than simply an internationalization of its business, Knoll helped bring the modernist International Style to postwar European consumers as a form of "American" design. Knoll International first opened a showroom in Paris in 1948.[68] An office in Stuttgart

followed in 1950, where ties to the firm of Hans Knoll's father were rebuilt.[69] In Italy, Knoll International used local suppliers such as well-established design furniture firms Cassina and Fantoni. Competitor Herman Miller observed that their European networks allowed Knoll to "have the jump on us" in Europe in terms of suppliers and markets.[70] Eventually, Knoll International opened showrooms in additional European cities including Brussels, Milan, Stockholm, and Zurich. Knoll became the face of modern American furniture abroad — and the company projected the signature "Knoll look" globally while allowing for localized product modifications.[71]

Knoll International profited directly from the Cold War competition over the consumer imagination. In 1951, the US Department of State ordered Knoll furnishings for ninety houses of American civil servants in Germany, and Knoll provided the interiors for several of the American cultural missions across West Germany.[72] Knoll International in Stuttgart refurnished the US consulates in Frankfurt, Düsseldorf, and Stuttgart as well as several embassies abroad, including those in Stockholm and Copenhagen.[73] These state contracts reflected a broader "cultural cold war" with which the American government tried to woo postwar Europeans.[74] Knoll became part of US efforts to utilize "good design" as a tool of cultural diplomacy, representing American goods abroad. The European roots of Knoll and its ties to European design modernism made the company particularly appealing to American administrators and European elites alike.

POSTWAR TRANSFERS:
DESIGN ÉMIGRÉS AS AGENTS OF "AMERICANIZATION"?

The end of World War II brought the United States into a position of unparalleled economic and political power. To consumer engineers, the American world of goods offered a unique selling point in the emerging Cold War competition. "The whole world admires and envies American products, American appearance, American quality," Raymond Loewy told students at Harvard University, "[and] we should and I believe we will take advantage to this receptive attitude." "Democracy," Loewy argued, "is hard to sell. No one has yet been able to make its high spiritual values of freedom, liberty, and self-respect a 'packaged' item [...] Democracy hasn't been merchandized. Until then, we must use substitute solutions. Foremost among them is the American product. The citizens of Lower Slobovia may not give a hoot for freedom of speech, but how they fall for a gleaming Frigidaire, a streamlined bus, or a coffee percolator."[75] As they returned after the war, many former émigrés heeded Lowey's call to make "modern" consumption a goal for Europe's postwar reconstruction.

The émigrés added a transnational dimension to the professionalization of marketing and design in postwar Europe. At conferences and through their consulting work they promoted new forms of consumer engineering, helping European companies and consumers adapt to a supposed new age of abundance. Raymond Loewy and other American designers spread their conception of marketing-oriented design among European colleagues.[76] Yet this did not amount to a simple postwar "Americanization" of European commercial design. Transatlantic impulses from designers such as Loewy were met with engrained domestic traditions in industrial and commercial modernism, which dated back to the interwar years and before. European fashion and design retained a significant cachet even at the height of the postwar "American century." Scandinavian modernist furniture, for example, fascinated US decorators during the 1950s, and Italian goods, from leatherware to automobiles, were in high demand.[77] Thus, while American designers and organizations wielded a new degree of influence, the commercial design field remained genuinely transatlantic during the postwar decades.

Nonetheless, Europeans were keenly interested in "American" innovations. Concerned about German competitiveness on the US market, German industry and government organized study tours to the United States for designers and industry representatives.[78] Industrialists such as Philip Rosenthal urged German design "purists" to embrace the commercial spirit of the United States. "Creating the desire to buy," Rosenthal argued, would serve as "the engine of a free economy."[79] Against critics of Loewy's commercial styling, proponents of American-style design countered that much contemporary work in the United States was informed by the ideal of "good form" and by the simple shapes that had motivated the Bauhaus.[80] In 1952, State Department official and former émigré Herwin Schaefer used a Darmstadt conference on industrial design to tout the role of the Museum of Modern Art in contemporary American design and its affinity to European modernism.[81]

Indeed, both International Style and organic design forms made inroads into postwar European consumer design.[82] As the consumer goods sector expanded, a number of firms — especially in the electronics industry and those specializing in furniture and housewares — began to emphasize industrial design in their production processes.[83] German design journals expressed keen interest in American designers and industry. Former émigrés played a role in this process of transatlantic exchange. Study tours to the United States featured visits with émigrés working for American companies and academic institutions, or as independent consultants.

One group of German professionals traveling to the United States, for example, visited the offices of Loewy and Peter Müeller-Munk to learn about commercial design consultancies. The group also toured the Institute of Design in Chicago, Knoll Associates, and such corporations as IBM, General Motors, and General Electric.[84] Visiting European professionals focused on the challenge of integrating designers into new corporate marketing strategies and on the professional education this required.

American design education was widely discussed in 1950s Germany. The design and advertising journal *Graphik*, for example, ran a long story on practice-oriented American design education in 1956, highlighting the impact of émigrés such as the Czech-born Antonín Heythum at the University of Syracuse.[85] A Stuttgart exhibition on industrial design education in the United States noted the influence of Bauhaus conceptions on contemporary American design, but also emphasized the close cooperation of American schools with large corporations.[86] The biggest institutional innovation in postwar German design education, the 1955 foundation of the Ulm Institute of Design (*Hochschule für Gestaltung*), was also heavily influenced by the American Bauhaus tradition. The school sought to reestablish Bauhaus education in Germany, and the prospect of American funding shifted its emphasis toward industrial design early on.[87]

The colorful design and packaging of the American world of consumer goods was closely tied to new marketing strategies. Europeans discussed the centrality of continuous model and color changes to US consumer products. Much like American advertising journals had once tracked European design developments during the interwar years, postwar West German design journals now looked across the Atlantic for new trends. They reported on émigré Walter Allner's graphic design at *Fortune* magazine and on the advertising work of Saul Bass, whose style had been influenced by György Kepes and László Moholy-Nagy.[88] As evidenced by the exhibitions discussed in this catalogue, the growing importance of packaging to consumer marketing was a recurring topic of transatlantic design reception. Italian-born designer and founder of the US Package Designer Council Frank Gianninoto was featured in several stories on new American packaging methods at a time when German package design was thought to lag behind internationally. As new packaging materials became available and self-service stores began to spread, concepts of brand image and corporate design garnered the attention of professionals in Western Europe as well.[89]

Retail design received similar attention by German professionals, whose trips to the United States occasionally included visits to the new enclosed shopping malls designed by Victor Gruen.[90] Back home, returning émigré Ferdinand Kramer reported on his experiences with American store design. In the age of self service, Kramer explained, the psychology of display was crucial: how goods were presented, and what visual arrangements guided customers through the store. Displays were supposed to trigger impulsive buying behavior in convenient and stimulating shopping environments.[91] New packaging formats came to Europe directly through American consultants such as Walter Landor, whose firm moved into various Western European markets by the late 1950s. Dutch companies, Landor's overseas partners claimed, were "keenly interested in American packaging designs" to make their products more competitive.[92] In Germany, he was in touch with porcelain manufacturer Rosenthal, brewing companies, and advertising agencies. While Europe remained a small part of his business at the time, the former émigré was part of the transatlantic reassessment of retail packaging.

As Greg Castillo has pointed out, exhibitions of consumer goods were used to show off the "soft power" of American mass consumption to Europeans during the Cold War.[93] These American displays often relied on the inclusion of émigré designers. Edgar Kaufmann Jr. of the Museum of Modern Art, for example, compiled international exhibitions that featured the modernist design styles that the émigrés had helped to popularize in the United States. A large ECA exhibition on household design in Stuttgart included contributions from the offices of Raymond Loewy, Peter Müller-Munk, and Knoll Associates. Émigrés Marli Ehrman and Anni Albers both had textiles included in the exhibition, and the wallpaper display showed a creation by György Kepes. Leading American-born designers were included in the exhibition, but the share of immigrants and émigrés was noteworthy. The exhibition featured Eva Zeisel and Peter Schlumbohm, German-American graphic designer Tommi Parzinger, Swedish-Americans Greta Grossman and Rolf Key-Oberg, Italian-American Francesco Collura, as well as the Austrian-American émigrés Otto Natzler and Ernst Lichtblau. Not all of American postwar design, to be sure, adhered to the modernist tradition, and these exhibitions provided European audiences with a distorted view of American consumer design. Yet their modernist slant and prominent inclusion of émigrés was calculated to appeal to the European elites who came to view them.

The very organization of these exhibitions, finally, also relied on European émigrés as transatlantic intermediaries. Next to Herwin Schaefer and architect Peter Blake, this included most prominently Cologne native Will Burtin. His work for the Traveling Exhibition Service (TES), itself headed by émigré art historian Henle Pope, is at the center of the present exhibition.[94] In their exhibits, Burtin and his collaborators did more than present an affluent American world of goods. They channeled a larger vision of reuniting a "shattered Western culture" — a notion that similarly inspired Walter Paepcke's Aspen design conferences in which Burtin was involved along with Herbert Bayer and other émigrés.[95] Industrial design had become a central element of American material culture by mid-century, but it would be a mistake to think of that design as a purely "American" phenomenon. In *Perspektiven*, the Ford Foundation's German-language periodical, art historian James Plaut argued in 1954 that American design was heavily influenced by transatlantic transfers, facilitated especially by European immigrants to the United States.[96] Following World War II, the émigrés then became part of an effort to sell these commercial designs to Western Europeans as both consumer products and as artifacts of a shared cultural tradition.

NOTES

1   This article draws on my forthcoming monograph: Jan Logemann, *Engineered to Sell: Émigrés and the Making of Consumer Capitalism* (Chicago: University of Chicago Press, 2018).

2   Roy Sheldon and Egmont Arens, *Consumer Engineering: A New Technique for Prosperity* (New York: Harper, 1932).

3   Sheldon and Arens, *Consumer Engineering*, 1.

4   Sheldon and Arens, 19.

5   See Lawrence Samuel, *Freud on Madison Avenue: Motivation Research and Subliminal Advertising in America* (Philadelphia: University of Pennsylvania Press, 2013); and Jan Logemann, "Consumer Modernity as Cultural Translation," in *Geschichte und Gesellschaft* (2017): 413–37.

6   See e.g. Regina Blaszczyk, *Imagining Consumers: Design and Innovation from Wedgwood to Corning* (Baltimore: Johns Hopkins University Press, 2002). On the rise of industrial design see esp. Jeffrey Meikle, *Twentieth Century Limited: Industrial Design in America, 1925–1939* (Philadelphia: Temple University Press, 2001).

7   See Raymond Loewy, *Never Leave Well Enough Alone* (New York: Simon & Schuster, 1953); and Internationales Design Zentrum Berlin, *Raymond Loewy: Pionier des Amerikanischen Industrie-Designs* (Munich: Prestel, 1990).

8   Raymond Loewy, "A.M.C. Speech," May 17, 1944, in Hagley Museum and Library, Loewy Archive, Box 21.

9   Ely Kahn, *Design in Art and Industry* (New York: Scribner's, 1936), 201.

10   See Jeffrey Meikle, "Geniestreiche, Werksentwürfe, Beraterverträge," in *Raymond Loewy: Pionier des Amerikanischen Industrie-Designs* (Munich: Prestel, 1990), 51–62.

11   See e.g. Margret Kentgens-Craig, *The Bauhaus in America: First Contacts 1919–1936* (Cambridge, MA: MIT Press, 1999).

12   Volker Fischer, "'Gute Form' made in USA: Design zwischen Europa und Amerika," in Bernd Polster, ed., *West Wind: Die Amerikanisierung Europas* (Cologne: DuMont, 1995), 66–78, here 66.

13   See e.g. Frederick Horowitz and Brenda Danilowitz, *Josef Albers: To Open Eyes* (London: Phaidon, 2009); and Anna Vallye, "Design and the Politics of Knowledge in America, 1937-1967," PhD Diss., Columbia University, 2011.

14   On the history of design education in the United States see Arthur Pulos, *The American Design Adventure: 1940–1975* (Cambridge, MA: MIT Press, 1988), 164–95. See also Alexander Dorner, "The Background of the Bauhaus," typescript [c. 1940], in Bauhaus Archive (= BhA), Folder 125 (Walter Gropius); and Rachel Delphia and Jewel Stern, *Silver to Steel: The Modern Designs of Peter Muller-Munk* (Munich: Prestel, 2015).

15   See e.g. Otto Kuhler, *My Iron Journey: An Autobiography of a Life with Steam and Steel* (Denver: National Railway Historical Society, 1967).

16   See Cherie and Kenneth Fehrman, *Postwar Interior Design: 1945–1960* (New York: Van Nostrand Reinhold, 1987).

17   See Virginia Gardner Troy, *The Modernist Textile: Europe and America 1890–1940* (Burlington, VT: Lund Humphries, 2006), esp. 132–37; and Martin Eidelberg, *Eva Zeisel: Designer for Industry* (Montreal: Le Château Dufresne, Musée des Arts Décoratifs, 1984).

18   On Moholy-Nagy's early career see e.g. Victor Margolin, *The Struggle for Utopia: Rodchenko, Lissitzky, Moholy-Nagy* (Chicago: University of Chicago Press, 1997). See also László Moholy-Nagy, *Vision in Motion* (Chicago: Paul Theobald, 1947).

19   E.g. for Schott Glassworks. László Moholy-Nagy to Alvar Aalto, February 9, 1932, Illinois Institute of Technology Archives, Acc. 2007.15 Alain Findeli, Box 4.

20   Sibyl Moholy-Nagy to László Moholy-Nagy, August 4, 1938, in Smithsonian Archives of American Arts, László Moholy-Nagy Papers, Reel 945.

21   See also Paul Betts, "New Bauhaus and School of Design, Chicago," in Jeannine Fiedler and Peter Feierabend, eds., *Bauhaus* (Cologne: Könemann, 2000), 66–73.

22   See Greg Ruth, "Walter Paul Paepcke," in Jeffrey Fear, ed., *Immigrant Entrepreneurship: German-American Business Biographies, 1720 to the Present*, vol. 4 (German Historical Institute, Washington, DC). Last modified May 27, 2014. http://www.immigrantentrepreneurship.org/entry.php?rec=67

23   See e.g. Agenda, Meeting of the Board of Directors, November 14, 1944, in University of Illinois Chicago, Daley Library, Institute of Design Collection, Box 1, Folder 5.

24   Minutes of the conference on "Industrial Design, a New Profession," held by the Museum of Modern Art for the Society of Industrial Designers, November 11–14, 1946, IIT Archives, Institute of Design Records, Box 1a.

25   Ibid., 59–60.

26   On Bayer see Gwen Finkel Chanzit, *Herbert Bayer and Modernist Design in America* (Ann Arbor: UMI Research Press, 1987). See also James Sloan Allen, *The Romance of Commerce and Culture* (Chicago: University of Chicago Press, 1983); and Patrick Rössler, *Herbert Bayer: die Berliner Jahre - Werbegrafik 1928–1938* (Berlin: Vergangenheitsverlag, 2013).

27   "Mittel zur Gestaltung der optischen Erscheinung einer Werbesache," typescript, December 15, 1927, Bauhaus Archive, BhA Bayer, Folder 1. See also Herbert Bayer, "Acceptance Speech Kulturpreis," Cologne, 1969, BhA Bayer, Folder 1.

28   On Dorland see Stefan Hansen, ed., *Moments of Consistency: Die Geschichte der Werbeagentur Dorland* (Bielefeld: Transcript-Verlag, 2004).

29   On the careers of Bayer and other Bauhaus artists during the NS regime cf. Winfried Nerdinger, ed., *Bauhaus Moderne im Nationalsozialismus* (Munich: Prestel, 1993), esp. 24-47.

30   See Alfred Barr to Bayer, September 28, 1937; and Barr to John McAndrew, n.d., BhA Bayer, Folder 2.

31   We know much about Bayer's activities after immigration from a comprehensive FBI background check documented as United States Civil Service Commission (USCSC), Case No. 1.22.57.4431. Here: FBI New York Office, Report, September 4, 1957.

32   See USCSC, Case No. 1.22.57.4431, Report of Investigation, July 8, 1957.

33   See Bayer to Gropius, November 28, 1941; and Gropius to Luce, December 1, 1941, in BhA Gropius, Folder 31.

34   USCSC, Case No. 1.22.57.4431, Report of Investigation, July 8, 1957.

35   "Herbert Bayer's Design Class," *A-D* 7 (June/July 1941) 18-32.

36   "Herbert Bayer, 85, Designer and Artist of Bauhaus School," *New York Times*, October 1, 1985.

37   Art Institute of Chicago, *Modern Art in Advertising: An Exhibition of Designs for the Container Corporation of America* (Chicago, 1945).

38   USCSC, Case No. 1.22.57.4431, Report of Investigation, June 14, 1957.

39   See Bernard Gallagher, "Walter Landor," in R. Daniel Wadhwani, ed., *Immigrant Entrepreneurship: German-American Business Biographies, 1720 to the Present*, vol. 5, German Historical Institute. November 8, 2012. http://immigrantentrepreneurship.org/entry.php?rec=69. On his use of consumer research see also Joseph Malherek, "Packaging Personality: Walter Landor and Consumer Product Design in Postwar America," in *Australasian Journal of American Studies* 31 (2012): 57–70.

40   Cf. Bobbye Tigerman, "Fusing Old and New: Émigré Designers in California," in Wendy Kaplan, ed., *California Design 1930–1965* (Cambridge, MA: MIT Press, 2011), 91–115.

41   "The Ultimate Image Maker," *San Francisco Focus*, August 1992, in Smithsonian Institution, Landor Design Collection (= LaP), Box 1.1, Folder: "Landor Publicity."

42   See Chapter Three in Walter Landor, "Autobiography (Draft)," in LaP Box 17.1, Folder: "WL Reminiscences."

43   "Milner Gray, A Profile," *Arts & Artist*, October 1986, 9–14, in LaP Box 17.1, Folder: "Milner Gray."

44   Walter Landor, "Personal History" n.d., in LaP Box 17.1, Folder: "WL Autobiographical."

45   On the development of the firm see e.g. "Chronology of Significant Dates in the History of Landor Associates," in LaP Box 1.1, Folder: "Landor Chronologies"; and "Decade highlights," LaP Box 1.1, Folder: "Landor Chronologies."

46   Walter Landor, "Personal History," n.d., in LaP Box 17.1, Folder: "WL Autobiographical."

47   Transcript of interview with Lewis Lowe (1990s) in LaP Box 1.1, Folder: "Lewis Lowe."

48   Walter Landor, "Why East Comes West for Design," *Good Packaging Yearbook* 19 (1958), n.p.

49   Hugh Schwartz, "Motivation Studies are Package Design Oriented," *Candy Industry Packaging*, n.d., in LaP Box 17.1.

50   Chapter on packaging research by Hugh Schwartz in "The Package in Marketing," book manuscript in LaP Box 19.2, Folder: "Packaging Design Book Files."

51   Walter Landor, "Good Design Does Not 'Date,'" *Designs*, September 1947 in LaP Box 17.1, Folder: "Articles by W.L." More generally: Diana Twede, "History of Packaging," in D. G. Brian Jones and Mark Tadajewski, eds., *The Routledge Companion to Marketing History* (Routledge: London, 2016), 115–28.

52   Walter Landor, "Design Moves Merchandise if it Moves People," *Good Packaging Yearbook* 18 (1957), 83.

53   Charlotta Heythum, "Ten Years – Knoll International in Germany," *Deutsche Bauzeitschrift*, October 1961 (translated by Else Stone), in Florence Knoll-Bassett Papers (= FKnP), Box 4, Folder 4, Smithsonian Institution, Archives of American Art.

54   See Brian Lutz, *Knoll: A Modernist Universe* (New York: Rizzoli, 2010); and Steven and Linda Rouland, *Knoll Furniture: 1938–1960*, 2nd ed. (Atglen, PA: Schiffer, 2005).

55   On the history of the Wilhelm and Walter Knoll companies see *Walter Knoll: Design Reloaded* (Herrenberg: Walter Knoll AG & Co., 2006).

56   Rouland, *Knoll Furniture*, 4.

57   See Barbara Tilson, "Plan Furniture 1932–1938: The German Connection," *Journal of Design History* 3 (1990): 145–55.

58   Toby Rodes, *Einmal Amerika und zurück: Erinnerungen eines amerikanischen Europäers* (Stuttgart: Huber, 2009), 169.

59   Sybil Moholy-Nagy to László Moholy-Nagy, September 7, 1937, in Sybil and László Moholy-Nagy Papers, Reel 945, Smithsonian Institution, Archives of American Art.

60   Margaret Warren, "Top-Flight Rating Comes in 10 Years to Home Furnishing Team," *Christian Science Monitor*, January 25, 1950, 6.

61   "Bickford's Rents 505 5th Avenue Unit," *New York Times*, March 21, 1940, 50.

62   See Lutz, *Modernist Universe*, 16–22; and Florence Knoll, "After Cranbrook," in FKnP Box 1, Folder 1.

63   See Bobbye Tigerman, "'I am Not a Decorator': Florence Knoll, the Knoll Planning Unit and the Making of the Modern Office," *Journal of Design History* 20.1 (2007): 61–74.

64   On Bertoia's work for Knoll see Katharine Elson, "Architect Designs New Furniture," *Washington Post*, March 24, 1957, F16.

65   See Rouland, *Knoll Furniture*, 16–29.

66   Sarah Booth Conroy, "So Cranbrook Married Bauhaus and We've Lived More Happily Ever After," *Washington Post*, February 6, 1972, H1.

67   See "Modern Design Doesn't Pay or Does it?" *Interiors*, March 1946; and Florence Knoll, "Early Designers," FknP Box 3, Folder 6.

68   Warren, "Top-Flight Rating."

69   See Rodes, *Einmal Amerika*, 166–71.

70   See Hugh De Pree, *Business as Unusual: The People at Herman Miller* (Zeeland, MI: Herman Miller, 1986), 69.

71   See Rodes, *Einmal Amerika*, 173.

72   See Heythum, "Ten Years."

73   Rodes, *Einmal Amerika*, 173.

74   On the cultural Cold War see Volker Berghahn, *America and the Intellectual Cold Wars in Europe* (Princeton: Princeton University Press, 2001).

75   Raymond Loewy, Harvard University Speech, March 22, 1950,

in HgA Loewy, Box 21.

76 For Dichter see e.g. Logemann, "Consumer Modernity," 478–35.

77 See e.g. Veronique Pouillard, "Keeping Designs and Brands Authentic: The resurgence of the post-war French fashion business under the challenge of US Mass Production," *European Review of History* 20 (2013): 815–35; and Per Hansen, "Networks, Narratives and New Markets: The Rise and Decline of Danish Modern Furniture Design, 1930–1970," *Business History Review* 80 (2006): 449–83.

78 A collaboration of the economics ministry with the industry association BDI, see German Federal Archives (=BuArch) B 102 / 34493 and B 102 / 21241.

79 Philip Rosenthal, "'Industrial Design' – Kunst oder Geschäft? Industrie und Kunst müssen Kompromiss finden," *Die Neue Zeitung,* September 27/28, 1952, 10.

80 See e.g. Hans Klaus, "Die Gute Form. Die Bedeutung der industriellen Formgestaltung," *VDI Nachrichten,* May 5, 1951, 3, in BuArch B 102 / 34493.

81 See *Internationale Diskussion über Industrielle Formgebung im Darmstädter Gespräch 1952 – "Mensch und Technik,"* vol. 3, (Darmstadt: Neue Darmstädter Verlagsanstalt, 1952), 29–33.

82 See Petra Eisele, "Zwischen 'Organic Design' und Nierentisch: Die 'organische Form' im Wirtschaftswunderland," in Breuer, ed., *Das gute Leben,* 157–65; and Fischer, "'Gute Form' made in the USA."

83 On West German industrial design see Christopher Oestereich, *"Gute Form" im Wiederaufbau* (Berlin: Lukas Verlag, 2000), 171–87.

84 Karl Otto, *Industrielle Formgebung in den USA* (Berlin: Berliner Industriebank, 1963).

85 Berthold Semper, "Formgebung im Spannungsfeld von Lehre und Praxis," in *Graphik: Werbung und Formgebung* 9, 1 (1956): 38–45.

86 See "Industrial Design Education USA" and "Das Pratt-Institut in New York," in *form* 6 (1959): 32–35.

87 On the Ulm Institute see e.g. Rene Spitz, *Hfg Ulm: Die politische Geschichte der Hochschule für Gestaltung, 1953–1968* (Stuttgart: Axel Menges, 2002).

88 See Eberhard Hölscher, "Walter Allner. Werbegraphik aus Amerika," in *Gebrauchsgraphik* 25, 12 (1954): 2–5; and Franz Wills, "Saul Bass," in *Graphik: Werbung + Formgebung* 9, 1 (1956): 31–34.

89 See e.g. special issue on packaging of *Graphik* 10, 3 (1957) and R. Leslie, "Frank Gianninoto," in *Graphik: Werbung + Formgebung* 9, 7 (1956): 348–51.

90 See Otto, *Industrielle Formgebung.*

91 Ferdinand Kramer, "Warenhäuser in den USA," talk at TH Aachen, August 1955; and Kramer, "Organisation und Funktion des Warenhauses," Nuremberg, March 1958, in Werkbund Archives Berlin, Kramer Papers, Box 4.

92 Joseph Bourdez to Walter Landor, July 30, 1958, in LaP, Box 18.2, Folder: "Holland."

93 See Greg Castillo, *Cold War on the Home Front: The Soft Power of Midcentury Design* (Minneapolis: University of Minnesota Press, 2010).

94 On Burtin see Margaret Re, "Will Burtin," in *Transatlantic Perspectives,* May 13, 2014; and Jack Masey and Conway Morgan, *Cold War Confrontations: US Exhibitions and Their Role in the Cultural Cold War* (Zurich: Lars Müller, 2008) 90–91, 104–06. See also Will Burtin, "Werbepackung in Amerika. Eine Ausstellung der Amerika-Häuser in Deutschland," exhibition catalogue, n.d. I am grateful to Margaret Re for sharing her copy of the catalogue with me.

95 Masey and Morgan, *Cold War Confrontations,* 14; and Re, "Will Burtin."

96 James Plaut, "Industrielle Formgestaltung in den Vereinigten Staaten," in *Perspektiven* 9 (Fall 1954), 112–30.

US Traveling Exhibits on Atomic Energy and Space Exploration

Emily A. Margolis and Stuart W. Leslie

"Cold War Modern" became the leitmotif for a generation of designers and architects on both sides of the iron curtain. Whether embodied in traveling exhibitions and world's fairs, housewares and model homes, or the iconic Cold War kitchen, mid-century modernism became a forceful projection of "soft power" at home and abroad.[1] Its doppelgänger, the harder edge of Cold War design, found expression in a parallel set of exhibitions on atomic power and space. Under the guise of "atoms for peace" and the peaceful exploration of outer space, these exhibitions also served as not-so-subtle proxies for Cold War superiority built upon the threat of nuclear weapons and the missiles capable of carrying them to their targets.

Intended, like their consumer-oriented counterparts, as stage sets for their respective economic and political systems, these exhibitions competed with one another in the developing world and in Western Europe, sometimes in isolation and other times head-to-head. They also toured their Cold War rivals. The famous "kitchen debate" between Richard Nixon and Nikita Khrushchev at the American National Exhibition in Moscow had its now-forgotten rejoinder in the Soviet National Exhibition in New York City's Coliseum, starring three Sputniks, a mockup of a Soviet space capsule, and a model of an atomic-powered icebreaker. The United States and the Union of Soviet Socialist Republics, as well as other nuclear nations, put together elaborate displays for meetings of the International Atomic Energy Agency in Geneva in 1955 and 1958 to showcase their progress in reactor design, fission and fusion energy, and nuclear medicine. The United States Information Agency (USIA) in collaboration with NASA mounted traveling exhibitions featuring the Mercury, Gemini, and Apollo spacecraft for displays in European science museums and as the centerpieces for the US pavilions at the world's fairs in Montreal and Osaka, much as the Soviets had done with Sputnik beginning at Expo 58 in Brussels.

The laboratories, industrial facilities, and testing locations that ushered in the nuclear and space ages — Oak Ridge National Laboratory, Marshall Space Flight Center, and the Nevada Test Site in the US, or Arzamas-16, Star City, and Semipalatinsk Test Site in the USSR

FIGURE 23 Erik Nitsche, "Nautilus," 1955. One of a series of posters commissioned by General Dynamics and printed in six languages for the "Atoms for Peace" exhibition in Geneva, Switzerland. *Cooper Hewitt, Smithsonian Design Museum/Art Resource, NY.*

— remained tightly guarded secrets, open only to those with the proper clearances and the need to know. So selected and unclassified examples of their work had to stand in for their accomplishments in international exhibitions, revealing just enough so that their doomsday machines would be, as Dr. Strangelove sardonically put it, "credible and convincing," and at the same time suggest how weapons of mass destruction might yet be beaten into plowshares of future prosperity. After all, an atomic reactor could power an icebreaker or a nuclear-armed submarine, supply medical isotopes or weapons-grade plutonium. Even a nuclear weapon might be repurposed for "peaceful nuclear explosions" intended to dig canals or dredge harbors at unprecedented speed and scale.

Exhibitions of "hard power" drew on the same stable of creative talent as did their "soft power" twins. Graphic designer Erik Nitsche's posters for American defense contractor General Dynamics became atomic-age classics and a surprise hit at the 1955 "Atoms for Peace" exhibition in Geneva **[FIGURE 23]**. Architect and visionary Buckminster Fuller adapted his geodesic domes to house US pavilions in industrial exhibitions and world's fairs across the globe. Will Burtin put together an in-house exhibit on atomic energy for the opening of Union Carbide's New York City headquarters building. Their designs, like the exhibitions themselves, concealed as much as they revealed, becoming the public face of otherwise secret enterprises. General Dynamics made its money building Nautilus submarines, Atlas missiles, and Convair strategic bombers — not the Triga research reactors prominently featured in one of Nitsche's posters. Fuller's radomes protected the defense radars of the Distant Early Warning Line. Union Carbide, in addition to its better-known chemical businesses, served as the managing industrial contractor for the Atomic Energy Commission's (AEC) Oak Ridge National Laboratory, which supplied enriched uranium and other crucial components for nuclear weapons.

NASA itself could be considered the civilian arm of the US aerospace industry. The contractors that designed and built its rockets and space capsules — McDonnell, Grumman, North American Aviation, among others — constituted a who's who of US military contractors. The launch vehicles that carried astronauts into space and eventually to the moon were modified intercontinental ballistic missiles originally designed to carry nuclear warheads. Ever conscious of its public image, NASA established its own art program and commissioned pieces from such diverse artists as Norman Rockwell and Robert Rauschenberg, and put their work on display at the National Gallery of Art.[2] NASA also set up traveling exhibits of strikingly imaginative design for museums and world's fairs, immersive environments that offered visitors the opportunity to sit in an actual astronaut's "training couch" and to see a moon rock displayed like the Hope Diamond.

The "industrial design" of nuclear power plants and space vehicles proved every bit as popular as the "soft power" displays of women's fashion, middle-class family lifestyles, and popular culture. Lines to see John Glenn's Mercury space capsule *Friendship 7* at the London Science Museum stretched around the block, while visitors waited several hours in the US Pavilion in Osaka for the chance to see a real moon rock. The US displays of "Atoms for Peace" in Geneva, including a working research reactor, attracted enormous crowds of scientists and laypeople alike. The "magic hands" displays of robotic arms to manipulate radioisotopes behind protective barriers were a huge draw whether in New Delhi, Geneva, or Moscow.

If anything, the agencies responsible for boosting US popularity and prestige abroad underestimated the appeal of American science and technology, especially in fields like nuclear energy and space. For foreign visitors those seemed to be the defining features of a Cold War superpower, perhaps more so than the latest kitchen gadgets, consumer electronics, modern suburban homes, or mass-market automobiles. What electric range could hold its own with a research reactor, what car with a space capsule? Where conventional exhibits offered a glimpse of the present, nuclear power and space exploration staked a compelling claim to the future.

FIGURE 24 President Eisenhower listening to an explanation of the working swimming pool reactor set up on site at the 1955 Geneva exhibition. Designed by Oak Ridge National Laboratory, the small research reactor drew large crowds and was later sold to Switzerland as part of the US "Atoms for Peace" program. *Courtesy Union Carbide Company.*

FIGURE 25 A full-scale mockup of Argonne National Laboratory's boiling water reactor on display at the 1958 Geneva exhibition. Designed as a power reactor capable of providing 5,000 kilowatts of electricity, Argonne's prototypes would train a generation of nuclear engineers from across the globe. *Courtesy United Nations.*

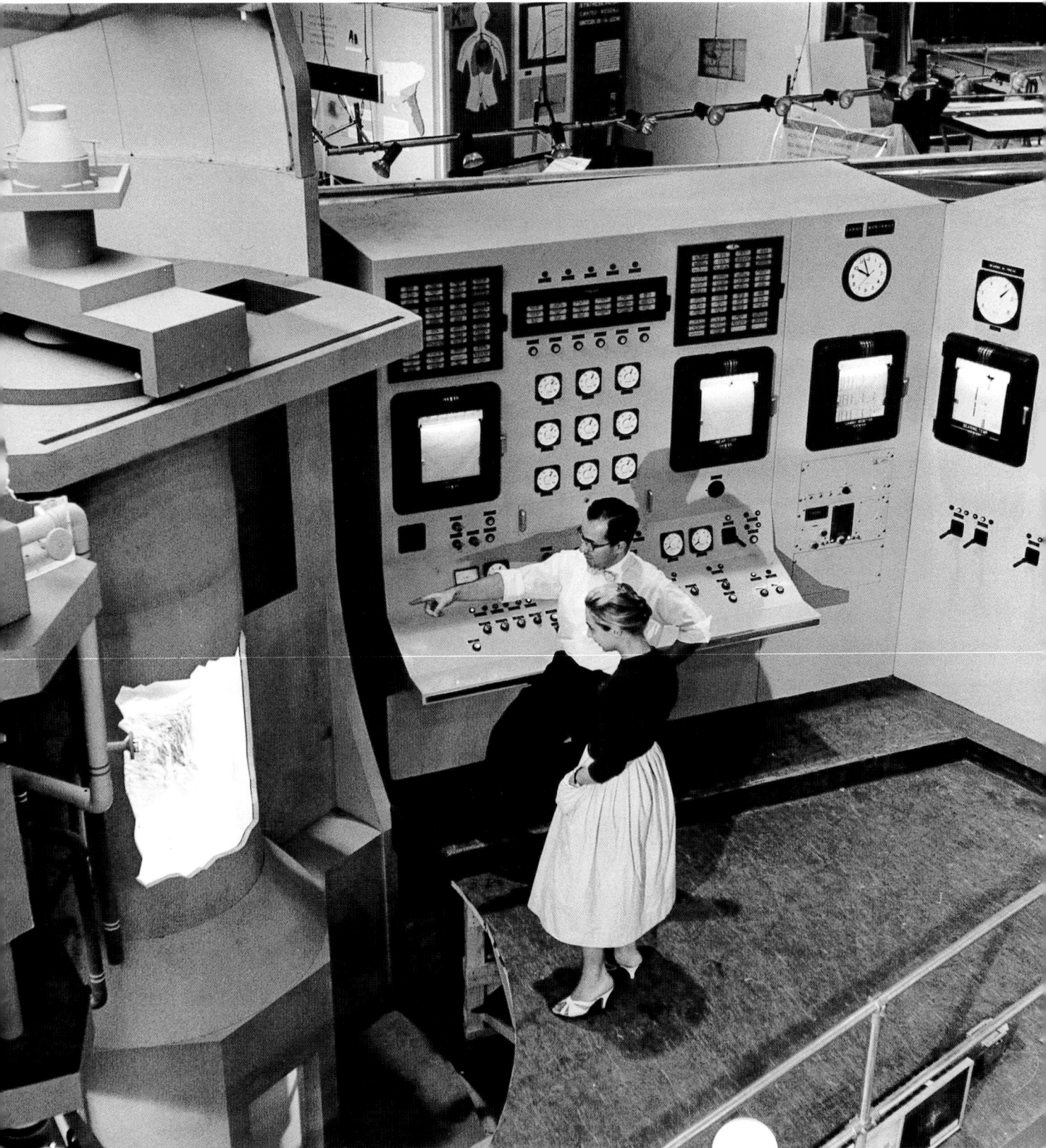

ATOMS FOR PEACE

President Dwight Eisenhower understood that all-out nuclear war could have no real victors and that the Cold War would be decided on the battlefield of ideas and propaganda. Early in his presidency he launched two key programs intended to win hearts and minds and to counter Soviet assertions that while it was building the society of the future the US had lapsed into a capitalist war machine.[3] In August 1953 Eisenhower set up the USIA "to understand, inform, and influence foreign publics in promotion of the US national interest, and to broaden the dialogue between Americans and US institutions and their counterparts abroad."[4] In December of the same year he announced what he called the "Atoms for Peace" initiative at a meeting of the General Assembly of the United Nations, offering to share US civilian nuclear expertise with allied and non-aligned nations and so "improve the material condition of peoples everywhere and enhance the prospect for peace."[5]

To spread that message, USIA subsequently organized a traveling "Atoms for Peace" exhibit in 1954 that visited Western Europe — Italy, Germany, Spain, the Netherlands, and the United Kingdom. The next year it stopped in India and Pakistan, and later in Brazil, attracting millions of visitors along the way.[6] In India, the most populous of the non-aligned countries and one with declared nuclear aspirations, USIA, under the leadership of Jack Masey, organized an "atomics" exhibit for the US Pavilion at the Indian Industries Fair in New Delhi. Industrial designer John Vassos, best known for his phonograph, radio, and television sets done for RCA, came up with a simple but striking pavilion, a single-story circular building with a circular drum on top capped with a ball-and-ring atomic model to highlight the feature attraction. Through photographs, explanatory texts, scale models, and interactive displays, the exhibit offered visitors a primer on nuclear power and medicine. Indian graduate students in physics, decked out in bright orange jumpsuits provided by Brookhaven National Laboratory (which sent a thirty-foot-high model of its latest graphite reactor) offered instruction in several languages, demonstrating the "magic hands" for handling radioactive materials, a Geiger counter, and a spacesuit. Masey gave Prime Minister Nehru (a strong proponent of a nuclear India) and new Soviet party leader Nikita Khrushchev personal tours of the exhibition.[7]

The Conference on the Peaceful Uses of Atomic Energy organized by the UN and held in Geneva, Switzerland, for two weeks in August 1955, gave international visibility to Eisenhower's idea. The AEC immediately recognized that a technical exhibit, including a working atomic reactor, would be a public relations coup and the perfect complement to the formal scientific talks, and asked about an appropriate display space at the Palais des Nations where the conference would be hosted. The United States took Salon XV, forty feet by one hundred feet. Once other delegations caught wind of the proposal, they insisted on their own exhibitions. Given limited space at the main venue, the US decided to split its display between official government exhibits at the Palais des Nations, aimed at the 1,400 scientific delegates, and popular and corporate exhibits at the Palais des Expositions downtown, intended for the general public.

The AEC, knowing next to nothing about explaining nuclear science to a broad audience, turned to Design and Production Inc., a firm that had done plenty of museums but had no experience with still-classified nuclear technology. After talking with nuclear scientists and engineers at Oak Ridge and the AEC, Design and Production laid out a suitcase-sized model of Salon XV that showed in detail the display cases, models, photographs, partitions, islands, and lighting and color schemes.[8] Arranged with the logic of a flow chart, the exhibition took the visitor from prospecting, mining, and processing uranium to the fabrication of fuel elements and then to models of different kinds of power reactors, with "sidebars" for such topics as instrumentation, radioisotopes, and nuclear medicine. The designers also included plenty of interactive displays. Visitors could try out Geiger counters or wait in line to test themselves on a hand-and-foot contamination monitor just like those in working nuclear facilities.

Lead designer Leonard Rennie crafted compelling visuals from some unlikely artifacts. He arranged a series of full-scale fuel elements by type of cladding material — aluminum, zirconium, and stainless steel — rather than by type of fuel or type of reactor, setting them against a black, concave backdrop that highlighted their distinctive shapes (plates, winged tubes, rods, and cylinders) and their bright metallic sheen.[9] Unique among the international displays, the fuel element panorama "attracted many scientists with cameras, measuring tapes, and notebooks, and Russian delegates more than any others."[10] The right lighting brought out the brilliant yellows, oranges, greens, and blues of thirty-two uranium samples and seventeen thorium samples arranged along facing panels that funneled visitors toward the fuel elements.

The tabletop (and larger) models of five experimental power reactors, some from AEC's own laboratories and others from its industrial contractors, took center stage. The massive material-testing reactor model nearly hit the ceiling of the spacious Salon, with six-inch human figures to add a sense of scale for the six-story structure.[11] Westinghouse brought a model of a pressurized water reactor that included miniature operating control rods and a sequence of lights to show how steam moved through the pressure vessel, heat exchanger, turbines, and generators. Oak Ridge's homogenous reactor and North American Aviation's sodium-cooled reactor used colored liquids infused with bubbles so visitors could follow the flow of fuel and coolants. For more details, viewers could consult cutaway drawings, photographs, flow diagrams, and text on the wall panels behind each model. The models had to be realistic and at the same time just inaccurate enough to mislead informed viewers hoping to discern still-classified details. As a historian of Britain's reactor models has pointed out, "the exhibits were designed to dissemble as much as disseminate."[12] The exhibition also included an actual reactor control panel with a working control rod, though it had to be operated by company representatives. Every visitor would have liked to try the ever-popular "magic hands," a kind of claw crane arcade game for the nuclear set, though even VIPs had to watch the experts handle "hot" materials remotely. Just outside the Salon the designers placed a cloud chamber constructed by the Radiation Laboratory at the University of California, Berkeley. The ghostly vapor tracks, up to five hundred at a time left by cosmic rays knocking electrons off of gas molecules, fascinated scientists and laypersons alike.

A total of 36,222 visitors toured the technical exhibition during its two-week run. The delegates, including a number of current or future Nobel laureates, already understood the technical details, but the exhibits had PhDs on hand to answer any hard questions. For everyone else, Design and Production trained a cadre of young multilingual guides. A brochure in the four official languages of the meeting — English, French, Russian, and Spanish — provided a clear overview of the US technical exhibits, leading off with a message of international cooperation from President Eisenhower, followed by short descriptions of each of the ten sections on the Salon floor.

The American showstopper, a full-scale research reactor, had to be located on the grounds of the Palais des Nations. Oak Ridge scientists had been thinking about such a display even before the Geneva conference had been officially announced. "Operating a research reactor of this type at the Geneva Conference will demonstrate one of the most important uses to which atomic fissionable materials can be put," the Oak Ridge scientists declared. "It will show that an efficient working reactor can be designed, constructed, and operated in complete safety without elaborate preparations or complicated facilities."[13] As an ideal nuclear ambassador they scaled-down a version of the Oak Ridge materials testing reactor from thirty megawatts to one hundred kilowatts so it could be broken down, transported by military cargo plane, and reassembled on site.[14]

The job of turning a spectacular scientific instrument into a memorable display fell to Donald Stewart, Union Carbide's corporate exhibits manager. When the Oak Ridge scientists told him a modular army barracks should be sufficient to house the reactor, Stewart had to educate them on the art of "three-dimensional selling." He came back with a modern twist on a classic Swiss chalet, using vertical wooden slats with large windows for illumination. Set on a small knoll in the gardens surrounding the Palais des Nations, Stewart's rustic gem domesticated a potentially unsettling technology. Stewart also mocked up the display panels surrounding the reactor, explaining fuel elements, radioisotopes, nuclear shielding and safety, a cross-sectional drawing of the reactor, and its many research applications, which his Union Carbide exhibit team turned into museum-quality displays in record time.[15]

Visitors had an unobstructed view of the "swimming pool" reactor's core, submerged in demineralized water at the bottom of a cylindrical steel tank, ten feet in diameter and twenty-two feet deep. A platform suspended over the tank held the mechanism for raising and lowering the control rods and offered a commanding podium for demonstrations. The control room, easily visible behind glass, had one-button operation so that visiting dignitaries such as President Eisenhower could power up the reactor as simply as possible [FIGURE 24]. On reaching full power, the reactor glowed the distinctive bluish-green of Cerenkov radiation that wowed the crowds. Union Carbide also organized a "reactor school" short course for young women from a local school, who could then guide visitors through the reactor display, another way of "domesticating" high-tech. The public waited in long lines for a tour of the reactor, and some 62,000 people saw it during its two-week run. Afterward the US sold the reactor to Switzerland for half of its cost to build, the first of a dozen similar US research reactors offered to friendly foreign countries and to US universities, where a future generation of nuclear scientists and engineers could train on them.[16]

Soviet scientists "had a good reputation among international exhibit-makers for their creative and inspired ways of popularizing science and technology"; Geneva would be no exception.[17] Understandably, the USSR delegation had demanded equal space, and the Soviet exhibits, like their American counterparts, ran the gamut from mining and fuel elements to industrial applications, agriculture (including an atomic-powered milking machine), cancer treatments, and radioisotopes. Of particular interest was a model of the first atomic reactor actually feeding power to a national electric power grid and its accompanying film, *First in the World*, that won praise for its high production value and exceptional score.

For sheer design imagination nothing at Geneva compared with Erik Nitsche's posters for General Dynamics. A major US defense contractor of nuclear-powered submarines and nuclear-armed bombers, General Dynamics had to figure out some way to advertise its achievements without giving away any secrets. Models being out of the question, General Dynamics hired graphic artist Erik Nitsche to create an eye-catching corporate display that soft-peddled its military businesses. Nitsche, a Swiss-born, transatlantic designer, had worked for many multinational clients such as Ciba and Hoffmann-La Roche. General Dynamics asked him to craft a visual identity for a highly diversified conglomerate. Printed lithographically in Switzerland, each poster proclaimed "Atoms for Peace" in six languages — English, Russian, French, German, Japanese, and Hindi — and somehow captured the essence of the company's core businesses without naming any of them. In one poster ("hydrodynamics"), a Nautilus submarine, recently completed by the General Dynamics Electric Boat division, emerges from its eponymous spiral shell more as harbinger of peaceful exploration than as a weapon of war. In another poster ("electrodynamics"), Nitsche superimposes a light bulb, the universal symbol of an inspiring idea, onto an azimuthal projection of the earth above the North Pole, atomic rings replacing conventional carbon filament as the new light of the world. In yet another ("nucleodynamics"), nuclear medicine plays out against a geometrical pattern of yellows, greens, blues, and reds, suggesting cells and their chemical structures. Distinctive enough to become known as prototypes of an emerging "atomic style," Nitsche's posters combined a refined modernist aesthetic with just enough realism to make the atomic future believable and welcoming. Nitsche's "Atoms for Peace" posters turned out to be graphic design classics and particularly popular with visitors from Switzerland, which Nitsche once called "a nation of posters." So well did Nitsche fulfill his client's expectations that General Dynamics put him to work as its in-house head designer for the next decade, crafting its corporate image in everything from its annual reports to its corporate jets, much like his IBM counterpart Paul Rand.[18]

Expo 58 in Brussels, the first Cold War world's fair, also showcased the peaceful atom. The Atomium, Expo 58's centerpiece, standing 335 feet tall, rescaled a stick-and-ball model of an iron crystal molecule to 165 billion times actual size. Given its official motto, "Atom=Hope," the Atomium's exhibits predictably highlighted the utopian promise of atomic energy, as did the national exhibits of many of the fair's participants, including the United States, USSR, Great Britain, France, and Belgium. As in Geneva, each country insisted on showcasing its own nuclear program. The

Atomium included space in four of its nine giant spheres for nuclear exhibits, though the US and the USSR decided to put their displays in their respective national pavilions, which faced off against one another in the fair's international section. Architect Edward Durell Stone's US Pavilion used a dramatic circular hub-and-spoke design with a sixty-foot-diameter oculus. Ivan Chermayeff and Tom Geismar, best known for their iconic corporate trademarks, did the graphics for "Main Street," a slice of everyday American life. Tucked away in a corner, Westinghouse constructed an atomic town of the future at model-railroad scale, alongside a much larger scale facsimile of the pressurized water reactor core that would power it. When the demonstrator pulled out the control rod the reactor glowed blue, and electricity, in the form of flashing lights, went coursing through the tabletop town's grid. The International Palace of Science included a small working reactor, but the clear message of the exposition was that national goals trumped supranational cooperation. The Atomium's nuclear exhibits wound up being so popular that updated versions would still be there a decade later.[19]

The Second International Conference on the Peaceful Uses of Atomic Energy, held in Geneva in 1958, was, like its predecessor, as much nuclear Olympiad as technical exhibition. To house it, the organizers constructed a temporary building near the Palais des Nations, with 90,000 square feet of exhibition space. In addition to updated displays of fission reactors, the US and the USSR brought models of recently declassified and still unproven fusion devices. Like their fission cousins, the prototype fusion reactors were spinoffs of still highly secret weapons programs. At Princeton, a satellite laboratory of Los Alamos working on hydrogen bomb designs had come up with an idea for confining plasma within a coiled figure-eight tube surrounded by an intense magnetic field. The Stellarator, looking like an industrial-strength Slinky, more than lived up to its astral name, alluding to the energy source of the stars, fusion. The USSR countered with its Tokamak, with a torus, or donut-shaped, confinement chamber. Since neither side knew much about the other's fusion program, the models attracted almost as much curiosity as the formal scientific papers.

The US exhibits took up almost half of the enormous hall. General Atomic, a new division of General Dynamics devoted to commercial nuclear power, brought its Triga, a small, fail-safe reactor developed for research and teaching purposes. Argonne National Laboratory set up a full-scale mock-up of its latest boiling-water reactor, including a control panel with enough gauges, dials, switches, and printouts for a science-fiction film. Both the US and USSR exhibits had far more sophisticated designs than back in 1955, with glowing simulated plasmas and deafening bursts that no one could ignore [FIGURE 25]. The Soviets also added the latest model of Sputnik to its display. AEC commissioner Lewis Strauss acknowledged that Sputnik "was a bare bid for prestige and interest, without apology, and it succeeded — at least as far as the general public was concerned."[20]

General Dynamics asked Nitsche for a second set of posters organized around the theme of "Exploring the Universe." As before, Nitsche's dazzling designs told a complex story at a glance and at the same time rewarded closer scrutiny. "Triga" gave the viewer a photorealistic peek at the reactor's core, with a backdrop of circles, in signature fission blue, mimicking the fuel and control rods and gradually brightening toward the center of radiant energy. "Nuclear Fusion" set a simple rectangular box at the center of a horizontal color gradient, with opposing arrows "pushing" against an intense red column to suggest the unimaginable pressures of hydrogen-helium fusion.

The US and the USSR also mounted strikingly similar nuclear exhibitions for their domestic audiences, no coincidence since the Americans and Russians had hosted exchanges of atomic displays and museological methods following the Geneva conferences. The Atomic Energy Pavilion at the VDNKh (Exhibition of the Achievements of the People's Economy) in Moscow and the American Museum of Atomic Energy in Oak Ridge offered their visitors a glimpse of a nuclear utopia just over the horizon. The VDNKh's logo showed heroic workers holding aloft an atomic nucleus. Opened in 1956, the atomic pavilion featured a working swimming-pool reactor similar to the US display in Geneva, a Russian version of "magic hands," and models and displays about Soviet power reactors, nuclear medicine, and nuclear science. The Soviets also organized a traveling exhibit, "The Atom for Peace," that toured major cities across the country.[21] The American Museum of Atomic Energy opened in 1949 "as an exhibition and educational center for advocating the peaceful uses of atomic energy," though paradoxically Oak Ridge remained very much a secret city.[22] Similar museums, with the same upbeat message, would subsequently open in Los Alamos, Sandia, and other highly secure nuclear facilities. The American Museum of Atomic Energy also sent its exhibits on the road in specially equipped bus caravans that stopped at high schools, county fairs, and community centers, and targeted local audiences with regional topics: radioactive isotopes for agriculture in Iowa, uranium mining in Arizona, nuclear power plants in Southern California. Of course everyone wanted a look at the "magic hands" and the "balloon suit" designed for radioactive protection.[23] Working with Disney to produce *Our Friend the Atom* (1957)

for its weekly show, the AEC reached a huge national television audience.

THE PEACEFUL USES OF OUTER SPACE

The space age rapidly eclipsed the atomic age. After the Soviet success with Sputnik at Expo 58 in Brussels, the US made space exploration a prominent theme of its traveling exhibitions and world's fair pavilions. Expo 58 had promised atoms for peace. In science museums, public plazas and state buildings, and at fairs in Seattle (1962), New York (1964–65), Montreal (1967), and Osaka (1970), the US offered a future vision of the "Peaceful Uses of Space" that showcased the American space program.

Over a period of three days in May 1962, nearly 25,000 people queued up outside of the London Science Museum to view a real spacecraft. The much-anticipated exhibition offered visitors a multisensory encounter with the US space program through *Friendship 7*, the capsule in which John Glenn Jr. became the first American to orbit the Earth. As historian J. B. Gouyon explains, the exhibit cultivated a sense of intimacy between visitors and American spacefarers, "making visitors part of the unfolding epic of the space age."[24]

Before museum patrons set eyes on the spacecraft, they listened to audio communications between Glenn and Mercury Mission Control. The three-minute excerpt placed the audience in the action, privy to the complexity of the mission and the complex of emotions it engendered. Once inside the exhibit, visitors were invited to ascend a small stairwell and peer down into *Friendship 7*. A spacesuit-clad mannequin, a stand-in for Glenn, was visible through a window that, for the purposes of the exhibition, was installed in place of the spacecraft's hatch. The curved panoramic photograph of the Earth further assisted visitors to imagine themselves as a part of the mission. The image would have been familiar from the short film on Glenn's mission screened in the museum's auditorium, which featured footage from a camera inside the spacecraft.[25] While the helmet of Glenn's spacesuit obscured some of his facial expressions, the audio revealed his elation at the "tremendous view" of Earth from orbit.[26] From London, *Friendship 7* continued on to tour twenty cities in Europe, the Middle East, Asia, and South America. Over four million people viewed the capsule in person, while another twenty million tuned in to local television coverage of the exhibition.[27] Its final stop was the world's fair in Seattle, Washington.

Only two years later, NASA produced another exhibit for national consumption, this time partnering with the Department of Defense to develop the US Space Park at the 1964–65 New York World's Fair. Unlike the traveling *Friendship*

FIGURE 26 Sunset at the US Pavilion in Montreal. Three Apollo parachutes are visible near the top of the dome, with suspended spacecraft in silhouette below. *Courtesy Chermayeff & Geismar & Haviv.*

7 exhibit, with its scripted experience, Space Park invited visitors to frolic among "products of the emerging space age," such as rockets, satellites, research planes, and spacecraft.[28] The asphalt and open air called out curiosity, not decorum. Fairgoers in New York had a chance to do what the Londoners never could — experience "spaceflight" inside of a Mercury mission simulator, equipped with a film depicting the Earth's rotating surface from an altitude of one hundred miles.[29]

Visitors could place their hands on the diverse artifacts, a mix of full-scale mock-ups and flight-flown hardware. Highlights included *Aurora 7*, the Mercury spacecraft in which Scott Carpenter orbited Earth, and *Gemini IV*, which arrived to the fairgrounds midway through the 1965 season after its June mission.[30] Also on display were mock-ups of the Command Module, Service Module, and Lunar Excursion Module for Project Apollo, which would become the centerpiece of American space displays for the next decade.[31] Looming large in the popular imagination, the spacecraft were physically dwarfed by the rockets that delivered them to space: Atlas, Titan II, and part of the first stage of the Saturn V.[32]

Between April and October 1967, over nine million visitors experienced the "American creative spirit" at the US Pavilion **[FIGURE 26]** at Expo 67 in Montreal.[33] The pinnacle of this spirit, as suggested by the pavilion's interior architecture, was the impending crewed mission to the moon. Prominently placed at the highest point within Buckminster Fuller's geodesic dome, the space exploration exhibit was the first major display along the route through the pavilion. As visitors ascended the longest escalator in the world toward the space exhibit, flanked on either side by a fifty-foot-tall banner reading USA and a giant mosaic of the American flag, there was no question as to which nation was en route to "Destination Moon," as the exhibit was called.[34]

The exhibit design encouraged admiration and appreciation, rather than engagement, by placing the trophies of American spaceflight just out of reach. Upon entering the exhibit, the fairgoer's gaze was drawn skyward to the space hardware suspended from the ceiling, including Mercury, Gemini, and Apollo spacecraft.[35] The latter appeared as if descending back to Earth, held aloft by three enormous orange-and-white parachutes. Below the spacecraft, visitors viewed wall cases featuring spacesuits, tools, and personal items astronauts brought into space, such as Wally Schirra's harmonica.[36] The exhibit **[FIGURE 27]** culminated in a lunar landscape populated with a mock-up of Surveyor, a robotic

FIGURE 27 The world's longest escalator deposited visitors at the entrance to "Destination Moon," which featured hardware from robotic and human space missions. The exhibit culminated in an imagined lunar landscape dominated by NASA's lunar module. *Courtesy Chermayeff & Geismar & Haviv.*

explorer, and the Lunar Module, but no spacesuits.[37] Armstrong's "small step" was still two years out.

The US Pavilion at Expo 70 in Osaka, Japan, elaborated the same immersive theme. As Cambridge Seven's exhibit designers (whose founding partners included Peter Chermayeff, Ivan's brother) explained, visitors to the US Pavilion would be "confronted with the raw material of experience; all that is demanded of him is participation. Not understanding. Not agreement. Participation."[38] When the gates of Expo 70 opened each morning, visitors ran to the United States Pavilion for a look at Apollo Sample 12055, a piece of basalt retrieved from the surface of the moon less than four months before the start of the fair.[39] The moon rock

was the crown jewel (literally displayed like a precious gemstone) of the space exploration exhibit, which celebrated America's moon landing program. Throughout the duration of the fair, eighteen of the sixty-four million visitors toured the US Pavilion.[40] On average 8,500 people passed through the displays each hour, sometimes waiting in queues for up to two hours to enter the building.[41]

The tremendous interest in the moon rock and the American space program was not merely a timely reaction to the recent moon landings, but rather the result of a multiyear campaign by USIA to promote Project Apollo across the globe. USIA assumed responsibility from the Department of State for facilitating US participation in international fairs

FIGURE 28 USIA and Cambridge Seven transported Expo 70 visitors from the fairgrounds to a tableau of the lunar landing site Tranquility Base, here built to scale with the aid of the US Army Topographic Command. *Courtesy of Chermayeff & Geismar & Haviv.*

and expositions.[42] At Osaka USIA presented the moon landing not as a triumphant American accomplishment but rather as a human endeavor pursued by America on behalf of all humankind.

Jack Masey, deputy commissioner general of design for the US Pavilion, remembers: "Participation was an opportunity, not so much, as in the past, to confront Communism but to present a positive image of American to the region." "In particular," he continued, the United States "needed to make the case for its policies in the Far East, where the escalation of the Vietnam War was a major concern."[43] The US Expo 70 advisory panel selected New York-based designers Chermayeff and Tom Geismar, and the architecture

firm Davis, Brody, and Associates, giving them instructions to collaborate on the kind of "total design" missing in earlier pavilions.[44]

USIA selected "Images of America" as the theme for the US Pavilion, with the understanding that the American images would have particular appeal to Japanese audiences. Chermayeff and Geismar developed seven distinct exhibit areas featuring American photography, painting, sports, space exploration, architecture, folk arts, and contemporary art.[45] USIA Director Leonard H. Marks outlined his agency's intentions for a space exploration display in the US Pavilion at Osaka: "We feel that emphasis should [...] be placed on accomplishments in the Apollo project, since the manned

lunar landing program is of the widest interest to audiences everywhere."[46] Authenticity was the paramount design principle of the space exploration exhibit. "The criteria we have followed in designing and assembling the space exploration exhibit is that actual flight-flown components should be shown whenever possible," Masey explained.[47] This subtly reinforced the distinction between American and Soviet society on the issue of transparency: the Soviet Pavilion included only models and replicas of its space technologies.

Without question, the space exploration exhibit was the most highly anticipated display in the US Pavilion, in part because it offered the real deal. Domestic and international news coverage heralded the authentic Apollo artifacts and the moon rock in particular.[48] Once inside the pavilion, an elliptical earth berm enclosed in an air-supported translucent fiberglass roof, the interior architecture compounded the excitement.[49] "The floor dividing the luminous enclosure," explained the official pavilion guidebook, "zigs and zags, projects and recedes so that exhibits may be seen above, below, and at eye level. Exhibition areas are arranged so that the visitor catches glimpses ahead, glances backwards at past exhibits."[50]

Glimmering satellites beckoned visitors from the sports exhibit — featuring the pavilion's second most popular object, baseball star Babe Ruth's locker — into the space exploration exhibit. The large, open space featured a constellation of satellites, spacesuits, and spacecraft suspended from the ceiling, with one example each of the Mercury, Gemini, and Apollo vehicles.[51] The Apollo 8 Command Module was displayed lowest to the ground **[FIGURE 29]**, hovering over a large mirror and enclosed by a protective barrier around which visitors congregated to examine the vehicle from all sides. Behind the spacecraft rose a two-story-high wall featuring a photograph of an astronaut's helmet stylistically rendered in yellow-and-orange horizontal lines. Large spherical satellites floated above the spacecraft, while the other satellites formed a column near the entrance to the exhibit. A single F1 engine, one-fifth of the assembly that powered the Saturn V rocket, was displayed at the foot of the stairwell.

Designers utilized wall cases to emphasize the human element of spaceflight. Between the first and second rooms of the exhibition, they placed two artifact groupings: the first featured life support systems and samples of freeze-dried astronaut food, while the second was dedicated to astronaut John Glenn who, in February 1962, became the first American to orbit the Earth in *Friendship 7*. Glenn was especially well liked in Japan, having participated in press conferences and meetings with students while vacationing there with his family in 1963.[52] Rounding the corner into the second room, a set of Mercury "couches" rested against the wall. These seats were fit to the bodies of the astronauts, and visitors were welcome to sit in them. It made for a tremendous photo opportunity.[53]

The second room was dominated by a full-scale recreation of Tranquility Base, the lunar landing site of Apollo 11 **[FIGURE 28]**. The US Topographic Command supplied an accurate model of the landscape, which USIA populated with a Lunar Module, mannequins dressed in Edwin "Buzz" Aldrin and Neil A. Armstrong's spacesuits, an American flag, and miscellaneous equipment, such as a camera and scientific tools. Tucked along the wall dividing the first two rooms was a display depicting the evolution of the spacesuit and a sampling of camera equipment used in space, against the backdrop of a stylized photograph of Earth rising above the lunar surface, this time in a mosaic of blue and orange pixels.[54] The arrangement of artifacts conveyed NASA's march of progress to the moon, which culminated in the moon rock, returned to Earth for display in the final room of the space exploration exhibit.[55]

The Saturn V rocket that delivered the Apollo astronauts into space was conspicuously absent from the US Pavilion. In the early stages of planning, USIA chief Leonard Marks imagined the rocket as the centerpiece of the space exploration exhibit, expressing to NASA administrator James E. Webb his belief that it would be "the undisputed smash of the

Exposition and the talk of Asia for decades to come."[56] Yet as the Vietnam War escalated, USIA had a change of heart regarding the most overtly militaristic technology of America's civilian space program. At the same time, NASA conveniently decided that transporting and installing a 363-foot-tall rocket on the Osaka fairgrounds might be too daunting logistically. Back home, NASA's strategy for presenting Project Apollo, and justifying it to American taxpayers, was to wow the public with its scale and complexity. The Saturn V was proudly displayed in various configurations in outdoor "rocket gardens" at NASA visitor centers. Its prelaunch home, the Vertical Assembly Building, then the largest building in the world, was the highlight of public tours of the Kennedy Space Center. As one visitor reflected: "It's hard to comprehend the size of an operation like this when you see it in the newspapers or on TV, but to see it firsthand you really have an appreciation for the enormity of the whole operation."[57] Abroad the USIA aimed to present the space program on a more human scale. So a singular F-1 engine became an eighteen-foot stand-in for the massive rocket.

In the space exploration exhibit at Expo 70, USIA told the story of how space travel and the moon were made habitable to men through the protective environments of spacecraft and spacesuits, with freeze-dried foods and tools compatible with zero gravity, and with personal mementos such as mission patches and musical instruments that brought humor and sentimentality to the lonely expanse of space. The selection of artifacts, the designers explained, aimed to "reveal that space technology must, in the final analysis, relate to human needs," so that visitors at Osaka could identify with the astronauts as people rather than American national heroes.[58] In emphasizing the universality of the moon landing, exhibit designers were careful not to tether the hardware to the American space program. The nation's name only appeared as decals on spacecraft, its flag stitched to spacesuits and planted on the Tranquility Base tableau. The only references to the program's state sponsor were embedded in the material culture of spaceflight rather than externally evoked, as in Montreal. The display downplayed the identities of the astronauts, all major celebrities in the US. In Osaka the display plaque read, "Here men from the planet Earth first set foot upon the moon July 1969, AD. We came in peace for all mankind." The astronaut's names appeared only as identifiers on spacesuits and couches, and their photographs were few and far between. Their grinning faces and last names had been key design elements at the Montreal fair only three years earlier.[59] By framing Project Apollo as an accomplishment that transcended men and nations, USIA encouraged visitors to imagine themselves as a part of the program.

FIGURE 30 Will Burtin's model of a uranium atom, the centerpiece of his 1961 "Atomic Energy in Action" exhibit designed for the lobby of the Union Carbide Building in New York City. Its ninety-two "electrons" — tiny lights mounted on thin steel rods — circled the nucleus in a mesmerizing electron cloud. *Photo © Ezra Stoller/Esto.*

Visitors were invited to see themselves, literally, in Project Apollo. Designers incorporated mirrored surfaces throughout the pavilion, in particular by covering the earth berm with reflective silver Mylar, which served as a backdrop for the exhibitions, as well as incorporating mirrored cubes as mounts for photographs. But in the space exploration exhibit, the hardware provided additional surfaces for reflection. Spheres of shining metal were suspended from the ceiling and in a column welcoming visitors. Of course the metallic satellites were naturally reflective, but it seems designers selected them for their form rather than function. In correspondence between USIA and the design team, the satellites are referenced not by name or purpose but by appearance.[60]

The Tranquility Base tableau also created an opportunity for visitors to imagine themselves on the lunar surface. The full-scale mock-up of the lunar landing site featured space-suit-clad mannequins depicting Neil Armstrong photographing Edwin "Buzz" Aldrin in the process of collecting lunar samples.[61] This scene reproduced, "as nearly as possible, the television view seen by the world of the Apollo 11 lunar exploration."[62] Witnessed the first time in the private setting of their homes, this scene helped deepen the personal connection visitors formed with Project Apollo.

ATOMIC ENERGY IN ACTION

As good as many of these atomic and space exhibitions had been, none of them came close to matching Will Burtin's "Atomic Energy in Action" developed for the opening of Union Carbide's new headquarters building in New York in 1961. Here a genuine design genius demonstrated what a "show of force" could look like if guided by a master's hand. With similar imagination, USIA exhibits might have risen above trade-show quality and become immersive works of art.

Burtin understood better than any designer of his generation how to make complex scientific principles comprehensible to almost anyone through vibrant interactive displays. His breakthroughs in "scientific visualization" for Upjohn pharmaceuticals included The Cell, a walk-through model of a human red blood cell brought to life at gigantic scale with a membrane of translucent plastic tubes and a "throbbing" nucleus; and The Brain, his equally audacious electro-mechanical marvel. To fill the massive lobby of its new headquarters building, a fifty-two-story skyscraper on Park Avenue designed by architect Gordon Bunshaft, Union Carbide commissioned Burtin to design a showcase for its most glamorous business, "probing the atom for you."[63]

Burtin came up with a multi-sectional visual script tracing nuclear fuel from ore to reactor, with a special focus on Union Carbide's contributions. In a note to himself, Burtin wrote: "Think of method to avoid overly texty demonstrations — do them with sound, light, etc. — related to the specific image about which the viewer wants information."[64] He took the life cycle of uranium as his organizing theme and the ball-and-stick model of the atom as his unifying visual motif. Burtin then subdivided the exhibit into kinetic sculptures illustrating key points of the script, surrounded by explanatory panels. At the top of the main escalator he put an enormous sculptural representation of an atom as a welcome sign, with images arranged on curved panels affixed to the electron orbits. In the prospecting and mining section, to complement aerial photographs of Union Carbide uranium mines in Colorado, Burtin built a freestanding "reactivity display." A dozen samples of uranium ores, mounted on large circular panels at the end of thin rods extending from a central spoke, revolved in front of a Geiger counter that indicated their radioactive content. In the center of the section on Union Carbide chemical products Burtin placed a molecular structure of colored spheres that stretched to the ceiling within an inverted pyramid of flaring rods, with the panels arrayed as fins around the base. Perhaps his most visually arresting sculpture was a working model of a uranium atom encased in a nine-foot-diameter plastic sphere [FIGURE 30]. Its ninety-two electrons, represented by tiny lights on thin steel rods, flew around the nucleus to create an utterly believable electron cloud. With a hands-on didactic flair Frank Oppenheimer would later develop for the Exploratorium science center, Burtin asked visitors to "go prospecting" with a Geiger counter and "to stake your claim" with a souvenir claim notice. His model of an atomic reactor let visitors start their own chain reaction: "A visitor pulled out a control rod, irradiating a nuclear pile that grew brighter as the rod withdrew; a soft hum grew louder and a Geiger counter clicked more urgently as its needle moved up the scale."[65] Whether climbing up the steps for a closer look at a Union Carbide swimming pool reactor or looking down at a model of Union Carbide's latest facilities in Oak Ridge, visitors found themselves in a dynamic, three-dimensional environment that

entertained as it educated. VVII Burtin's "temporary" exhibit for Union Carbide proved so popular that it ran for five years, until the company finally sold the building.

These exhibits now survive only in aging photographs, postcards from a future that never quite arrived. As the atomic age and the space age slowly fade into memory, so has the confidence that once characterized an era of seemingly limitless possibility. After the disasters of Three Mile Island and Chernobyl, *Challenger* and *Columbia*, uncritical exhibits on the world's fair model seemed out of touch with current realities. Even official government atomic museums at Oak Ridge, Los Alamos, and Sandia National Laboratories, and their counterparts in the USSR, had had to face up to public concerns about the environment and public health. The emerging information age may offer endless consumer choice, but it no longer asks citizens to commit themselves to the collective aspirations that defined the Cold War at home and abroad.

NOTES

1   David Crowley and Jane Pavill, eds., *Cold War Modern: Design, 1945–1970* (London: V & A, 2008); Greg Castillo, *Cold War on the Home Front: The Soft Power of Midcentury Design* (Minneapolis, MN: University of Minnesota Press, 2010); Ruth Oldenziel and Karin Zachmann, eds., *Cold War Kitchen: Americanization, Technology, and European Users* (Cambridge, MA: MIT Press, 2011).

2   Anne Collins Goodyear, "The Relationship of Art to Science and Technology in the United States: Five Case Studies, 1957–1971" (Dissertation, University of Texas at Austin, 2002).

3   Kenneth Osgood, *Total Cold War: Eisenhower's Secret Propaganda Battle at Home and Abroad* (Lawrence, KS: University of Kansas Press, 2006).

4   Jack Masey and Conway Lloyd Morgan, *Cold War Confrontations: US Exhibitions and Their Role in the Cultural Cold War* (Baden, Switzerland: Lars Muller Publishers, 2008), 34.

5   Ira Chernus, *Eisenhower's Atoms for Peace* (College Station, TX: Texas A&M University Press, 2002).

6   Michael L. Krenn, *The History of United States Cultural Diplomacy* (New York: Bloomsbury, 2017), 107; Andrew James Wulf, *U.S. International Exhibitions During the Cold War* (Lanham, MD: Rowman and Littlefield, 2015), 57.

7   Masey and Morgan, *Cold War Confrontations*, 48–49.

8   Laura Fermi, *Atoms for the World* (Chicago: University of Chicago Press, 1957), 68.

9   The International Conference on the Peaceful Uses of Atomic Energy, vol. 1 (Geneva, August 8–20, 1955), 261, accessed April 24, 2018, https://www.osti.gov/opennet/servlets/purl/16295117/16295117.pdf.

10 Fermi, *Atoms for the World*, 140.

11 Fermi, 143.

12 Alison Boyle, "Communicating While Concealing: Exhibiting Britain's Atomic Piles, 1949–1960" (paper presented at International Committee for the History of Technology, Porto, Portugal, 2016).

13 "Background Data: The United States Exhibit Reactor," Union Carbide and Carbon Corporation delegate dossier.

14 Frank Munger, "Did that airplane swallow a nuclear reactor," *Atomic City Underground*, accessed May 3, 2018, http://knoxblogs.com/atomiccity/2012/03/03/did_that_airplane_swallow_a_nu/.

15 Fermi, 99–104.

16 Fermi, 99–109.

17 Sonja D. Schmid, "Celebrating Tomorrow Today: The Peaceful Atom on Display in the Soviet Union," *Social Studies of Science* 36 (June 2006): 338.

18 Steven Heller, "Erik Nitsche: The Reluctant Modernist," *Typotheque*

(November 29, 2004), accessed April 23, 2018, https://www.typotheque. com/articles/erik_nitsche_the_reluctant_modernist.

19   Stuart W. Leslie and Joris Mercelis, "Expo 58: Nucleus for a New Europe," in Arthur Molella and Scott Knowles, eds., *World's Fairs in the Era of the Cold War: Science, Technology, and the Culture of Progress* (Pittsburgh: University of Pittsburgh Press, 2019).

20   Robin Herman, Fusion: *The Search for Endless Energy* (New York: Cambridge University Press, 1990), 56. Herman has an excellent description of the 1958 exhibition.

21   Schmid, "Celebrating Tomorrow Today," 342–45.

22   Arthur Molella, "Exhibiting Atomic Culture: The View from Oak Ridge," *History and Technology* 19 (2003): 211–26.

23   Accessed May 12, 2018, http://www.coldwarla.com/atoms-for-peace-mobile-exibits.html.

24   Jean-Baptiste Gouyon, "Making Science at Home: Visual Displays of Space Science and Nuclear Physics at the Science Museum and on Television in Postwar Britain," *History and Technology* 30, no. 1-2 (2014): 47.

25   Gouyon, "Making Science at Home," 49.

26   NASA, *Friendship 7*, film, accessed May 5, 2018, https://www.youtube.com/ watch?v=ON0YrkC-OL4.

27   Teasel Muir-Harmony, "Project Apollo, Cold War Diplomacy and the American Framing of Global Interdependence" (Dissertation, Massachusetts Institute of Technology, 2014), 86.

28   NASA, *U.S. Space Park*, film, 1965, accessed May 5, 2018, https://www. youtube.com/watch?v=CtwJlXVG_-g.

29   "Exhibit Layout," *NYWF64.com*, accessed May 5, 2018, http://www.nywf64. com/spacpark05.shtml.

30   Laurence R. Samuel, *The End of Innocence: The 1964–1965 New York World's Fair* (Syracuse, NY: Syracuse University Press, 2007), 177.

31   NASA, *U.S. Space Park*, film, 1965.

32   Samuel, *The End of Innocence*, 176.

33   Masey and Morgan, *Cold War Confrontations*, 324; Asa McKercher, "The Art of Soft Power at Expo 67: Creative America and Cultural Diplomacy in the US Pavilion," *Journal of Curatorial Studies* 5, no. 3 (2016): 377.

34   McKercher, "The Art of Soft Power at Expo 67," 377.

35   Ibid.

36   "Space Exhibit Survey," n.d., Space Exhibit-NASA, Container 4, General Records of the United States Information Agency, Record Group 306, National Archives at College Park, College Park, MD.

37   McKercher, "The Art of Soft Power at Expo 67," 377.

38   Quoted in Daniela Sheinin, "Kookie Thoughts: Imagining the United States Pavilion at Expo 67 (or How I Learned to Stop Worrying and Love the Bubble)," *Journal of Transnational American Studies* 5, no. 1 (2013): 5.

39   Masey and Morgan, *Cold War Confrontations*, 354.

40   Martin J. Manning, "Fairs! Fairs! Fairs! The United States Information Agency and U.S. Participation in World Fairs Since World War II," *Popular Culture in Libraries* 2, no. 3 (1994): 14.

41   David Anderson, "Memories of Expo '70," 4.

42   For a history of USIA administration and programs, see Nicholas J. Cull, *The Cold War and the United States Information Agency: American Propaganda and Public Diplomacy, 1945–1989* (Cambridge, UK: Cambridge University Press, 2008); Manning, "Fairs! Fairs! Fairs! The United States Information Agency and U.S. Participation at Worlds Fairs Since World War II," *Popular Culture in Libraries* 2, no. 3 (1994): 7.

43   Masey and Morgan, *Cold War Confrontations*, 352–53.

44   USIA, Press Kit, "U.S. Pavilion: Advisory Panel Members," Folder: Japan World Exposition in Osaka (EXPO 70), UJ-190000-01, Archives Department, National Air and Space Museum, Smithsonian Institution, Washington, DC.

45   USIA, Press Kit, "U.S. Exhibits: Theme and Contents," Guide Exhibit, Container 1, General Records of the United States Information Agency, Record Group 306, National Archives at College Park, College Park, MD.

46   Leonard Marks, USIA Director, to Thomas O. Paine, NASA Administrator, October 24, 1968, Space Exhibit-NASA, Container 4, General Records of the United States Information Agency, Record Group 306, National Archives at College Park, College Park, MD.

47   Jack Masey, USIA, to Deke Slayton, Chief of the Astronaut Office, May 6, 1969, Space Exhibit-NASA, Container 4, General Records of the United States Information Agency, Record Group 306, National Archives at College Park, College Park, MD.

48   Muir-Harmony, "Project Apollo, Cold War Diplomacy and the American Framing of Global Interdependence," 224–25.

49   USIA, Press Kit, "U.S. Pavilion: Architectural Characteristics," Folder: Japan World Exposition in Osaka (EXPO 70), UJ-190000-01, Archives Department, National Air and Space Museum, Smithsonian Institution, Washington, DC.

50   USIA, Official Guidebook, Brochure Mailings, Container 4, General Records of the United States Information Agency, Record Group 306, National Archives at College Park, College Park, MD.

51   Expo '70 marked a return to Japan for *Friendship 7*, which toured Japan as part of a global USIA-sponsored goodwill tour. See Muir-Harmony's "Project Apollo," Chapter 2: "From Spacecraft to Icon: *Friendship 7*'s Fourth Orbit." For a discussion of the first tour stop at the London Science Museum, see Gouyon's "Making Science at Home," 37–60.

52   Jack Masey to Frederick C. Durant III, Assistant Director of Astronautics at the National Air and Space Museum, May 16, 1969, Space Exhibit (Smithsonian), Container 5, General Records of the United States Information Agency, Record Group 306, National Archives at College Park, College Park, MD; Muir-Harmony, "Project Apollo," 123–24.

53   Associated Press Archive, "US Astronauts Visit the US Pavilion at Expo '70," March 25, 1970, accessed May 5, 2018, https://www.youtube.com/ watch?v=cJ-ScKXHmw8.

54   Exhibition photographs, Folder: Apollo Project, Exhibits, Osaka Expo '70, OA-250222-80, Archives Department, National Air and Space Museum, Smithsonian Institution, Washington, DC; Official U.S. Pavilion Guide, Folder: Japan World Exposition in Osaka (EXPO 70), UJ-190000-01, Archives Department, National Air and Space Museum, Smithsonian Institution, Washington, DC.

55   USIA, Press Kit, "U.S. Pavilion: Participants," Folder: Japan World Exposition in Osaka (EXPO 70), UJ-190000-01, Archives Department, National Air and Space Museum, Smithsonian Institution, Washington, DC.

56   Leonard Marks, USIA Director, to James E. Webb, NASA Administrator, July 15, 1968, Space Exhibit-NASA, Container 4, General Records of the United States Information Agency, Record Group 306, National Archives at College Park, College Park, MD.

57   "100,000th Visitor Impressed," *Spaceport News* 5, no. 34 (October 13, 1966): 3, Kennedy Space Center Archives.

58   USIA, Press Kit, "U.S. Exhibits: Space Exploration," Folder: Japan World Exposition in Osaka (EXPO 70), UJ-190000-01, Archives Department, National Air and Space Museum, Smithsonian Institution, Washington, DC.

59   Masey and Morgan, *Cold War*, 331.

60   Jack Masey to Julian Scheer, NASA Assistant Administrator for Public Affairs, August 4, 1969, Space Exhibit-NASA, Container 4, General Records of the United States Information Agency, Record Group 306, National Archives at College Park, College Park, MD.

61   Patricia Ezell, USIA Program Officer, to Tom Geismar, October 27, 1969, Space Exhibit General Design, Container 5, General Records of the United States Information Agency, Record Group 306, National Archives at College Park, College Park, MD.

62   Masey to Scheer, August 4, 1969, Space Exhibit-NASA, Container 4, General Records of the United States Information Agency, Record Group 306, National Archives at College Park, College Park, MD.

63   R. Roger Remington and Robert Fripp, *Design and Science: The Life and Work of Will Burtin* (London: Lund Humphries, 2007).

64   Will Burtin, Working Memorandum, Will Burtin Archive, The Atom in Action, Box 9.6, Rochester Institute of Technology.

65   Remington and Fripp, *Design and Science*, 98.

PLATE 1   Eszter Haraszty   Printed by Printext,   Screen print, linen
           Fibra   produced by Knoll Textiles   36 ¼ × 25 in.
                                    1953

PLATE 2 Philip Johnson Arundell Clarke Ltd. Cotton print
Van Dyke Squares C. 1953 173 ¼ × 52 in.
(repeat height: 29 ⅛ in.)

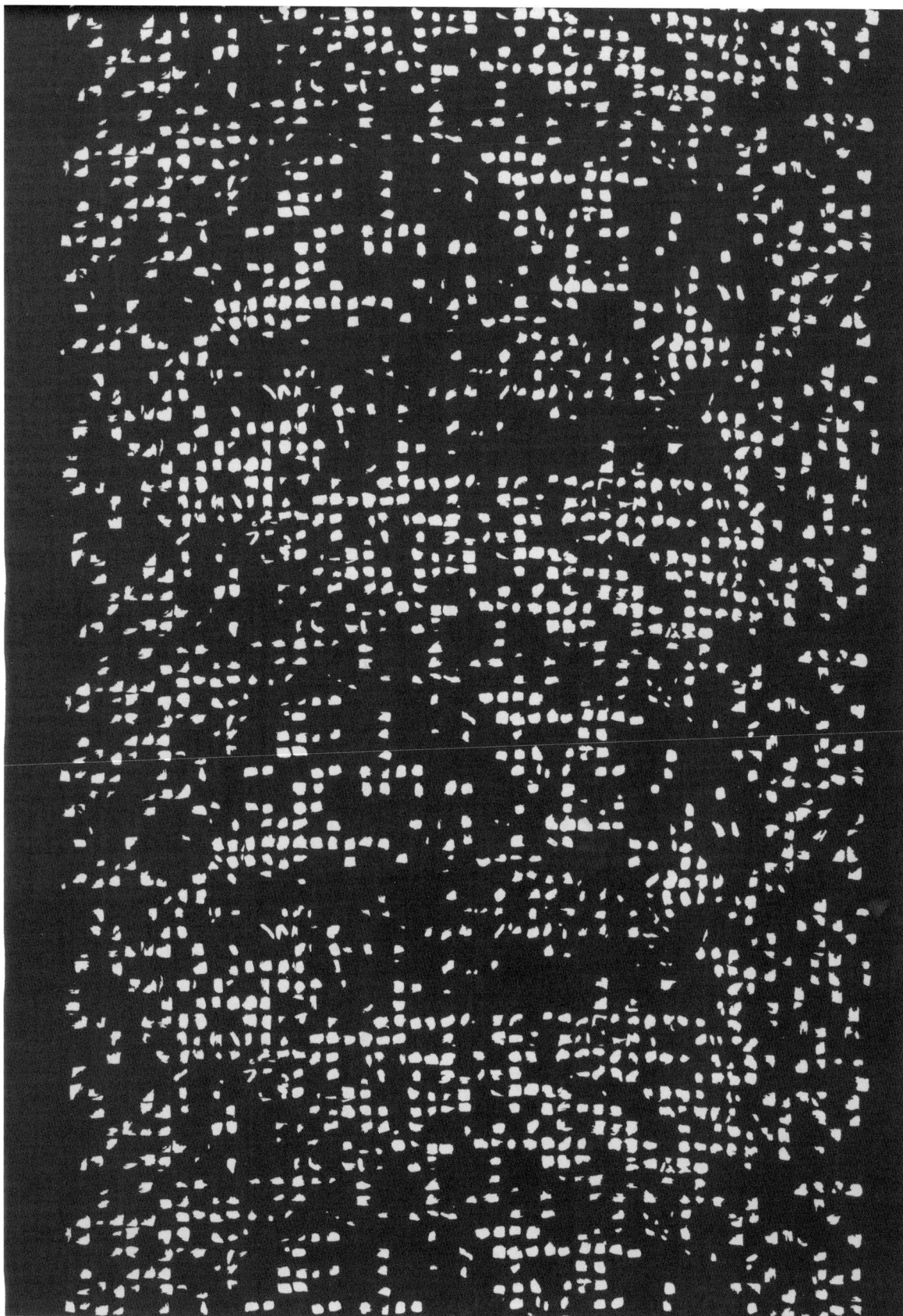

PLATE 3   Ross Littell   Laverne Originals   Batiste
         Border Riff #3   c. 1948   64 ½ × 46 in.

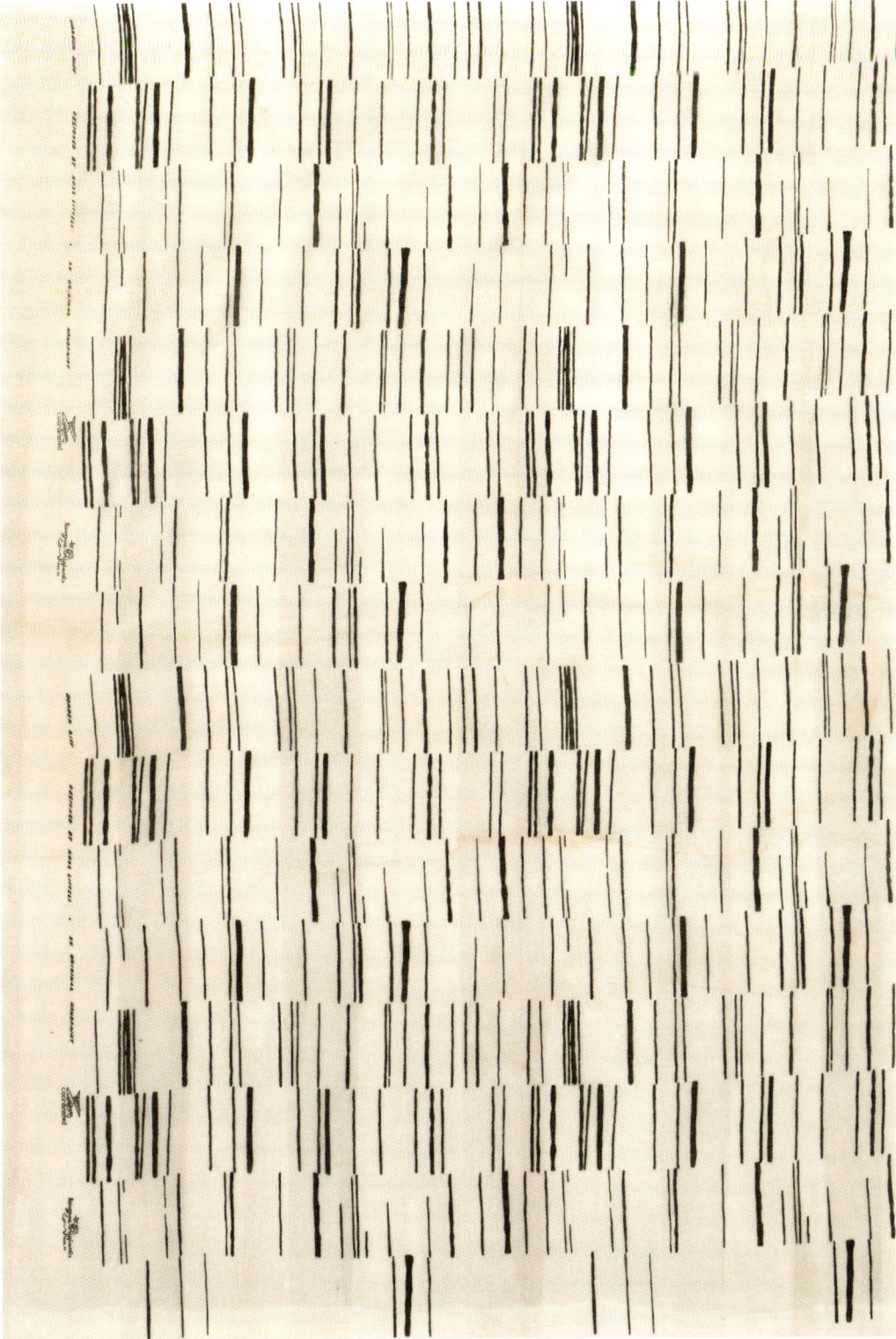

PLATE 4   Angelo Testa   Knoll Associates Inc.   Screen print, linen
         Campagna   c. 1951   69 × 52 ½ in.

PLATE 5   D. D. and Leslie Tillett   D. D. and Leslie Tillett Inc.   Screen print,
           Walnuts   c. 1950   plain weave cotton
                                        69 × 52 ½ in.

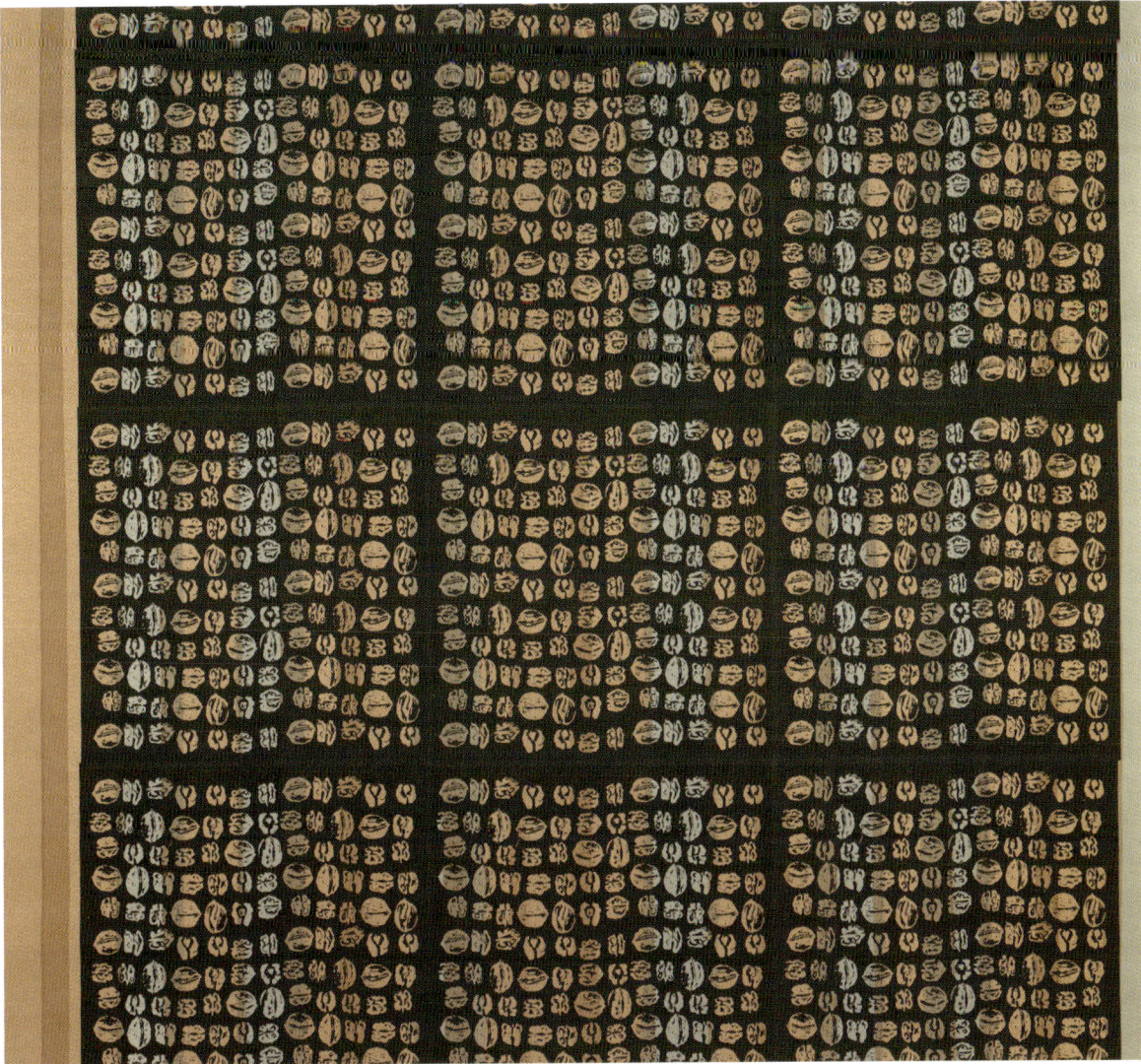

PLATE 6   Noémi Raymond   Knoll Textiles   Print, linen
           Chinese Coin   1948   51 ¾ × 25 ⅛ in.

PLATE 7   Eszter Haraszty   Knoll International Inc.   Screen print,
           Tracy   1952   plain weave cotton,
                                                                     rayon blend
                                                                     119 ⅝ × 48 in.

PLATE 8   Portia LeBrun   Piazza Prints Inc.   Screen print, paper (facsimile)
           Balloons   1950–51   30 $^{15}\!/_{16}$ × 27 $^{9}\!/_{16}$ in.

PLATE 9   Ben Rose   Ben Rose Inc.   Screen print (facsimile)
           Foliation II   1946, reprinted 1988   121 ½ × 49 ⅛ in.

PLATE 10 **Aesop's Fables**   Herndon Papers   Screen print, paper (facsimile)
                             1953   36 × 29 ¹⁵⁄₁₆ in.

PLATE 11 Marion Dorn Katzenbach and Warren Inc. Screen print, paper (facsimile)
Master Drawings 1951 49 ¼ × 28 ¾ in.

PLATE 12 Ilonka Karasz
Ducks and Grasses

Katzenbach and Warren Inc.
1940–50

Unused wallpaper sample
backed on cardboard mat
(facsimile)
31 ½ × 27 ¾ in.

PLATE 13   Nancy McClelland   Nancy McClelland Inc.   Screen print, paper (facsimile)
          George Washington   1950–60   23 ¼ × 22 in.

PLATE 14   William Justema (?)   Katzenbach and Warren Inc.   Screen print, paper (facsimile)
           Mosaic   1950–51   19 $^{15}/_{16}$ × 29 $^{15}/_{16}$ in.

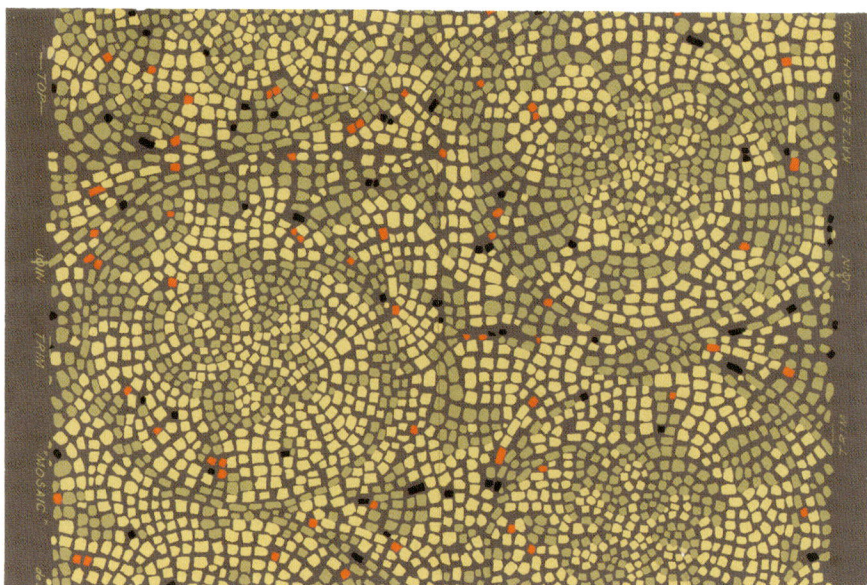

PLATE 15   Will Burtin   Mass Production   Photograph: Ezra Stoller
            Containers   and Design Issues (front)
            & Packaging   1951

PLATE 16   Will Burtin   Purchase Appeal and Grabbing   Photograph: Ezra Stoller
           Containers   Attention (back, detail)
           & Packaging   1951

PLATE 17   Will Burtin   Technical Resourcefulness   Photograph: Ezra Stoller
           Containers   (front, detail)
           & Packaging   1951

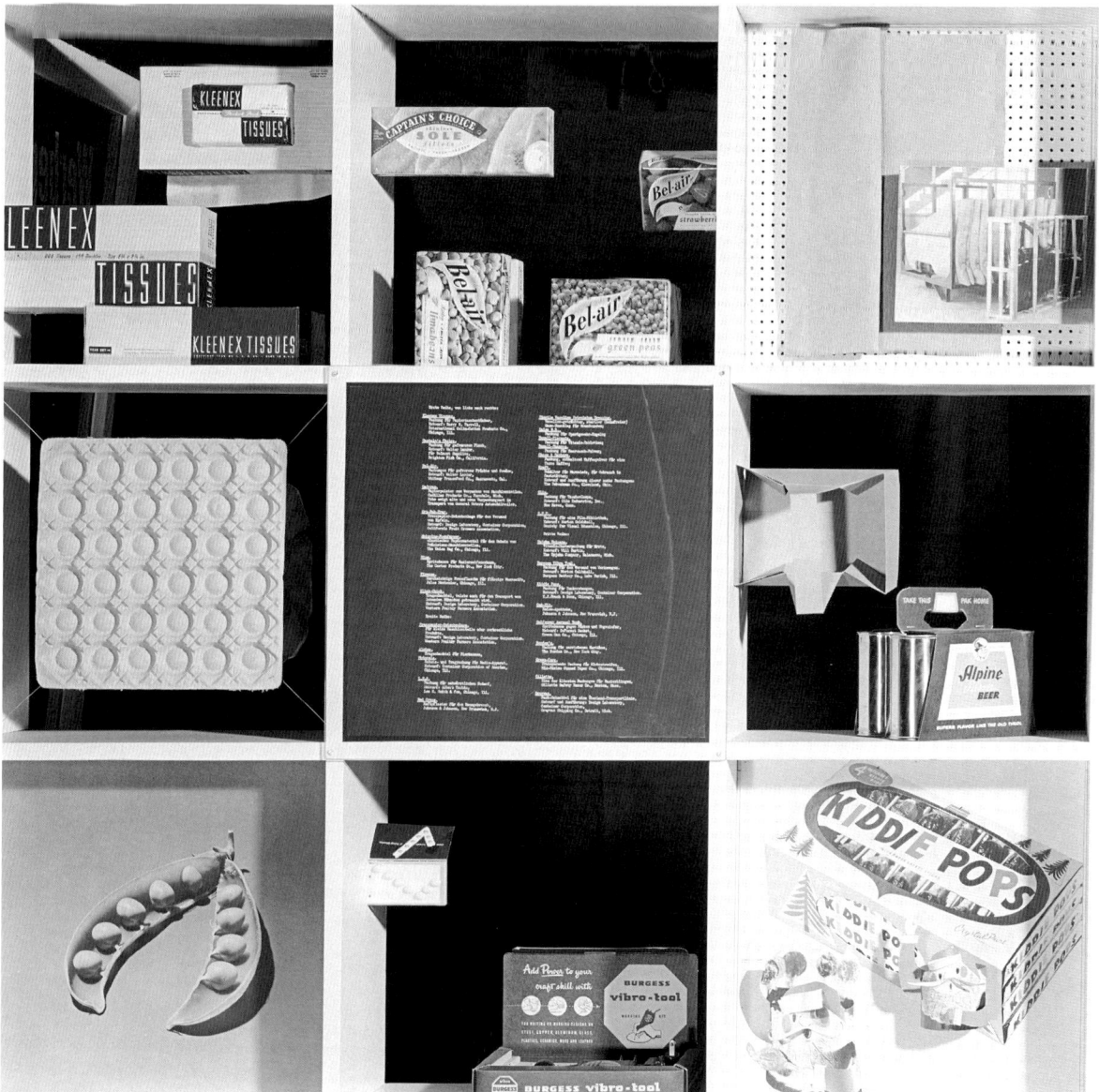

Exhibition Checklist

**ECONOMIC RECOVERY PLAN
(ERP) POSTERS**

PFC Joseph M. Hasselbeck
George C. Marshall House
October 1, 1950
Altered photographic reproduction
from original black and white
42 × 42 in.
*U.S. Information Agency, National
Archives and Records Administration,
College Park, MD (306-BN-171-1)*

Reyn Dirksen
All Our Colours to the Mast
c. 1950
Lithograph
29 ½ × 21 ½ in.
*Collection of George C. Marshall
Foundation, Lexington, VA*

Pierre Gauchat
*Inter-European Prosperity, Inter-
European Cooperation*
c. 1950
Lithograph
29 ¾ × 21 ½ in.
*Collection of George C. Marshall
Foundation, Lexington, VA*

Alfredo Lalia
To Rise and Live Better
c. 1950
Lithograph
27 ⅛ × 19 ⅛ in.
*Collection of George C. Marshall
Foundation, Lexington, VA*

Mario Puppo
Untitled
c. 1950
Lithograph
29 ¾ × 21 ½ in.
*Collection of George C. Marshall
Foundation, Lexington, VA*

Gaston Van den Eynde
*By the Marshall Plan, Inter-European
Cooperation for a Higher Standard
of Living*
c. 1950
Lithograph
20 × 28 in.
*Collection of George C. Marshall
Foundation, Lexington, VA*

Alban Wyss
Rebuilding Europe
c. 1950
Lithograph
29 ½ × 21 ⅝ in.
*Collection of George C. Marshall
Foundation, Lexington, VA*

Walter Hofmann
A United Europe Brings Prosperity
c. 1950
Lithograph
30 × 21 ½ in.
*Collection of George C. Marshall
Foundation, Lexington, VA*

Erik Oelmebo
*Collaboration for Peacefulness and
High Living Standards*
c. 1950
Lithograph
29 ¾ × 21 ½ in.
*Collection of George C. Marshall
Foundation, Lexington, VA*

Fabien Vienne
Inter-European Cooperation
c. 1950
Lithograph
29 ½ × 21 ½ in.
*Collection of George C. Marshall
Foundation, Lexington, VA*

Louis Emmerick
*Europe, Cooperation Means
Prosperity*
c. 1950
Lithograph
29 ½ × 21 ¾ in.
*Collection of George C. Marshall
Foundation, Lexington, VA*

Andre Golven
New Sap, Better Life
c. 1950
Lithograph
29 ½ × 21 ¾ in.
*Collection of George C. Marshall
Foundation, Lexington, VA*

Brian E. Dear
*Prosperity. The Fruit of Co-Operation.
European Recovery Programme.*
c. 1950
Lithograph
29 ¾ × 21 ⅝ in.
*Collection of George C. Marshall
Foundation, Lexington, VA*

Alfred Lutz
*Inter-European Cooperation for
Better Living*
c. 1950
Lithograph
29 ¾ × 21 ½ in.
*Collection of George C. Marshall
Foundation, Lexington, VA*

Rudolf Korunka
Inter-European Cooperation
c. 1950
Lithograph
29 ½ × 21 ¾ in.
*Collection of George C. Marshall
Foundation, Lexington, VA*

**Leonard Ray Horton
and Ronald Sandifort**
E.R.P. You Hold the Key
c. 1950
Lithograph
28 ⅜ × 18 ⅜ in.
*Collection of George C. Marshall
Foundation, Lexington, VA*

Kurt Krepcik
We Are Building a New Europe
c. 1950
Lithograph
29 ½ × 21 ¾ in.
*Collection of George C. Marshall
Foundation, Lexington, VA*

I. Spreekmeester
*Whatever the Weather, We Only
Reach Welfare Together*
c. 1950
Lithograph
29 ½ × 21 ⅝ in.
*Collection of George C. Marshall
Foundation, Lexington, VA*

Kennan Temizan
All the Same
c. 1950
Lithograph
29 ½ × 21 ¾ in.
*Collection of George C. Marshall
Foundation, Lexington, VA*

**ECA FILMS
ECONOMIC COOPERATION
ADMINISTRATION**

*Marshall Plan at Work
in Western Germany*
1950
Film, black and white, sound
13 minutes
*Collection of George C. Marshall
Foundation, Lexington, VA*

**HICOG (High Commission
for Germany)**
Me and Mr. Marshall
1949
Film, black and white, sound
13 minutes
*Collection of George C. Marshall
Foundation, Lexington, VA*

FLORENCE KNOLL
**Textilien aus U.S.A. | Contemporary
American Textiles**
"Contemporary American Textiles" is
a self-lit, eight-by-sixteen-by-
twenty-four-foot modular
aluminum-framed pavilion with a
drop-in floor. Fourteen double-sided
panels hung by straps and braced by
cross wires are suspended from this
frame. Each panel is assembled
from American designed and
manufactured patterned and woven
textiles stitched together into
geometric compositions.

———
Projected Textiles
Panel 1
Serge Chermayeff
Navajo #1
L. Anton Maix Fabrics, NY
1952
Screen print, linen
34 ¼ × 51 in.
*Committee on Architecture and
Design Funds. The Museum of Modern
Art. Digital image © The Museum
of Modern Art/Licensed by SCALA/
Art Resource, NY*

Alexander H. Girard
Small Squares
Herman Miller Textiles, MI
1953
Screen print, silk
105 ½ × 50 in.
*Promised gift of George R. Kravis II,
7065.119-1.2015. Photo: Matt Flynn
Photo credit: Cooper Hewitt,
Smithsonian Design Museum/
Art Resource, NY*

Don Wight
Garden of Glass
Quaintance Fabrics, NY
c. 1950
Cotton print
78 ½ × 44 ½ in.
*Anonymous gift. The Museum
of Modern Art. Digital image ©
The Museum of Modern Art/Licensed
by SCALA/Art Resource, NY*

Stig Lindberg
Apples
Knoll Inc.
c. 1950
Screen print, plain weave cotton
51 ⅝ × 49 ¼ in.
*Gift of Mae Lamar Festa, 1992-125-
1-a. Photo: Matt Flynn. Cooper Hewitt,
Smithsonian Design. Museum Photo
credit: Cooper Hewitt, Smithsonian
Design Museum/Art Resource, NY*

Philip Johnson
Van Dyke Squares
Arundell Clarke Ltd., NY
c. 1953
Cotton print with discharge
173 ¼ × 52 in.
Gift of Arundell Clarke, 1956-150-8. Photo: Matt Flynn. Cooper Hewitt, Smithsonian Design Museum. Photo credit: Cooper Hewitt, Smithsonian Design Museum/Art Resource, NY

Eszter Haraszty
Tracy
Knoll International Inc.
1952
Screen print, plain weave cotton, rayon blend
119 ⅝ × 48 in.
Courtesy Knoll Inc. Photo credit: Collection of Cranbrook Art Museum, Bloomfield Hills, MI

———

Panel 2, Inside
Hourglass (Field), Air
Knoll Textiles

Double Triangles, Black & White
Alexander Girard, 1952 (originally designed for Herman Miller)
Maharam

Crossroads, Iris
Knoll Textiles

Journey, Twist
Knoll Textiles

Journey, Hot Pink
Knoll Textiles

Pullman, Atrium
Inspired by Kerry Linen, 1953
Knoll Textiles

Tryst, Blue Star
Knoll Textiles

Alter Ego, Splash
Based in part on a 1947
Toni Prestini design
Knoll Textiles

Alter Ego, Key Lime
Based in part on a 1947
Toni Prestini design
Knoll Textiles

Eclat Weave, Black (black and white)
Based on a 1974 Anni Albers print
Knoll Textiles

Milestone, Blackberry
Knoll Textiles

———

Panel 2, Outside
Hourglass (Field), Air
Knoll Textiles

Small Dot Pattern, Charcoal
Designed by Ray Eames, 1947
Maharam

Tivoli, Sanctuary
Knoll Textiles

In Stitches, Neon Stitch
Knoll Textiles

Firefly, Watercolor
Knoll Textiles

Alter Ego, Garnet
Based in part on a 1947
Toni Prestini design
Knoll Textiles

Feeling Plaid, Feeling Inspired (blue/green weave)
Knoll Textiles

Juno, Azurite
Knoll Textiles

Journey, Twist
Knoll Textiles

Utmost, Tomato
Knoll Textiles

Venue, Noir
Knoll Textiles

———

Panel 3, Inside
Looking Glass (Field), Ice
Inspired by 1950s fiberglass casement textiles
Knoll Textiles

Commuter Cloth, Slicker
Knoll Textiles

Commuter Cloth, Clementine
Knoll Textiles

Commuter Cloth, Sorbet
Knoll Textiles

Commuter Cloth, Clementine
Knoll Textiles

Nylon Webbing, Purple
Strapworks

———

Panel 3, Outside
Looking Glass (Field), Ice
Inspired by 1950s fiberglass casement textiles
Knoll Textiles

Commuter Cloth, Slicker
Knoll Textiles

Commuter, Slicker
Knoll Textiles

———

Panel 4, Inside
Hopsack (Field), Buff
Knoll Textiles

Presto, Blue Chip
Knoll Textiles

Modern Tweed, Shetland
Knoll Textiles

Catwalk, Festive
Knoll Textiles

Chroma, Iris
Knoll Textiles

Feeling Plaid, Feeling Happy
Knoll Archive inspired
Knoll Textiles

Little Devil, Lizard
Based on *Devil*, a 1951
Marianne Strengell design
Knoll Textiles

Mini Stitch, Bittersweet
Knoll Textiles

———

Panel 4, Outside
Hopsack (Field), Buff
Knoll Textiles

Little Devil, Canary Yellow
Based on *Devil*, a 1951
Marianne Strengell design
Knoll Textiles

Uni-Form, Ivy
Knoll Textiles

Fibra, Brown/Camel
Based on a 1953
Eszter Haraszty design
Knoll Textiles

Intrigue, Tempting
Knoll Textiles

Classic Boucle, Aegean
Knoll Textiles

Zen Wave, Koi
Knoll Textiles

Hourglass, Tart
Knoll Textiles

———

**Panel 5
(semi-sheer fabrics)**
Entice, Ivory
Knoll Textiles

Escala, White
Knoll Textiles

Caravan, Mirage
Knoll Textiles

Fila, Chalk
Knoll Textiles

———

Panel 6, Inside
Hourglass (Field), Air
Knoll Textiles

Cato, Fire Red
Knoll Textiles

Tara, Nocturne
Knoll Textiles

Cato, Yellow
Knoll Textiles

Sashiko, Mizu
Knoll Textiles

———

Panel 6, Outside
Hourglass (Field), Air
Knoll Textiles

Calypso, Spearmint
Knoll Textiles

Knoll Felt, Tangerine
Knoll Textiles

Overture, Regal
Knoll Textiles

Melange, Flannel
Knoll Textiles

**Projected Textiles
Panel 7**
D. D. & Leslie Tillett
Walnuts
D. D. & Leslie Tillett Inc.
c. 1950
Screen print, plain weave cotton
69 × 52 ½ in.
Gift of Seth Tillett and Nicole Rauscher, 2015-16-12. Cooper Hewitt, Smithsonian Design Museum. Photo credit: Cooper Hewitt, Smithsonian Design Museum/Art Resource, NY

Marianne Strengell
Textile
c. 1950
Screen print, plain weave cotton
97 ⅝ × 48 in.
Cooper Hewitt, Smithsonian Design Museum. Gift of Marianne Strengell, 1984-111-74. Photo: Matt Flynn Cooper Hewitt, Smithsonian Design Museum. Photo credit: Cooper Hewitt, Smithsonian Design Museum/ Art Resource, NY

Angelo Testa
Campagna
Knoll Associates Inc.
c. 1951
Screen print, linen
69 × 52 ½ in.
Gift of Nicholas A. Pappas, FAIA, 2002-14-3. Photo: Matt Flynn © Smithsonian Institution Cooper Hewitt, Smithsonian Design Museum. Photo credit: Cooper Hewitt, Smithsonian Design Museum/Art Resource, NY

Bernard Rudofsky
Fractions
Schiffer Prints
c. 1949
Screen print, twill weave cotton
50 × 51 in.
Gift of Berta Rudofsky, 1991-101-1. Photo: Matt Flynn. Cooper Hewitt, Smithsonian Design Museum. Photo credit: Cooper Hewitt, Smithsonian Design Museum/Art Resource, NY

Noémi Raymond
Chinese Coin
Knoll Textiles
1948
Print, linen
51 ¾ × 25 ⅛ in.
Gift of Mae Lamar Festa. 1991-157-S. Photo: Matt Flynn © Smithsonian Institution Cooper Hewitt, Smithsonian Design Museum. Photo credit: Cooper Hewitt, Smithsonian Design Museum/ Art Resource, NY

Ross Littell
Border Riff #3
Laverne Originals, NY
c. 1948
Batiste
64 ½ × 46 in.
*Gift of the manufacturer. The Museum
of Modern Art. Digital image © The
Museum of Modern Art/Licensed by
SCALA/Art Resource, NY*

———

Panel 8, Title Wall
Lorelei, Tinsel
Knoll Textiles

———

Panel 9, Inner Left Wall
Indigo Selvage, Dark Blue
Cone Denim

Radiance, Caraway
Based on *Puli*, a 1951
Marianne Strengell design
Knoll Textiles

———

Panel 10, Inner Center Wall
Helios, Daisy
Knoll Textiles

Helios, Nectarine
Knoll Textiles

———

Panel 11, Inner Right Wall
Uni-Form, Fresco
Knoll Textiles

Knoll Felt, Cadet
Knoll Textiles

———

Panel 12, Inner Ceiling
Entice, Ivory
Knoll Textiles

Caravan, Mirage
Knoll Textiles

———

Panel 13, Ceiling Left Corner
Fila, Chalk
Knoll Textiles

———

Panel 14, Ceiling Right Corner
Looking Glass, Ice
Knoll Textiles

———

Mobile
Stretch Appeal, Red
Knoll Textiles

Stretch Appeal, Avocado
Knoll Textiles

———

AMERIKA HAUS | AMERICA HOUSE
Studio Müller-Blase
Felix Müller and Karl Oskar Blase
*Industrial Art and Printing
in the U.S.A., America House, Berlin*
1954
Color screen print (facsimile)
36 ¾ × 27 ¼ in.
*Photo credit: Prints & Photographs
Division, Library of Congress,
LC-DIG-ds-07680*

Stefan P. Munsing
*American Household Appliance,
America House, Munich*
1951
Color screen print (facsimile)
36 ¾ × 27 ¼ in.
*Courtesy of the Estates of
Stefan P. and Juliana D. Munsing,
all rights reserved. Photo credit:
Prints & Photographs Division, Library
of Congress, LC-DIG-ds-07678*

Studio Müller-Blase
300 Years of American Glass
1954
Color screen print (facsimile)
36 ¾ × 27 ¼ in.
*Photo credit: Prints & Photographs
Division, Library of Congress,
LC-DIG-ds-07681*

Studio Müller-Blase
American Home Appliances
1952
Color screen print (facsimile)
36 ¾ × 27 ¼ in.
*Photo credit: Prints & Photographs
Division, Library of Congress,
LC-DIG-ds-07679*

Unknown photographer
*Window Displays of the
New Amerika Haus Always
Attract the Attention
of Passersby*
November 24, 1952
Photographic reproduction
Dimensions variable
*US Information Agency, National
Archives and Records Administration,
College Park, MD (306-CS-1D-3)*

Unknown photographer
*Location of Information Centers and
Bookmobiles in Western Germany*
January 1952
Photographic reproduction
36 × 47 ½ in.
*US Information Agency, National
Archives and Records Administration,
College Park, MD (306-CS-3A-16)*

TOM LEE
**Tapeten aus USA | Contemporary
American Wallpapers**
Research yielded no photographs,
sketches, or installation instructions
documenting Lee's presentation
of wall coverings designed and
manufactured in America.

Piranesi
Piazza Prints Inc., NY
1952
Screen print, paper (facsimile)
76 × 29 ¹⁵⁄₁₆ in.
*Gift of Piazza Prints Inc., 1954-1-2.
Photo: Matt Flynn. Cooper Hewitt,
Smithsonian Design Museum
Photo credit: Cooper Hewitt,
Smithsonian Design Museum/
Art Resource, NY*

Saul Steinberg
Wedding Picture
Piazza Prints Inc., NY
1950
Screen print, paper (facsimile)
27 ⁵⁄₁₆ × 30 ¹⁵⁄₁₆ in.
*Gift of Harvey Smith, 1950-126-2.
Photo: Matt Flynn. Cooper Hewitt,
Smithsonian Design Museum.
Photo credit: Cooper Hewitt,
Smithsonian Design Museum/
Art Resource, NY*

Saul Steinberg
Views of Paris
Piazza Prints Inc., NY
1946–1950
Screen print, paper (facsimile)
44 ⅞ × 29 ¹⁵⁄₁₆ in..
*Gift of Harvey Smith, 1950-126-4-b.
Photo: Matt Flynn. Cooper Hewitt,
Smithsonian Design Museum.
Photo credit: Cooper Hewitt,
Smithsonian Design Museum/
Art Resource, NY*

Portia LeBrun
Balloons
Piazza Prints Inc., NY
1950–51
Screen print, paper (facsimile)
30 ¹⁵⁄₁₆ × 27 ⁹⁄₁₆ in.
*Gift of Jessup Inc., 1958-115-31.
Photo: Matt Flynn. Cooper Hewitt,
Smithsonian Design Museum
Photo credit: Cooper Hewitt,
Smithsonian Design Museum/
Art Resource, NY*

Ben Rose
Time Capsule
Ben Rose Inc., IL
c. 1954, reprinted 1988
Screen print (facsimile)
118 ½ × 51 ⅞ in.
*Gift of Mr. and Mrs. Ben Rose
(through The Art Institute of Chicago),
1989-62-10. Cooper Hewitt,
Smithsonian Design Museum
Photo credit: Cooper Hewitt,
Smithsonian Design Museum/
Art Resource, NY*

Ray Komai
Masks
Laverne Originals
1948–49
Screen print, paper (facsimile)
46 × 53 in.
*Costume Council Fund
(AC1998.86.1). Los Angeles County
Museum of Art
Digital image © 2018 Museum
Associates/LACMA/Licensed
by Art Resource, NY*

William Justema (?)
Mosaic
Katzenbach and Warren Inc.
1950–51
Screen print, paper (facsimile)
19 ¹⁵⁄₁₆ × 29 ¹⁵⁄₁₆
*Gift of Katzenbach and Warren Inc.,
1952-88-6. Photo: Matt Flynn
Cooper Hewitt, Smithsonian Design
Museum. Photo credit: Cooper Hewitt,
Smithsonian Design Museum/Art
Resource, NY*

Ilonka Karasz and William Justema
Chicken Wire
Katzenbach and Warren Inc.
1949
Screen print, paper (facsimile)
17 ¹¹⁄₁₆ × 29 ⅛ in.
*Gift of Katzenbach and Warren Inc.,
1949-46-1-9. Photo: Matt Flynn
Cooper Hewitt, Smithsonian Design
Museum. Photo credit: Cooper Hewitt,
Smithsonian Design Museum/
Art Resource, NY*

Marion Dorn
Master Drawings
Katzenbach and Warren Inc.
1951
Screen print, paper (facsimile)
49 ¼ × 28 ¾ in.
Photo credit: Historic New England

Ben Rose
Foliation II
Ben Rose Inc., IL
1946, reprinted 1988
Screen print (facsimile)
121 ½ × 49 ⅛ in.
*Gift of Mr. and Mrs. Ben Rose
(through The Art Institute of Chicago),
1989-62-2. Photo: Matt Flynn
Cooper Hewitt, Smithsonian Design
Museum. Photo credit: Cooper Hewitt,
Smithsonian Design Museum/
Art Resource, NY*

Aesop's Fables
Herndon Papers
1953
Screen print, paper (facsimile)
36 × 29 ¹⁵⁄₁₆ in.
*Gift of The Wallpaper Magazine,
1953-198-12. Photo: Matt Flynn
Cooper Hewitt, Smithsonian Design
Museum. Photo credit: Cooper Hewitt,
Smithsonian Design Museum/Art
Resource, NY*

George Nelson
Stimulus Fabrics: Chips
Schiffer Prints
1949
Screen print (facsimile)
108 × 52 in.
Museum purchase from General
Acquisitions Endowment Fund,
2015-19-3. Photo: Matt Flynn.
Cooper Hewitt, Smithsonian
Design Museum

Nancy McClelland
George Washington
Nancy McClelland Inc.
1950–60
Screen print, paper (facsimile)
23 ¼ × 22 in.
Photo credit: Historic New England

Ilonka Karasz
Ducks and Grasses
Katzenbach and Warren Inc.
1940–50
Unused wallpaper sample backed
on cardboard mat (facsimile)
31 ½ × 27 ¾ in.
Photo credit: Historic New England

Alexander Calder
"Calder #1" Textile (Model No. 1-145)
Laverne Originals
1949
Rayon, fiberglass (facsimile)
55 × 49 ½ in.
Gift of Mrs. David M. Stewart, 1984
(1984.565). The Metropolitan
Museum of Art, New York, NY.
Image copyright © The Metropolitan
Museum of Art. Image source:
Art Resource, NY

WILL BURTIN
Werbepackung in Amerika |
Containers & Packaging
"Containers & Packaging" is
composed of three framed,
double-sided wooden rectangles,
each four by eight by one and a half
feet, equally divided into eighteen
compartments. Each compartment
housed containers and packages
designed and manufactured in
America, replicated here using Ezra
Stoller's photographs of Burtin's
original exhibit. Burtin included a
label that followed MoMA's "Good
Design" format, listing product
name, designer, and manufacturer;
the same format is followed here.

Courtesy of Carol Burtin Fripp.
Photo credit: © Ezra Stoller/Esto

Purchase Appeal
and Grabbing Attention
Front
First row, from left to right:
Simoniz
Floor polish container
Design: Lester Beall
Simoniz Company of Chicago,
Chicago, IL

McGavin's
Waxed-paper bag for white bread
Design: Paul Rand
McGavin's Bakeries,
Vancouver, BC

El Producto
Father's Day cigar packaging
Design: Paul Rand
G. H. P. Cigar Company,
New York, NY

Bab-O
Packaging for scouring powder
Design: Paul Rand
The B. T. Babbit Co.,
New York, NY

EZE-Hang
Container for wallpaper
Design: Design Laboratory,
Container Corporation of America
E.Z.E. Home Furnishers,
Chicago, IL

Brach
Packaging for candy
Design: Lester Beall
E. J. Brach & Sons,
Chicago, IL

Zymacap
Package for vitamin capsules
Design: Will Burtin
The Upjohn Company,
Kalamazoo, MI

Second row:
Martin Senour
Package and folder for color samples
Design: Morton Goldsholl
Martin Senour Paints,
Chicago, IL

Shur Edge
Package for carving knives
Design: Design Laboratory,
Container Corporation of America
American Kitchen Equipment Co.,
Evanston, IL

El Producto
Cigar wrapper made
of synthetic material
Design: Paul Rand
G. H. P. Cigar Company,
New York, NY

Santa Claus
Gift packaging
Design: Saul Steinberg
Neiman Marcus Department Store,
Dallas, TX

Presto
Pocket pack for suede shoe cleaner
The Woolworth Co.,
New York, NY

Brach's Thin Mints
Box for peppermint candies
Design: Lester Beall
E. J. Brach & Sons,
Chicago, IL

Woolco
Packaging for straight pins
and safety pins
The Woolworth Co.,
New York, NY

Tot 50
Package for small stapler
Speed Products Co.,
Long Island City, NY

Disney
Hatbox for men's hats
Design: Paul Rand
Disney Hats Inc.,
New York, NY

Third row:
Sunkist
Orange peel as packaging
California Fruit Growers Association

Stafford
Box for nightgowns
Design: Paul Rand
Goodman-Theiss Inc.,
New York, NY

Petri
Wine bottles and labels
Design: Walter Landor
Angelo Petri Vineyards,
San Francisco, CA

Indian
Gift packaging
Design: Alma Shon
Neiman Marcus Department Store,
Dallas, TX

Brach "Totem Pole"
Box for chocolates
Design: Design Laboratory,
Container Corporation of America
E. J. Brach & Sons,
Chicago, IL

Pabco
Can for wood stain
Design: Walter Landor,
The Paraffine Companies Inc.,
San Francisco, CA

Back
First row, from left to right:
Villa
Packaging for candy
Design: Design Laboratory,
Container Corporation of America
E. J. Brach & Sons, Chicago, IL

Factories and Products
Protective envelope
for color negatives
Design: Morton Goldsholl
Container Corporation of America,
Chicago, IL

EZE-Hang
Container for wallpaper
Design: Design Laboratory,
Container Corporation of America
E. Z. E. Home Furnishers,
Chicago, IL

El Producto
Father's Day cigar packaging
Design: Paul Rand
G. H. P. Cigar Company,
New York, NY

Bab-O
Packaging for scouring powder
Design: Paul Rand
The B. T. Babbit Co.,
New York, NY

Country Club
Packaging for
fruit-flavored ice cream
Design: Paul Rand
Country Club Ice Cream Company,
Patterson, NJ

McGavin's
Waxed paper bag for white bread
Design: Paul Rand
McGavin's Bakeries,
Vancouver, BC

Simoniz
Floor polish container
Design: Lester Beall
Simoniz Company of Chicago,
Chicago, IL

Second row:
Abbott
Packaging for capsule medicine
Design: Harry H. Farrell
Abbott Laboratories,
Chicago, IL

Christmas
Gift wrapping
Design: Alma Shon
Neiman-Marcus Department Store,
Dallas, TX

Rosemarie Reid
Box for bathing suits
Design: Saul Bass
Rosemarie Reid Swimsuits,
Los Angeles, CA

Cremex
Container for a cosmetic hand cream
Design: Saul Bass
Sandra Cassil,
Los Angeles, CA

Barri-Cigars
Container for chocolate cigars,
Barricini Candies,
New York, NY

Air-Wick Mist
Spray against kitchen odors
Design: Paul Rand
Seaman Brothers,
New York, NY

Martin Senour
Package and folder for color samples
Design: Morton Goldsholl
Martin Senour Paints,
Chicago, IL

———
Third Row:
Pabco
Can for wood stain
Design: Walter Landor
The Paraffine Companies Inc.,
San Francisco, CA

Coolfoam
Box for pillows
Design: Design Laboratory,
Container Corporation of America
Dayton Cushion Co.,
Dayton, OH

Brach's Wafer Mints
Box for peppermint candies
Design: Lester Beall
E. J. Brach & Sons,
Chicago, IL

Steuben Glass
Protective box for valuable glasses
Design: Steuben Glass
Design Department
Steuben Glass Inc.,
Corning, NY

Coty
Small palette for jewelry
Coty Inc.,
New York, NY

Pond's
Pocket packaging for facial tissues
Design: Lester Beall
Pond's Extract Co.,
New York, NY

Diamond
The nutshell as package
Diamond Nuts Inc.,
San Francisco, CA

———
**Technical
Resourcefulness**
Front
First row, from left to right:
Kleenex Tissues
Box for facial tissues
Design: Harry H. Farrell
International Cellu-Cotton
Products Co.,
Chicago, IL

Captain's Choice
Box for frozen fish
Design: Walter Landor
for Belmont Supplies
Brighton Fish Co., CA

Bel-Air
Boxes for frozen fruits and vegetables
Design: Walter Landor
Whitney Frozen Food Co.,
Sacramento, CA

Cadwrap
*Paper cushioning
for packing machinery parts*
Cadillac Products Co.,
Ferndale, MI
*Photo shows old and new ways
of packing and shipping spare parts
for General Motors cars*

Kys-Pak-Tray
*Pressed paper layer separators
for shipping apples*
Design: Design Laboratory,
Container Corporation of America
California Fruit Growers Association

Shipping Reenforcer
*Flexible paper material to protect
precision machine parts*
The Union Bag Co.,
Chicago, IL

Rise
Aerosol dispenser for shaving cream
The Carter Products Co.,
New York, NY

Finesse
*Transparent soft bottle
for liquid shampoo*
Jules Montenier,
Chicago, IL

Slick-Chick
*Carrying case, also used
for shipping live chickens*
Design: Design Laboratory,
Container Corporation of America
Western Poultry Farmers
Association

———
Second Row
Pressed paper layer separator
*For small machine parts
or fragile products*
Design: Design Laboratory,
Container Corporation of America
Western Poultry Farmers
Association

Alpine
Carrying case for beer bottles

Motorola
*Protective and carrying case
for radio equipment*
Design: Container
Corporation of America,
Chicago, IL

L.S.2.
Case for dental supplies
Design: Albert Yochim
Lee S. Smith & Son,
Chicago, IL

Red Cross
Adhesive bandages for home use
Johnson & Johnson,
New Brunswick, NJ

**Sterile Vaseline
Petrolatum Dressing**
*Sealed, sterile,
Vaseline-laden gauze for burns*

Daisy B.B.
*Box for bullets
for sporting weapons*

Rexall Plenamin
Box for vitamin pills

Rexall Shampoo
Box for powdered shampoo

Chase & Sanborn
*Container holding ground
coffee for one cup of coffee*

Kraft
*Marmalade containers
for use in restaurants*
The Dobeckmun Co.,
Cleveland, OH

Olin
Box for a flashlight
Design: Olin Industries Inc.,
New Haven, CT

S.V.E.
Box for a film library
Design: Morton Goldsholl
Society for Visual Education,
Chicago, IL

———
Third row
Upjohn Unicaps
Sample vitamin package for doctors
Design: Will Burtin
The Upjohn Company,
Kalamazoo, MI

Burgess Vibra Tool
Packaging for shipping tools
Design: Morton Goldsholl
Burgess Battery Co.,
Lake Zurich, IL

Kiddie Pops
Packaging for suckers
Design: Design Laboratory,
Container Corporation of America
E. J. Brach & Sons,
Chicago, IL

Cut-Kit
First-aid kit for travelers
Johnson & Johnson,
New Brunswick, NJ

Gulfspray Aerosol Bomb
Aerosol spray for mosquitoes and bugs
Design: DeForest Sacket
Crown Can Co.,
Chicago, IL

Borden's
Tin can for grated hard cheese
The Borden Co.,
New York, NY

Green-Core
*Transparent packaging
for adhesive tape*
Mid-States Gummed Paper Co.,
Chicago, IL

Gillette
*One of the oldest packages
for razor blades*
Gillette Safety Razor Co.,
Boston, MA

Grayvan
*Packing container for an
overland shipping company*
Design and production:
Design Laboratory, Container
Corporation of America
Greyvan Shipping Co.,
Detroit, MA

———
Back
First row, from left to right:
Hang-Mor
Packaging for metal clothes hangers
Design: Design Laboratory,
Container Corporation of America
Smith & Wesson,
Flint, MI

Armour
Wrap for smoked meat products
Design: Raymond Loewy Associates
Armour & Co.,
Chicago, IL

Aero-Shave
*Aerosol dispenser
for shaving cream*
Boyle Midway Co.,
Cranford, NJ

Cadwrap
*Paper cushioning for packing
of machine parts*
Cadillac Products Co.,
Ferndale, MI

Bel-Air
Frozen fruit and vegetable packaging
Design: Walter Landor
Whitney Frozen Food Co.,
Sacramento, CA

Kleenex Tissues
Packaging for paper facial tissues
Design: Harry H. Farrell
International Cellu-Cotton Products
Co., Chicago, IL

———
Second row:
Olin
Packaging for flashlight
Design: Olin Industries Inc.,
New Haven, CT

S.V.E.
Container for a film library
Design: Morton Goldsholl
Society for Visual Education,
Chicago, IL

Motorola
*Protective and carrying case
for radio equipment*
Design: Design Laboratory,
Container Corporation of America
Motorola Radio Corporation,
Chicago, IL

Alpine
Carrying case for beer bottles
Design: Design Laboratory,
Container Corporation of America
Alpine Beer Co.,
Grand Rapids, MI

*Various bottles and
containers made out of plastic*

Scotch Tape
Packaging for cellophane tape
DuPont, Wilmington, DE

Egg carton
For American wholesale and retail use
Design: Design Laboratory,
Container Corporation of America,
Chicago, IL

Third row:
Container for overseas shipping
*This experimental automobile travels
in its own tool box*
Design and production:
General Motors Corporation,
Detroit, MI

Stak-Lok-Lug
Carton for shipping grapes
Design: Design laboratory,
Container Corporation of America
California Fruit Growers Association

Borden's Golden Whip
Aerosol can for whipped cream

Borden's Grated Cheese
Package for grated hard cheese
The Borden Co.,
New York, NY

Asti
Tissue paper wrap for wine bottles
Design: Walter Landor
Italian Swiss Colony Wines,
Sacramento, CA

Burgess Vibra Tool
Packaging for shipping tools
Design: Morton Goldsholl,
Burgess Battery Co.,
Lake Zurich, IL

American bottles and canning jars,
produced before 1850, and probably
used during the great wagon trains
to the west (from the collection of
Fred A. Chappell, Kalamazoo, MI)

**Mass Production
and Design Issues**
Front
First row, from left to right:
Kodak
Packaging for photographic material
Eastman Kodak Company,
Rochester, NY

Para Pure
Jars or cans with lids for moth balls
Reefer Galler Inc., NY

Delco Remy
Packaging for auto parts
Delco Remy Division,
General Motors Corporation,
Anderson, IN

Evenflo
Packaging for baby products
Design: Design Laboratory,
Container Corporation of America
The Pyramid Rubber Co.,
Ravenna, OH

Thor
Packaging for tools
Design: Design Laboratory,
Container Corporation of America
Independent Pneumatic Tool Co.,
Aurora, IL

Second row:
Kodak
Packaging for photographic material
Eastman Kodak Company,
Rochester, NY

Eagle
Cans for assorted screws
The Woolworth Co.,
New York, NY

Ballantine
Carrying case for beer bottles
Design: Lester Beall
P. Ballantine & Sons,
New York, NY

G.M.
*Packaging for machine parts
for automobiles*
Design: Design Department,
General Motors Corporation,
Detroit, MI

Thor
Packaging for tools
Design: Design Laboratory,
Container Corporation of America
Independent Pneumatic Tool Co.,
Aurora, IL

Third row:
Cortalex
Pocket packaging for medicinal tablets
Design: Will Burtin
The Upjohn Company,
Kalamazoo, MI

FoMoCo
*Packaging for all kinds
of automobile parts*
Design: Design Laboratory,
Container Corporation of America
Ford Motor Company,
Detroit, MI

Kotex
Packaging for hygienic products
Design: Harry H. Farrell
The Kotex Co.,
Chicago, IL

A. B. Dick
Packaging for office supplies
Design: Design Laboratory,
Container Corporation of America
The A. B. Dick Co.,
Chicago, IL

Back
First row, from left to right:
Thor
Packaging for tools
Design: Design Laboratory,
Container Corporation of America
Independent Pneumatic Tool Co.,
Aurora, IL

Evenflo
*Packaging for supplies
for small children*
Design: Design Laboratory,
Container Corporation of America
The Pyramid Rubber Co.,
Ravenna, OH

Farrington
Carton for sheets and bedding
Design: Design Laboratory,
Container Corporation of America
Farrington Mills Inc.,
New Bedford, MA

De Luxe
Packaging for paper for office use
Design: Design Laboratory,
Container Corporation of America
Michigan Paper Co.,
Flint, MI

Italian Balm
Packaging for skin cream
Design: Harry H. Farrell
Campana Corporation,
Batavia, IL

Kodak
*Packaging for
photographic supplies*
Design: Design Department,
Eastman Kodak Company,
Rochester, NY

Second row:
Thor
Packaging for tools
Design: Design Laboratory,
Container Corporation of America
Independent Pneumatic Tool Co.,
Aurora, IL

G.M.
*Packaging for machine parts
for automobiles*
Design: Design Department,
General Motors Corporation,
Detroit, MI

Ballantine
Carrying case for beer bottles
Design: Lester Beall
P. Ballantine & Sons,
New York, NY

Eagle
Cans for assorted screws
The Woolworth Co.,
New York, NY

Wrigley's Gum
Pack for chewing gum
Wrigley Jr.,
Chicago, IL

Beechies
Chewing gum package
The Beechnut Packing Co.,
Canajoharie, NY

Kodak
*Packaging for
photographic supplies*
Design: Design Department,
Eastman Kodak Company,
Rochester, NY

Third row:
A. B. Dick
Packaging for office supplies
Design: Design Laboratory,
Container Corporation of America
A. B. Dick Co.,
Cincinnati, OH

Kotex
Packaging for hygienic products
Design: Harry H. Farrell,
The Kotex Co.,
Chicago, IL

FoMoCo
Packaging for car parts
Design: Design Laboratory,
Container Corporation of America
Ford Motor Company,
Detroit, MI

Shott
Packaging for a folding chair
Design: Design Laboratory,
Container Corporation of America
Balcrank Inc.,
Cincinnati, OH

**FLORENCE KNOLL
ELECTRONIC DISPLAY**
Photographer unknown
Florence Knoll Portrait
7 didactic panels
*Black-and-white photograph courtesy
Knoll Inc.*

Florence Knoll
*Knoll Showroom,
575 Madison Ave, NY, NY*
View of installation
featuring Barcelona chairs
and ottoman designed by
Ludwig Mies van der Rohe
1951
*Courtesy Knoll Inc. Photo credit:
Robert Damora © Damora Archive,
all rights reserved Knoll Archives*

Florence Knoll
Paste-up for Cowles Publication
Courtesy Knoll Inc.

Florence Knoll
*Knoll Showroom,
601 Madison Avenue, NY, NY*
View of installation with
Womb Chair by Eero Saarinen,
string screen by Herbert Matter,
and textile display
1948
*Courtesy Knoll Inc. Photo credit:
Robert Damora © Damora Archive,
all rights reserved*

Herbert Matter
*Knoll Inc. Advertisement
Featuring Stig Lindberg's Apples,
Astrid Sampe's Stripes, and
Noémi Raymond's Chinese Coins*
1948
Courtesy Knoll Inc.

Florence Knoll/Knoll Planning Unit
Office for CBS President,
John A. Schneider
1965
Courtesy Knoll Inc. Photo credit:
Robert Damora © Damora Archive,
all rights reserved

Amerika Haus
America Haus Interior with
Knoll-manufactured Seating
Man reading a book at Amerika Haus
Augsburg Library, Germany
c. 1950
Gelatin silver print (photographic
reproduction)
8 ¼ × 6 ⅞ in.
Image courtesy Prints & Photographs
Division, Library of Congress,
LC-DIG-ds-07675

Angelo Testa
Campagna
Knoll Associates Inc.
c. 1951
Screen print, linen
69 × 52 ½ in.
Gift of Nicholas A. Pappas, FAIA,
2002-14-3. Photo: Matt Flynn ©
Smithsonian Institution Cooper Hewitt,
Smithsonian Design Museum. Photo
credit: Cooper Hewitt, Smithsonian
Design Museum/Art Resource, NY

Florence Knoll Bassett
Knoll Exhibit
Philadelphia Museum of Art
2004
Courtesy Knoll Inc. Photo credit:
Philadelphia Museum of Art

D. D. and Leslie Tillett
Printed Textile
(Chrysanthemum pattern)
1947–81
Silk print, plain weave
221 × 52 ⅜ in.
Courtesy Seth Tillett. Photo credit:
Philadelphia Museum of Art, Gift
of Seth Tillett, 201217946

Eszter Haraszty
Fibra
Printed by Printext,
produced by Knoll Textiles
1953
Screen print, linen
36 ¼ × 25 in.
Gift of Mae Lamar Festa, 1991-157-
6,a,b. Photo: Andrew Garn. Cooper
Hewitt, Smithsonian Design Museum.
Photo credit: Cooper Hewitt,
Smithsonian Design Museum/Art
Resource, NY

Noémi Raymond
Squares, Blobs, Speckles
Cyrus Clark Co. Inc., NY
Before 1941
Cotton print
89 × 46 in.
Gift of the designer. The Museum
of Modern Art. Digital image © The
Museum of Modern Art/Licensed
by SCALA/Art Resource, NY

TOM LEE
ELECTRONIC DISPLAY
Tom Lee Portrait
Undated
Sarah Tomerlin Lee and Tom Lee
Collection, nysidar_2013_01,
Box 9, Folder 9, New York School
of Interior Design, New York, NY
(stamped on back "Photograph by
Rawings"); image courtesy of the
NYSID Archives & Special Collections

Tom Lee
Bonwit Teller Window Display
1940s
Sarah Tomerlin Lee Archives,
New York School of Interior Design,
NY. Photo credit: Worsinger; image
courtesy of the NYSID Archives
& Special Collections

Tom Lee
Drawings, Various Designs
for Golden Jubilee Floats
1941–1970s
Sarah Tomerlin Lee Archives,
New York School of Interior Design,
NY; image courtesy of the NYSID
Archives & Special Collections

Tom Lee
Lever House Christmas Carousel
c. 1950s
Sarah Tomerlin Lee and Tom Lee
Collection, nysidar_2013_01, Box 13,
Folder 6, New York School of Interior
Design, NY; image courtesy of the
NYSID Archives & Special Collections

Tom Lee
Lever House Shopping Display
1953–57
Sarah Tomerlin Lee and Tom Lee
Collection, nysidar_2013_01, Box 13,
Folder 7, New York School of Interior
Design, NY; image courtesy of the
NYSID Archives & Special Collections

Tom Lee
Photograph and Visa Memo,
Moscow Exhibit Beauty Salon,
Moscow Fashion Show
c. 1958
Sarah Tomerlin Lee Archives,
New York School of Interior Design,
NY; image courtesy of the NYSID
Archives & Special Collections

Tom Lee
Photograph and Visa Memo,
Moscow Exhibit, Fashion Show
c. 1958
Sarah Tomerlin Lee Archives,
New York School of Interior Design,
NY; image courtesy of the NYSID
Archives & Special Collections

Ilonka Karasz
Page from a Sample Book (Arches)
Katzenbach and Warren Inc.
1948
Mezzotone print, paper
11 ¼ × 8 ¹¹⁄₁₆ in.
Gift of Katzenbach and Warren Inc.,
1959-134-1-16. Photo ©
Smithsonian Institution. Cooper Hewitt,
Smithsonian Design Museum. Photo
credit: Cooper Hewitt, Smithsonian
Design Museum/Art Resource, NY

Ilonka Karasz
Drawing
c. 1950
Watercolor and crayon on paper
47 ¼ × 29 ½ in.
Gift of Katzenbach and Warren Inc.,
1964-37-10-a,b. Photo: Matt Flynn
© Smithsonian Institution Cooper
Hewitt, Smithsonian Design Museum.
Photo credit: Cooper Hewitt,
Smithsonian Design Museum/Art
Resource, NY

William Katavolos, Douglas Kelley,
Ross Littell, and Alton Kelley
Side Chair
Laverne Inc., New York, NY
1952
Steel, plastic
31 ½ × 21 ⅜ × 24 in.
Gift of the manufacturer. The Museum
of Modern Art. Digital image © The
Museum of Modern Art/Licensed by
SCALA/Art Resource, NY

WILL BURTIN
ELECTRONIC DISPLAY
Photographer unknown
Will Burtin as Art Director
of "Fortune" magazine
1945
Photograph
Courtesy of Carol Burtin Fripp
Photo credit: RIT Cary Graphic Arts
Collection, Wallace Center, Rochester
Institute of Technology

Will Burtin
"Nose attack" spread, pp. S28-S29.
WWII Gunnery manual: Position
Firing, May 1944, Designed for the
U.S. Office of Strategic Services
Courtesy of Carol Burtin Fripp
Photo credit: RIT Cary Graphic Arts
Collection, Wallace Center, Rochester
Institute of Technology

Will Burtin
The Cell Exhibit
1958
Courtesy of Carol Burtin Fripp
Photo credit: RIT Cary Graphic Arts
Collection, Wallace Center, Rochester
Institute of Technology

Will Burtin
Will Burtin Narrating the Brain
Exhibit at the 1960 American
Medical Association Meeting
1960
Courtesy of Carol Burtin Fripp
Photo credit: RIT Cary Graphic Arts
Collection, Wallace Center, Rochester
Institute of Technology

Will Burtin
Paper ribbon detail representing
industry of Kalamazoo, Michigan.
Kalamazoo...Eine Mittelstadt in
Mittelwesten exhibit, Berlin Fair
1958
Courtesy of Carol Burtin Fripp
Photo credit: RIT Cary Graphic Arts
Collection, Wallace Center, Rochester
Institute of Technology

Morton and Millie Goldsholl
Installation view of the exhibition
"Good Design." The Museum
of Modern Art, New York
November 27, 1951, through
January 27, 1952.
Digital image © The Museum of
Modern Art/Licensed by SCALA/
Art Resource, NY

Walter Landor
Bel-Air packaging for
frozen fruits and vegetables
Whitney Frozen Food Co.,
Sacramento, CA
Photo credit: Landor Design
Collection, Archives Center,
National Museum of American History,
Smithsonian Institution

Paepcke/Container Corporation
of America
Poster, Ben Shahn/John Locke
"Great Ideas of Western Man"
Art © Estate of Bernarda Bryson
Shahn/Licensed by VAGA, New York,
NY. Photo credit: University of Illinois
at Chicago, Special Collections &
University Archives

Biographies of Key Figures
CHELSEA MERTON AND MARGARET RE

Anni Albers

Anni Albers (née Fleischmann, 1899–1994) is generally regarded as the most influential textile designer of the twentieth century.[1] She was the first weaver to have a solo exhibition at the Museum of Modern Art in New York; her books *On Designing* and *On Weaving* are considered seminal works in the field of textile design; and her work continues to be reproduced by manufacturers today.[2]

Albers was from an affluent family; her mother was from a German-Jewish publishing family, and her father was a furniture manufacturer.[3] She began studying painting with impressionist painter Martin Brandenburg when she was seventeen, but was discouraged from further pursuit of painting by Oskar Kokoschka, who believed that Albers "would have been better off as a housewife and a mother."[4] In 1922, Albers then spent two unfulfilling months in the School of Arts and Crafts (Kunstgewerbeschule) in Hamburg — she enrolled in the Weaving Workshop at the Bauhaus later that same year. At the Bauhaus, Albers studied under Paul Klee, although she asserted that his influence was less in the classroom and more through observing his work.[5] Albers received a Bauhaus diploma in 1930 after developing a woven cellophane wall covering to replace the dark, heavy velvet used for acoustic dampening in concert halls. Inspired by a cap that she had purchased in Florence, her wall treatment absorbed sound but also beautifully reflected light.[6] At the Bauhaus, Anni met her husband, Josef Albers, an accomplished painter and the first student to attain the status of Master. Together they immigrated to the United States in 1933, following the decision to close the Bauhaus. They were invited to teach at Black Mountain College in North Carolina, where Anni established the Weaving Workshop.

Albers's work is characterized by bold geometric patterns, textures, and innovative uses of both conventional and unconventional materials, often melding industrial needs with traditional weaving methods. She found the discipline of weaving liberating, and preferred working with abstract imagery, relying instead on the materials themselves to provide visual interest. For her, the most important factor in creating a textile was its intended function.[7] That said, she believed that art and design were essential to the human experience.[8] After the death of her husband in 1976, Albers shifted her focus to printmaking, a medium at which she was said to be "prolific."[9] CM

Evelyn Anselevicius

Born and raised in Oklahoma, American weaver Evelyn Anselevicius (née Hill, 1925–2003) was best known for creating large, textural, three-dimensional tapestries for display in public spaces. She studied under Josef Albers at Black Mountain College, and later at the Institute of Design in Chicago, where she met her husband George Anselevicius, a Lithuanian-born architect and educator. She briefly worked at Knoll Textiles as the director of the handweaving studio. Her handwoven textiles were shown in the international "Good Design" exhibition at the Museum of Modern Art in New York City in 1953, and later in "Wall Hangings," from February 25 to May 4, 1969, which featured work that was "in no way concerned with the pictorial aspects of weaving."[10]

Anselevicius was described by her husband as "a strong woman [known for] her commitment to her work."[11] Although most of her pieces were around six by seven feet, she is best known for working on enormous tapestries commissioned for display in public spaces. For example, she created a sixty-five-by-sixteen-foot tapestry for the Colorado School of Mines, a nineteen-by-twenty-four-foot tapestry for the Crown Center Hotel in Kansas City, and a thirty-five-by-forty-foot piece for the West Building of the BMO Harris Financial Corporation Headquarters in Chicago — a unique project, as this was the first building project in the United States to include commissioned artwork.[12] Her tapestries have an unusually three-dimensional quality about them and "often are constructed of beading, feathers, and metal fibers."[13] They frequently feature giant faces. Anselevicius, who had a longtime love of Mexican weaving, worked with "wool that was spun and dyed in Mexico," and often wove her biggest projects "on the ten-foot-wide looms in the artist colony at San Miguel de Allende in Guanajuato, Mexico."[14] CM

Richard Lee Brecker

US Department of State officer Richard Lee Brecker (1921–2005) identified propaganda as "a major weapon in the Cold War arsenals on both sides of the Iron Curtain," calling it a "new and conscious arm of contemporary diplomacy."[15] Brecker attended Yale University, where he was an editor for the *Yale Daily News* and wrote lyrics and music for dramatic performances. Following service during World War II as a member of the US Marine Corps attached to the Office of Strategic Service, Brecker spent several years in advertising, radio, and politics. He joined the Foreign Service in 1948, serving for eight years. Initially assigned to the American Consulate General in India as vice counsel and information officer,[16] Brecker also acted as chief of the exhibitions branch for the US Department of State (later the United States Information Service) as officer in charge of the 1954 US exhibition at the International "Atoms for Peace" conference held in Geneva, and as briefing officer for the secretary of state. After leaving government service, Brecker, who co-owned a flag manufacturing company, again spent a number of years in advertising before establishing Brecker & Merryman, in 1973, a New York City–based management consultant firm that specialized in human resources management and communications.[17] MR

Will Burtin

Typographer, designer, and educator, Wilhelm "Will" Burtin (1908–1972) was a master at visually organizing information to make complex ideas more easily understood. A prominent German émigré who contributed to the growth of modernism in the United States during the mid-twentieth century, Burtin studied graphic and industrial design at the Kölner Werkschulen (Cologne Academy of Fine and Applied Arts) in Germany. He completed a four-year training program in typesetting at the Handwerkskammer Köln in 1926, and in 1928 he opened his commercial studio, where he designed advertisements, publications, posters, displays, and exhibitions.[18] His surviving early work includes *Kristallspiegelglas*, a booklet on the use of glass in architecture, with text by Bauhaus directors Walter Gropius and Ludwig Mies van der Rohe.[19]

In 1938, facing demands that he serve as design director for the Nazi Ministry of Propaganda, Burtin fled to the United States with his Jewish wife, Hilde (née Munk).[20] While he began his American career designing a logo for his immigration sponsor and cousin-in-law Max Munk, an aeronautical pioneer and fellow émigré,[21] Burtin's first significant job within the United States was to design the Federal Works Agency's exhibit for the US Pavilion at the 1939 World's Fair. For this exhibit, Burtin created a modular system that was easy to assemble, crate, and ship.[22]

Drafted into the US Army in 1943 as an enlisted man and assigned to the Office of Strategic Services, Burtin designed training manuals for aerial gunners — books that used diagrams to teach soldiers who were often semiliterate or illiterate.[23]

Released from military service in 1945 at the request of publisher Henry Luce, Burtin became the art director of *Fortune* magazine.[24] His layouts, which artfully combined photographs, illustrations, and text, reflected a buoyant postwar optimism. One example is his 1947 photo essay "The American Bazaar: A picture gallery of the chief activity of Americans — selling things to one another."[25]

To Burtin, people were the most important element in the design process. Effective visual communication depended on the audience's physical, emotional, and intellectual response and comprehension. Burtin presented this design philosophy in his 1948 traveling exhibit "Integration, the New Discipline in Design," which linked new and unexpected materials to the design aesthetics and influences of avant-garde European design.[26]

In 1949, Burtin started Will Burtin Inc.[27] The company designed print materials, containers and packaging, corporate identities, and exhibits. Clients included major publications (*Architectural Forum* and *Fortune* magazines), pharmaceutical companies (Upjohn and Scope), Fortune 500 companies (Union Carbide and Eastman Kodak), and the US government.

Burtin, who continued working with the Traveling Exhibition Service after designing "Containers & Packaging," designed exhibits that traveled within the United States and abroad. These included Upjohn Pharmaceutical's "The Cell" (1958)28 and "The Brain" (1960),[29] Union Carbide's Atom (1961),[30] and exhibits for the United States Information Agency (USIA). "Kalamazoo—and how it grew" (1957), an exhibit that presented examples of American middle-class life in a midsized Midwestern city to English, Scottish, and German audiences, is one example of a Burtin-designed USIA exhibit.[31]

Burtin died of cancer in 1972. His daughter, Carol, and his second wife, the Austrian-born graphic designer Cipe Pineles, survived him.[32]   MR

This biography was originally published in "Will Burtin," Transatlantic Perspectives, 2019.

Serge Chermayeff
Born Sergei Ivanovich Issakovich in Grozny, Azerbaijan, Serge Chermayeff (1900–1996) was an architect, interior designer, and furniture designer. The son of a wealthy Jewish family, Chermayeff studied in England from a young age. He began painting at the age of ten at the Royal Drawing Society School, which he attended for three years before enrolling at the prestigious Harrow School. After leaving school, he had a series of colorful jobs: in 1917 he became an interpreter for Major-General Sir Charles Murmansk; from 1918 to 1923 he worked as journalist for the Amalgamated Press in London, which, "because of his taste for jazz and ballroom dancing," led to a position as the editor of *Dancing World* magazine.[33]

In 1928 he became the director of the Modern Art Department for the London firm Waring & Gillow, where he organized the first exhibition of modern furnishings in England. It was at Waring & Gillow that he began designing furniture.[34] Despite having no formal training in architecture, in 1930 he opened an architecture firm with Erich Mendelsohn. He never held a license as an architect, and would instead draw a design and allow contractors to execute it, doing the same with his furniture designs.[35]

In 1940, Chermayeff immigrated to the United States. He first worked as an architect in California, then became a professor of design and chair of the design department at Brooklyn College in New York. In 1946, Walter Gropius recommended him for the position of president of the Institute of Design in Chicago. He resigned from this position, "in protest at the Institute's loss of autonomy," when the Institute of Design was merged with the Illinois Institute of Technology.[36] However, he continued to teach: in 1952 at MIT; from 1953 to 1962 at Harvard; and from 1962 until his retirement, in 1970, at Yale. As a professor, he encouraged a multi-disciplinary approach to design; he and his students could often be found at local jazz clubs, exploring the relationship between jazz music, dancing, and design.[37] He had a lifelong passion for designing urban environments, and was especially concerned with how design impacted communities and urban environments.[38]   CM

Morton and Millie Goldsholl
Morton (1911–1995) and Millie Goldsholl (née Monat, 1920–2012) were Chicago-based designers and advertising professionals, best known for their experimental filmmaking that combined design with commercial advertising. Mildred — a passionate artist from childhood — grew up in Freeport, New York, but moved to Chicago with her family at sixteen. She met Morton Goldsholl at a factory where she was working in accounting. Morton, a package designer who had created print materials and packaging for the Museum of Modern Art's "Good Design" exhibition and Walter Paepcke's Container Corporation of America, had aspired to study painting, but recalled: "That dream dissolved in the nightmare of a depression and factory work for too many years."[39] Morton encouraged Millie to pursue design at Paepcke's "newly formed" Institute of Design, which was "the first school in Chicago to offer a design degree."[40] Millie studied architecture, but was encouraged to explore other mediums, and fell in love with filmmaking. Although Mort continued to design packaging during the day, he attended seminars at the school with Millie, where both gravitated to seminars and classes with Hungarian painter, experimental filmmaker, and former Bauhaus professor László Moholy-Nagy. Moholy-Nagy's teachings profoundly impacted the rest of the Goldsholl's careers; they established Goldsholl Design & Film Associates in 1955, which historian Amy Beste notes "drew upon the model of Moholy-Nagy's Bauhaus, encouraging experimentation and aesthetic innovation, but in a competitive commercial environment."[41] They notably hired a significant number of Institute of Design alumni, especially in their film department.[42]

The Goldsholls produced a prodigious number of films that embodied the spirit of modernism. Goldsholl Associates is credited with "bringing the avant-garde aesthetics […] into nontheatrical film and commercial advertising […] with its 'design-in-film' — playful, constructivist collages, stylized graphic animation, and dazzling light displays in industrial films, television ads, title sequences, and short independent art films."[43] Although Morton created a number of logos that continue to be used today, including the iconic Motorola *M*, both he and Millie seemed most enamored with the process of design, rather than the product; the

Chicago Institute of Design included the following quotation in his biography. "I enjoy my work immensely, but seldom the results. The playtime in design is the most joyful experience — the wasted moments in scribbles, dribbles, and scratches that formulate thoughts into ideas and dreams into action. [...] The problem is to get the final design to match the fleeting idea. The big dreams about the great work of art can too easily be dissipated in the practicalities."[44]   CM

Elizabeth Gordon

Best known as the editor of *House Beautiful* from 1939 to 1964, Elizabeth Gordon (1906–2000) was an American magazine editor, writer, and staunch critic of modern design. Gordon was born in Indiana to a strict and devout Methodist family; her education at the University of Chicago was her first taste of independence, despite having her mother along as a "permanent chaperone."[45] Gordon developed a passion for journalism, in part because it allowed her to conduct research — at which she was particularly skilled — and pursue knowledge. Following her graduation, Gordon and her new husband, engineer and magazine publisher Carl Hafey Norcross, moved to New York, where she cut her teeth in the publishing world. Her work was rigorously researched; before publishing her groundbreaking 1960 special issues of *House Beautiful* dedicated to Japanese design and *shibui,* Gordon apparently conducted five years of research and took seven trips to Japan.[46]

Gordon had exacting taste for design and a rigid editorial agenda; her primary goal was to shape American ideas about taste, especially as it pertained to the American home. She is perhaps best known for her controversial 1953 article "The Threat to the Next America," in which she criticized the state of modern design and those who practiced and promoted ideas which she considered to be contrary to American values — whether that was in response to a perceived threat to her status as a tastemaker or a desire to promote design that was attainable for all is a matter of scholarly debate.[47] She was very critical of what she called "the mystical idea that 'less is more,'" which took aim at practitioners of Bauhaus-style functionalism and, most especially, those who immigrated to the United States and popularized it.[48] Gordon instead promoted what

she considered a "good modern" that "provided a 'humanistic' alternative to the 'clinical' International Style."[49]   CM

Eszter Haraszty

Eszter Haraszty (1920–1994) was a Hungarian-born textile and interior designer best known for her use of vibrant color and flowers in her designs — especially her signature Iceland poppy, which "she replicated on textiles, ceramics, and stained glass."[50] She was a forerunner in the pervasive "flower power" style of the 1960s, and was described in a 1999 *New York Times* article about her redesigned Thonet settee as "an Age of Aquarius heroine."[51] Haraszty studied at the University of Fine Arts in Budapest and worked as a costume designer before immigrating to the United States in 1946. She worked under Marianne Strengell until becoming director of Knoll Textiles in 1949. She used color masterfully and took great risks with its use — Knoll's signature pink-and-orange stripe was Haraszty's.[52] Her *Knoll Stripe* (1951) and *Fibra* (1953) were exhibited in the Museum of Modern Art's "Good Design" show.

She resigned from Knoll in 1955 and opened an independent design studio in New York in 1958, before unexpectedly moving to Los Angeles with her husband, a television producer. In 1960, she began experimenting with embroidery, which would become her life's passion. In 1962, her home was featured in a spread in *Life* magazine; it featured not only her lavish embroidery but also works that she collected from her travels around the world, and pieces from other designers reimagined in her own style.[53] In addition to the interior, she also designed the landscape, planting fifty varieties of plants over "every inch of her two acres."[54] Her home was also featured in a ten-page spread in the May 1966 issue of *House Beautiful.*

Haraszty won five gold medals from the Association of Interior Designers for textile designs. She taught design at the University of California, Los Angeles, and was the author of three books on embroidery design.   CM

Peter Harnden

Peter Harnden (1913–1971) was an architect and exhibition designer best known for his work on Marshall Plan programs designed to promote an American lifestyle in postwar Germany. Harnden was born in London to a United

States Foreign Service Officer, and was trained as an architect at the Yale School of Architecture. He served as a captain in the US Army Corps of Engineers, of the Ninth Army Intelligence section in Germany following Nazi defeat. Here he married Marie Illarionovna Vassiltchikov, a former Belarusian princess whose family had fled the Bolshevik Revolution for Weimar Germany and who had served as an informant for the anti-Nazi resistance while working as an assistant in the German Foreign Ministry's Information Office. Rather than returning to Washington following his assignment, Harnden remained in Europe, settling near Paris with his family.

Harnden's first foray into promoting the "American way of life" was as director of exhibition programs at the Office of Military Government in US-occupied Germany (OMGUS). His first exhibition, "How America Lives," was a disappointment, but only because they hadn't dreamed big enough — the exhibition was lacking in demonstrations of real innovation and technology.[55] Harnden was selected to curate the Mutual Security Agency's 1952 "We're Building a Better Life" exhibition, which featured a model home curated with modern American gadgets and interiors by modern designers. This exhibition was a runaway success. Harnden then was hired as the director of the Office of International Trade Fair's European Trade Fair Program. The purpose of this program was to directly combat the influence of Soviet Russia in Europe through the use of cultural exhibitions. In this position, Harnden "produced a new generation of US exhibitions on a shoestring budget by artfully editing a grab bag of material donated by businesses into thematically coherent installations."[56] Harnden later designed exhibitions with his design partner, Italian architect Lanfranco Bombelli — together they were responsible for "the interior exhibits for the United States Pavilion at the Brussels World's Fair of 1958."[57]   CM

Ilonka Karasz

Ilonka Karasz (1896–1981) was one of the most prolific and influential designers of the twentieth century; her work was ubiquitous, spanning textiles, wallcoverings, furniture, toys, and illustration. Karasz studied at the Royal School of Arts and Crafts in Budapest, and immigrated to the United States in 1913. She worked first as a graphic designer and illustrator for avant-garde periodicals in Greenwich Village, and she taught textile design at the Modern Art School. She was an active member of both the immigrant and artist communities in New York, and was a founding member of the Society of Modern Art, the goal of which was "to keep in touch with modern European tendencies" at a time when travel to Europe was "freighted with difficulties, and thereby encourage the development of the Modern Movement in this country."[58] In addition, Karasz "served on the Society of Modern Art's Service Bureau, which advised American companies on how to apply modern art and design to promotional material."[59] In 1920 she married Dutch chemist Wilhelm Nyland.

Karasz often drew inspiration from her native Hungary; her work, and most especially her vivid florals, were inspired by Hungarian peasant arts. Her practice was remarkably multidisciplinary; although trained as an illustrator, she often worked as a batik artist, and she was known for designing to the smallest detail of spaces, which might include furniture, ceramics, and silver. She consistently pushed the boundaries of her materials: she was involved with the DuPont Rayon Company's endeavor to produce better quality synthetic fiber; and was commissioned by the Aluminum Company of America to create a wallcovering utilizing that material.[60] She was "one of the earliest designers and one of few women to design textiles for planes and automobiles — types of transportation that had come to epitomize modernity."[61]

Karasz was one of the few textile designers producing modern woven textiles on the Jacquard loom, combining traditional methods with modern designs.[62] Notably, she was one of the first designers to incorporate child development theory into spaces designed for children. She became well known for creating practical and aesthetically appealing spaces that could stimulate learning and growth in children, thus "combining [her] goals as a modern designer with her practical knowledge as a mother."[63] CM

Katzenbach and Warren Inc.

Best known for its collaborations with modern designers as well as its exclusively licensed reproductions for Colonial Williamsburg, Katzenbach and Warren Inc. was an American Wallpaper manu-

facturing firm co-founded in 1928 by Lois and W. Whittredge Katzenbach.[64] Their commissioned and manufactured wallpapers are represented in collections internationally, and include pieces by Henri Matisse, Alexander Calder, and longtime contributor Ilonka Karasz, who was with the company for several years in the 1950s — the heyday of modern wallpaper design.

The Katzenbachs were inspired to establish their own firm after a trip to Italy and Paris, where they saw both Roman wall decorations and modern wallpapers being used in ways they had never seen in the United States, where typical wallpapers were "still strongly influenced by the over-embellished Victorian patterns that had been so popular a generation or two before."[65] They first imported wallpapers from Europe, and then commissioned designs by fashion designer Paul Poiret to be manufactured by their new company.[66] They aspired to both update wall coverings, which they felt had an unjustly old-fashioned reputation in the United States, and increase their durability with modern materials and printing techniques.

The Katzenbachs also demonstrated a nuanced understanding of how to display wallpaper; in a 1948 exhibition, rather than diminish the appeal of the bold patterns, they displayed wallpapers "around a series of 'corners,' combining two different wallpapers with appropriately modern furniture, painting, and sculpture."[67] Their seminal work, *The Practical Book of American Wallpaper*, expanded upon these ideas, and featured images of designed spaces with wallpapers as well as black-and-white photographs of wallpapers that they manufactured. Katzenbach and Warren wallpapers continue to be produced today. CM

Juliet Kepes

Juliet Kepes (née Appleby, 1919–1999) was a British painter, sculptor, author and illustrator of children's books, including the Caldecott Honor Book *Five Little Monkeys* (1952). Kepes was noted for her "use of expressive, almost calligraphic brushwork, colour, and overall design qualities."[68] She studied at Brighton School in the late 1930s, and later at the New Bauhaus, where her husband, Hungarian painter György Kepes, had been invited to teach in 1937.

Kepes predominantly designed for children. She wrote books, painted murals, and designed textiles and environments.

She often collaborated with her husband on these projects; the playroom that they designed for their daughter was recreated for the Museum of Modern Art's "Century of the Child: Growing by Design, 1900–2000" exhibition in 2012.[69] Her children's books were regularly featured in the *New York Times;* frequent reviewer Ellen Lewis Buell wrote of *Beasts From a Brush* (1955): "There are a suggestion of Picasso, a reminiscence of cave men's paintings and of the Orient, but Mrs. Kepes's style is essentially her own, and her draftsmanship is superb."[70]

Her work has been featured in more than twenty-five solo exhibitions as well as several joint exhibitions with her husband. She received a citation from the Society of Illustrators for *Frogs Merry* (1961).[71] CM

Florence Knoll

Florence Knoll (née Schust, 1917–2019) once declared, "I am not a decorator. The only place I decorate is my own house."[72] She studied architecture and design at the Cranbrook Academy of Art alongside other design professionals closely associated with American modernism.[73] In 1937 she attended London's Architectural Association, returning to the United States at the start of World War II to complete her architecture degree at the Illinois Institute of Technology in 1941. Knoll had ties to Bauhaus directors Walter Gropius and Mies van der Rohe; and Bauhaus master Marcel Breuer, with whom she studied and worked.[74]

In 1942 she joined Harrison & Abramovitz, where she met Hans Knoll, the émigré son of a German industrialist who manufactured furniture designed by Bauhaus and Werkbund artisans. She designed interiors for the H. G. Knoll Company on a freelance basis before joining the company in 1943. The couple married in 1946, and the H. G. Knoll Company was renamed Knoll Associates in recognition of both their marriage and the financial investment made by Florence in the company. She also provided the company with its creative vision, establishing the Knoll Planning Unit in 1944. Dissatisfied with the fabrics available for use on furniture, she founded Knoll Textiles in 1947.[75]

Florence Knoll and the Planning Unit revolutionized modern corporate interiors. After determining user need and workflow, they designed unified, functional interior spaces. Outfitted with low-profile furniture custom designed for specific needs, these spaces used bright colors and texture as ornament. The press dubbed this the "Knoll Look."[76] Knoll Inc. promoted this distinctive approach that "stresses the collaboration of the architect, designer, and technician"[77] through regional show-rooms that offered design services and sold sofas, desks, chairs, sideboards, and tables — products that remain available today.

The "Knoll look," which was an essential part of the American portrait as presented by the US Department of State, influenced European design. In 1951, Knoll Inc., oper-ating outside of the United States as Knoll International, was asked to furnish US government housing in Germany, Amerika Haus interiors, and several US embassies. By the 1960s, Knoll International was designing corporate interiors in Germany and other parts of Europe.[78]

Florence Knoll became president of Knoll Inc. in 1955 after Hans's death. She married Harry Bassett in 1958 and retired in 1965. In 1972, the Musée des Arts Décoratifs in Paris organized "Knoll au Louvre."[79] The Philadelphia Museum of Art presented a 2004 exhibition of furni-ture and interiors designed by Knoll herself.[80] New York City's Museum of Modern Art included her work in six exhi-bitions. She passed away in 2019.[81] MR

Walter Landor

Born Walter Fritz Joseph Landauer to a German-Jewish family in Munich, Walter Landor (1913–1995) was an industrial designer and pioneer in marketing, brand-ing, and package design. His company, Walter Landor and Associates, grew to prominence in the 1950s and 1960s through its innovative use of market research, which capitalized upon Landor's uncanny understanding of the relationship between consumer and product as a tool for developing lasting corporate identities. Landor studied under Milner Gray at the Goldsmith College of Art in London, but left school in order to accept a position designing plastic packages. In 1935 he started his first company with Gray and Misha Black, an exhibition specialist.[82] Landor claimed to have learned how to design from his colleagues in London. In 1936, at the age of twenty-three, Landor became the youngest Fellow of the Royal Society of Industrial Arts in Great Britain. It was then that he changed his name to reflect his "new identity" as an Englishman.[83]

Landor grew up around images of modernity in a household where "the ideas of the Werkbund and the Bauhaus"[84] were prominent. His family often visited museums and galleries in Munich, and his uncle was a publisher who sent Landor and his sister "art books and design magazines that contained some of the latest Werkbund and Bauhaus publications."[85] Landor's father was an architect, and although Landor himself claimed to have "absolutely no talent" for the technical aspects of architecture, much of his earliest work was designing branded environments in San Francisco.[86]

Landor came to the United States to assist with the design of the British Pavilion at the 1939 New York World's Fair. Sensing the rising tides of war in Europe, Landor decided to spend six months traveling the United States; impressed by the creativity and opportunity in San Francisco, he decided to stay. He became a member of the faculty at the California College of Arts and Crafts, where he met his wife Josephine Martinelli. Together they started his namesake company Walter Landor and Associates in 1941,[87] now known as Landor & Associates.

Landor, who held that design was "a tool to express the client's selling strat-egy,"[88] was very concerned with creating lasting connections between consumers and products. He believed in setting aside personal aesthetics and in pretesting his firm's products in order to gauge public reception and design effectiveness. In a 1985 commencement address he advised graduates that good design was "a prob-lem-solving activity" in which "consumers [are] your boss."[89] CM

Laverne Originals

Estelle and Erwine Laverne were painters, interior designers, and designers and manufacturers of furniture, wallpaper, and textiles via their company Laverne Originals. Erwine Laverne (1909–2003) and Estelle Lester (1915–1997) met in 1932 while studying as painters under Hans Hofmann at the Art Student's League in New York. Estelle Lester was the daughter of a jewelry designer; Erwine's father was a painter of murals, mostly in religious spaces, who would "enlist his sons to paint the backgrounds."[90] They started Laverne Originals in 1942 with an empha-sis on wallpaper and textiles.[91]

In the beginning, most of their retail items were designed by a team employed

or contracted by the Lavernes. These included textile designs by Alexander Calder, György Kepes, Ray Komai, and Alvin Lustig; and furniture designs from collaborations between William Katavolos, Ross Littell, and Douglas Kelley, like the ubiquitous "T" chair.

In the late 1950s, the Lavernes began manufacturing their own furniture designs. The most well known of these was the "Invisible Group" of furniture: elegant, curvy, and completely transparent chairs produced in clear acrylic, the likes of which had never been seen in modern design.[92] This fugitive material was in keeping with their perspective on design: in an interview with the *New York Times,* Erwine Laverne remarked that "the most important element in rooms is people, not furniture."[93] Even within their own retail space, furniture was apparently used by the staff until it was requested, rather than have a customer be overwhelmed by a large number of pieces on display.

Erwine Laverne's work often incorpo-rated abstract interpretations of natural textures; his hand-painted faux marble gained him international recognition.[94] Estelle's work showed impressive variety, ranging from geometric patterns to figural paintings, pulling influences from folk art, nature, and other artists; her most famous piece, *Fun to Run* (1948), which was displayed in the Metropolitan Museum of Art, draws inspiration from Matisse's *Dance* (1910) and also demonstrates the influence of Hoffman, who wrote that "space is filled with movement."[95]

After years of litigation regarding the zoning of their screen-printing practice, and due to Estelle's declining health (she had a form of multiple sclerosis that rendered her unable to walk), they were forced to close Laverne Originals, then Laverne International, in 1964.[96] CM

Tom Lee

Heralded as one of New York's best "display men,"[97] and famed for his window and store interior displays, Thomas Bailey Lee (1910–1971) packaged a unique brand of American identity for international audiences. The son of an American diplomat, Lee spent his childhood in Vermont, Brazil, Portugal, Great Britain, and Australia. He joined Macy's design studio when he was nineteen, and later became display director for Bonwit Teller. Lee served overseas with the Office of Strategic Services and with the US Army Air Corps' first school of camouflage during World War II. In 1947 he establishing Tom Lee Ltd., an interior and industrial design firm, and went on to design what he called "spectaculars."[98] These included sets and costumes for musical comedies and burlesque shows; salons, factories, and packaging for the beauty and fashion industries; product showrooms for the Chicago Merchandise Mart; torchlight parades for the Fifth Avenue Association of Retailers; and window displays for Lever House.[99]

Working with the Traveling Exhibition Service (TES), Lee designed "American Wallpapers" in 1951. He also created other TES exhibits: a 1952 exhibition on the American motion picture industry; and a 1954 display that presented the history of American theater. Lee contributed to the design of two US government–sponsored international exhibits that must have met his definition of "spectacular": the United States Pavilion at Brussels's Expo 58 and the 1959 American National Exhibition in Moscow.[100]

At the American National Exhibition, Lee was responsible for the design of the "Fashion Industries Presentation." This display included a fashion show that took place four times a day under large-scale, colorful, plastic umbrellas. American men, women, and children strolled the runway wearing American-manufactured clothing that was promoted as readily available for purchase within the United States at a variety of prices. As part of this display, Lee mounted shoes to a revolving eighteen-foot-wide Ferris wheel that furthered the concept of personal choice. Lee also contributed a showroom titled "For Women Only" that presented lingerie and hosiery. This included a beauty parlor, where select women publicly experienced personal care treatments.[101]

In the mid-1950s, Lee, who also served as display director for Bergdorf Goodman, a luxury department store, entered the field of hotel design. He designed more than a dozen hotels, including Colonial Williamsburg's Motor Lodge, the Shah of Iran's Teheran Hilton, the President Hotel in Johannesburg, and the Inn-on-the-Park in Toronto.[102]

Lee died in a car crash at the height of his career, which may be why he is not better known. His widow, Sarah Tomerlin Lee, continued Tom Lee Ltd. after his death.[103] MR

Dorothy Liebes

Called "the mother of modern weaving,"

Dorothy Liebes (1897–1972) was a textile designer who brought California to the forefront of modern design through her pioneering use of artisan production techniques to create modern textiles for interiors. Born in Santa Rosa, California, Liebes learned to weave at the Jane Addams Hull-House in Chicago, and continued to weave on a loom that she purchased while studying art education at the University of California at Berkeley. In order to continue to evolve her craft, she sold small pieces to pay for trips to Europe; historian Alexa Griffith Winton suggests that "[Elsa] Gullberg's interest in allying art and industry and [Paul] Rodier's highly textured fabrics in a simple, modern style both appear to have greatly influenced her."[104] Liebes, unhappy in her marriage to a man who didn't support her ambition, used weaving as an outlet and began to seek out professional opportunities. In 1935, she and her husband split; by 1937, she had established her own design studio, which was so successful it was quickly outgrew its space.

Liebes's work was identifiable by the "Liebes Look": vibrant textiles woven with unusual materials, inspired by her childhood in beautiful Northern California. She made a name for herself by cornering a niche market in the design field: one-of-a-kind, hand-woven textiles produced by commission for architecture and interiors. Liebes's pieces were singular and groundbreaking both for her use of unusual materials and for her melding of art and design. She was well known for her beautiful and vibrant color work, which she achieved through a partnership with a Greek master dyer, who was able "to give her often unorthodox materials the striking colors for which she became famous."[105] She was an advocate for weaving as a "creative, practical, and therapeutic hobby," which could be done in the home quickly and easily, and for very little money.[106] She served as the home furnishings consultant for DuPont from 1955 to 1971, and was instrumental in their campaign to popularize synthetics in the United States. CM

Raymond Loewy

Raymond Loewy (1893–1986) is often called the father of industrial design; he was a pioneer in branding and marketing, his work spanned multiple disciplines and industries, and he was a co-founder of the Society of Industrial Design. Loewy was born in Paris and raised in France.

At fifteen, he designed, patented, and produced a rubber-band-powered model airplane.[107] Loewy studied engineering at the École de Lanneau in Paris, but his studies were interrupted by the outbreak of the First World War; he "served with distinction as an officer of engineers."[108] Both of his parents died during the influenza epidemic of 1919, after which time he immigrated to the United States.

Loewy worked as a fashion illustrator for *Vogue*, *Harper's Bazaar*, and *Vanity Fair* in New York before getting his start in advertising. He designed a "cutting edge" ad campaign for the White Star line in 1928 that "evoked style and emotion in a surrealistic register, the copy deftly appealing both to the wealthy, who sought exclusivity, and to the 'economical,' who required assurance that they too would be treated well."[109] In 1929, Loewy established an immensely successful private design firm in New York; before filing for bankruptcy in 1977, his firm designed iconic product packaging for Lucky Strike, several Studebaker automobiles, the Exxon logo, streamlined locomotives for the Pennsylvania Railroad, a Greyhound bus, a number of Frigidaire products, and a space station. Loewy famously consulted on the redesign of Air Force One during John F. Kennedy's presidency after declaring the original design "gaudy"; Kennedy apparently personally collaborated with Loewy on the final design, and Loewy neither accepted a fee for his services nor disclosed his involvement in the project until 1967.[110] CM

Jack Masey

Jack Masey (1924–2016) was an American exhibition designer best known for his work with the United States Information Agency's Office of International Trade Fairs. Born in Brooklyn and raised in poverty by an injured World War I veteran and a seamstress, Masey attended the High School of Music and Art on a scholarship. At nineteen he was drafted into service in World War II; he served as part of the Camouflage Engineers' Ghost Army, an 1,100-man unit of designers and artists who used sound engineering and special effects to obfuscate troop numbers.[111] Following his discharge, he studied architecture and graphic design at Yale. In the early 1950s, he was recruited by the State Department to work for Eisenhower's newly formed United States Information Agency (USIA), which sponsored American cultural exhibitions that promoted the "American way of life" — and by extension democracy — abroad. Masey worked as an exhibition designer for the USIA for almost thirty years.

Masey is most famous for being in charge of "procurement and coordinating design and construction" for the 1959 American National Exhibition in Sokol'niki Park, Moscow, which became the staging ground for the famous 1959 "kitchen debate" between then Vice President Richard Nixon and Soviet Premier Nikita Khrushchev. Masey believed in the power of images, rather than words, in cementing ideas in people's minds; he used modern art, fashion, and functioning high-end appliances to demonstrate the USIA's image of American life. Despite criticism over some of the exhibitions, especially the art shows, Masey asserted that they never pulled pieces, because it "showed the Soviets that we paint what we want — nobody dictates to us."[112] Masey received Presidential Design Awards for his work as the project manager for exhibitions at the Ellis Island Museum and the Statue of Liberty Museum in 1979. MR

George Nelson

Known as one of the fathers of American modernism, George Nelson (1908–1986) was an architect, writer, industrial designer, design theorist, and exhibition designer. Nelson was born in Hartford, Connecticut, and studied architecture at Yale University, where he was awarded the Rome Prize, "which provided a ... stipend to study at the American Academy in Rome, where he lived from 1932–34."[113] While in Rome, Nelson interviewed twelve significant architects and wrote a series of biographies that highlighted his skill as a writer. He became an associate editor at *Architectural Forum* magazine in the mid-1930s; he also taught architecture at Columbia University, and co-owned an architecture firm in New York, which closed at the beginning of World War II. In 1945, Nelson's Storagewall, "the first modular storage system and a forerunner of systems furniture," was featured in *Life* magazine.[114] The Storagewall concept caught the attention of D. J. De Pree, the founder of Herman Miller, who hired Nelson as the company's design director in 1947. He maintained his relationship with Herman Miller for more than twenty-five years.

During his tenure at Herman Miller, Nelson established his own design firm,

George Nelson & Associates, which won the gold medal for the US Information Agency exhibition at Sao Paolo's international biennial Exposition in 1957. In 1958, Nelson was hired as the lead designer for the American National Exhibition in Moscow, set to open in June 1959, which was the stage of one of the most famous Cold War exchanges, Vice President Richard Nixon and Soviet Premier Nikita Khrushchev's "kitchen debate" in the "Splitnik" model kitchen. In 1992, Nelson was posthumously awarded a medal from the American Institute of Graphic Arts in recognition of his contributions to design. CM

Walter Paepcke

Walter Paepcke (1896–1960) was a prominent US industrialist and philanthropist. He was born in Chicago to an upper-middle-class family; his father, a German emigrant, owned a lumber mill and packaging company. Paepcke studied economics and history at Yale, and became president of Chicago Mill and Lumber Company in 1921 following the death of his father. In 1926, he established the Container Corporation of America, which was an extension of a paper container production project that he had started during World War I. Encouraged by his wife, Elizabeth, a painter who had studied at the Art Institute of Chicago, Paepcke hired designers, rather than commercial artists, to produce advertising campaigns for his company — a major "advertising milestone" that "combined culture and commerce."[115] The Container Corporation of America was wildly successful; "by the late 1940s, [it] had become the largest domestic producer of paper containers."[116]

Influenced by his parents' love of music and literature, Paepcke was a great supporter of the arts. He "served as a trustee or as a member of the board of directors for the University of Chicago, the Art Institute of Chicago, the Chicago Orchestral Association, the Cliff Dwellers Club, the Great Books Foundation, and the Encyclopaedia Britannica."[117] In 1944, Paepcke used his business expertise and capital to assist Hungarian painter, experimental filmmaker, and former Bauhaus professor László Moholy-Nagy in establishing the Institute of Design in Chicago. In 1950, after staging a successful celebration of the two-hundredth birthday of Johann Wolfgang von Goethe, the Paepckes founded the Aspen Music Festival and Institute for Humanistic

Studies, which was "to be an intellectual and cultural center of continuing education."[118] They are credited with turning Aspen into a major travel destination and resort town. CM

Annemarie Henle Pope

Before immigrating to the United States in 1932, Annemarie Henle Pope (1907-2001) had already earned a PhD with a study of German baroque sculpture. Her continued education in the US included post-graduate work in museum studies with Harvard University's Paul Sachs during the depths of the Depression. A 1935 Elmhirst Foundation fellowship supported her travel and research at various North American museums. She joined the Seattle Art Museum around 1939, where she served as assistant director for two years. Pope then worked as assistant director of the Portland Art Museum from 1941–42 before relocating to Washington, DC, during World War II.[119]

Pope served as assistant director in charge of exhibitions from 1947–51 for the American Federation of Arts (AFA), a national association of museums that circulates traveling exhibits as a service to its member institutions.[120] In 1950, the AFA, which relocated its headquarters from Washington, DC, to New York City in 1952, organized a set of US government–funded exhibits in support of the German reorientation program.[121] Pope described these "very small"[122] exhibits as "presented in their own boxes in which they traveled."[123] Married to John Alexander, director of the Freer Gallery of Art, Pope declined to move with the AFA.[124]

Smithsonian Institution Director Alexander Wetmore hired Pope to start the Traveling Exhibition Service (TES). In all likelihood, Pope, as TES chief, relied on the experience she gained with the AFA in developing the State Department–funded TES program that sent exhibits of American art, architecture, and design to Germany and Austria. Pope described these exhibits as "very well researched by the very best people in the country."[125]

Considered the "First Lady of International Art,"[126] Pope founded the International Exhibitions Foundation in 1965, serving as its president and organizing more than 140 traveling exhibits before her retirement in 1988. The governments of Sweden, Denmark, Norway, West Germany, Italy, and Britain honored Pope for this work.[127] The granddaughter of anatomist Jacob Henle and the sister of photographer Fitz Henle and virologist Werner Henle, Pope, who was of Jewish descent, left no direct survivors.[128]   MR

Noémi Raymond

Noémi Raymond (née Pernessin, 1889–1980) was a painter, sculptor, illustrator, and textile designer known for her warm, vivid interiors, as well as her dedication to mentorship and collaboration. Raymond was born in Cannes and raised in New York, where she attended the prestigious Horace Mann School. She was trained in graphic design at Columbia University under John Dewey and Arthur Wesley Dow, "who were instrumental in her introduction to Japanese art and design," and later studied painting at the École de la Grande Chaumière in Paris.[129] In 1914, Noémi married Antonin Raymond, a painter and architect from Bohemia. Because of Noémi's status in the New York art world, the Raymonds were able to secure apprenticeships with Frank Lloyd Wright. They both contributed to Frank Lloyd Wright's Imperial Hotel in Tokyo: Antonin served as the project architect, and Noémi worked "on its decorative art design elements."[130] It was in Japan that the Raymonds would make their mark on design history "as interpreters of Japanese and American culture."

In 1922, the Raymonds opened a Tokyo-based design firm in which, through the exploration of Japanese culture and interpretation of American culture in Japan, they would develop "their own personal voice."[131] In the late 1930s, the Raymonds returned to the United States in order to avoid the oncoming war. They established themselves as mentors to an emerging generation of designers with the New Hope Experiment, a farm and artist community where they would offer classes, apprenticeships, and boarding.[132] They would later return to Japan to assist in reconstruction efforts following the war.

Although they were internationally acclaimed designers in their own time, "the Raymonds have remained under the radar mostly because a majority of their projects were in Japan, and few are extant."[133] Although she primarily designed interiors, modern scholarship portrays Raymond as instrumental to her husband's architecture, noting that it is nearly impossible to separate her influence from her husband's design.[134] Noémi Raymond's work has been featured in a

number of exhibitions worldwide, including several retrospectives on modern design, and the "Good Design" exhibition at the Museum of Modern Art in New York. Her work is maintained in museum collections internationally.   MR

Bernard Rudofsky

Bernard Rudofsky (1905–1988) was an architect, curator, exhibition designer, fashion designer, writer, and critic best known for his controversial exhibitions at the Museum of Modern Art (MoMA) in New York. Rudofsky completed master's degrees in architecture and engineering and a doctorate in technical sciences from the Technische Hochschule in Vienna.[135] He was a Ford, Fulbright, and Guggenheim Fellow, and taught at Yale, MIT, Cooper-Hewitt, and at the Royal Academy of Fine Arts in Copenhagen. His wallpaper and textile designs were included in both of the "Good Design" shows at MoMA.

Rudofsky's work, both in writing and design, was concerned with exploring functionalism, utility, and humanity. He ventured into fashion design with Bernardo Sandals, a company that he started with his wife, Berta, which produced sandals "designed to allow the foot complete freedom" — this after he "made scathing attacks on the footgear accepted by modern women" in his controversial 1944 MoMA exhibition "Are Clothes Modern?"[136] His 1964 exhibit "Architecture without Architects" was similarly subversive, displaying photographs of vernacular, non-pedigreed architecture from Rudofsky's world travels. He collaborated with Peter Harnden on the United States' critically unsuccessful contribution to the 1958 Brussels World's Fair, an exhibition titled "Islands for Living," which eliminated the impactful American model kitchen and instead included a daily ready-to-wear fashion show, where "before walking an atrium runway, European models in American outfits posed amid [...] their Eames leather and rosewood recliner, George Nelson desk, antique Shaker chair, and an assemblage of other domestic objects ranging from upscale to oddball."[137]   CM

Herwin Schaefer

Herwin Schaefer immigrated to the United States from Germany in 1937. He studied in Chicago, his mother's birthplace, in New York, and at Harvard University where, in 1944, he earned

a PhD with a dissertation on medieval architecture. After a brief period as a German language instructor, in 1945 Schaefer joined the Museum of the Rhode Island School of Design in the Department of Decorative Arts. In 1947 he was offered a position as an assistant curator at the Museum of Modern Art (MoMA) in the Department of Architecture and Design. He left MoMA in 1949, when he was appointed assistant director of design at Boston's Institute of Contemporary Art.[138]

Anxious to learn how his family had survived the war,[139] Schaefer joined the Department of State in 1951. He was assigned to the American High Commission for Germany (HICOG) as chief of the exhibitions section. Within Germany, Schaefer was responsible for organizing, promoting, and circulating State Department–sponsored exhibits through trade shows, museums, educational institutions, and the Amerika Haus program.

Schaefer, who held that people are first and foremost interested in their own lives, argued against art museums presenting exhibits and artifacts that made no connection with the everyday. Advocating for the importance of industrial design and domestic architecture, Schaefer proposed that the art museum try "to guide and educate"[140] the visitor's aesthetic preferences so as "to increase his discrimination in the choice of the simple utensils and furnishings"[141] used to furnish the home.

Schaefer wrote in a 1953 issue of the international design annual *Idea* that American design reflected a politically free country founded upon a belief in a "self-created life." He argued that such "freedom of creation" in search of "the most rational" and "most beautiful forms for tools and appliances" was supported by the "ideas of the Bauhaus" that came to the United States beginning in the 1930s."[142]

In 1954, Schaefer joined the University of California at Berkeley as a professor in what is now the College of Environmental Design. Schaefer started the Morrison Library's Graphic Arts Loan Collection.[143] This program, which invites UC Berkeley community members to borrow original art, reflects Schaefer's belief in the importance of connecting aesthetic choices with everyday life.   MR

Saul Steinberg

Cartoonist, architect, and graphic designer

Saul Steinberg (1914–1999) was born in Romania to Russian-Jewish parents. His father owned a printing and bookbinding shop where he produced product packaging. Steinberg was unable to study architecture at the University of Bucharest because of the small quota of Jewish students allowed into the program, and therefore enrolled in the architecture school at the University of Milan in 1933.[144] As a student, he contributed "cartoons to the twice-weekly Italian humor newspaper *Bertoldo* and soon became one of the paper's most popular artists."[145] Steinberg was awarded his architectural degree in 1940, but was unable to work due to anti-Semitic laws. He spent six weeks in an internment camp, and finally fled Italy in 1941. He went first to New York, then to the Dominican Republic, where he remained for a year, contributing drawings to *The New Yorker* before receiving a US visa in 1942.

Steinberg is best known for his *New Yorker* covers — he credited his precise lines to his background in architectural drafting — but "only about a quarter of his output comprises magazine and other commercial work."[146] His work regularly featured architectural motifs. Steinberg's goal "was to draw like a child who never stopped drawing that way even as he aged and his subject matter became not childish."[147] His textile and wallpaper designs, described as "quirky" and "mischievous," were enormously popular and extremely influential.[148] One of his enduring legacies is the classification of his work: his hand is technical and skilled, his subjects smart and sophisticated, but critics continue to question the legitimacy of a cartoonist as an artist.[149] CM

Angelo Testa

Born in Springfield, Massachusetts, to Italian emigrant parents, Angelo Testa (1921–1984) was a painter, sculptor, and weaver known for his textile and wallpaper designs. He first attended the New York School of Fine and Applied Arts, and later studied archaeology at the University of Chicago. In 1945 he became the first graduate of the Institute of Design in Chicago, where he studied under László Moholy-Nagy, architect George Fred Keck, and weaver Marli Ehrman. In 1947, Testa established his own design firm, Angelo Testa & Co. Starting out, he had little capital, and was responsible for nearly every aspect of his business; he apparently even delivered his designs to his

clients.[150] Although his only showroom was a modest one in Chicago, his clients included Herman Miller and Knoll Associates.[151] He also designed wallpapers and rugs, and was a gifted painter and sculptor.

Testa was a pioneer in silk-screened textiles in the United States.[152] He favored "linear and geometric forms, commonly associated with his Bauhaus training."[153] He was primarily interested in designing for mass markets, "particularly for large institutional facilities such as hotels, schools, and dormitories."[154] In 1947, *New York Times* home editor Mary Roche noted that Testa "knows how to inject into a simple composition of lines and squares the pleasant vitality too often lacking in the bizarre attempts of less able artists."[155] CM

The Tilletts

D. D. and Leslie Tillett were a husband-and-wife textile design team, best known for their innovative and energetic prints that were used in interiors and worn by First Lady Jacqueline Kennedy. Doris "D. D." Doctorow (1917–2008), the daughter of Russian emigrants, studied drawing at the Art Students League in New York City under George Grosz and Vaclav Vytlacil. In 1944 *Harper's Bazaar* sent her to Mexico to photograph the textiles of the fabric printing workshop Artes Tillett, where she met British textile designer Leslie Tillett (1915–1992). Tillett's family "had been in the textile industry for generations in England."[156] D. D. decided to remain in Mexico, where she learned silk-screening in an artists' colony. The couple returned to Manhattan in 1946 and opened House of T fabrics in a carriage house that was large enough to accommodate both production and retail space and the raising of their family.[157]

The Tilletts designed custom textiles as well as textiles for mass production, both for use in interiors and fashion. Their prints adorned the likes of First Lady Jacqueline Kennedy, who both wore their designs and used them in her summer home. Kennedy remained a close friend and later hired the Tilletts to help design the interior of the Greek villa she was building with her second husband; she also helped fund their Manhattan storefront.[158] The Tilletts taught screen-printing for Design Works, a program envisioned by Senator Robert Kennedy, which helped revitalize the Bedford Stuyvesant neighborhood in D. D.'s native Brooklyn "while

providing employment to a dozen members of the community."[159] A 2012 exhibition at the Museum of the City of New York portrayed the Tilletts as being the predecessors of contemporary independent designers; they are remembered for maintaining "complete artistic control of their work and [selling] locally or in their own shop."[160] CM

NOTES

1   "Anni Albers," National Museum of Women in the Arts, accessed June 27, 2017, https://nmwa.org/explore/artist-profiles/anni-albers; Madeleine Luckel, "A New Exhibition Explores Anni Albers's Textiles, Among Other Things," *Vogue*, February 4, 2017, accessed June 27, 2017, http://www.vogue.com/article/anni-albers-textiles-americas-small-great-objects-yale; Rita Reif, "Anni Albers, 94, Textile Artist and the Widow of Josef Albers," *New York Times*, May 10, 1994.

2   Rita Reif, "Anni Albers."

3   Ulrike Müller, *Bauhaus Women: Art, Handicraft, Design* (Paris: Flammarion, 2009), 51.

4   Ibid.

5   Oral history interview with Anni Albers, July 5, 1968, Archives of American Art, Smithsonian Institution.

6   Ibid.

7   Ibid.

8   Ibid.

9   Rita Reif, "Anni Albers."

10   "Wall Hangings," MoMA press release, February 25, 1969.

11   Paul Logan, "Weaver Evelyn Anselevicius Left Powerful Tapestries Worldwide," *Albuquerque Journal*, July 12, 2003.

12   Laurence B. Mussio, *A Vision Greater than Themselves: The Making of the Bank of Montreal, 1817–2017* (Montreal: McGill-Queen's University Press, 2016), 121.

13   Rita Reif, "Tapestries? Well, Not in the Classic Sense," *New York Times*, March 8, 1971.

14   Logan, "Weaver Evelyn Anselevicius."

15   Richard L. Brecker, "Truth as a Weapon of the Free World," *The Annals of the American Academy of Political and Social Science* 278 (November 1951): 1.

16   Richard L. Brecker, "The New Arm of Diplomacy: The Role of Propaganda in International Relations," *Foreign Service Journal* 29, no. 8 (August 1951): 23.

17   Obituary, *New York Times*, April 3, 2005.

18   Herbert A. Strauss and Werner Röder, "Burtin, Will," *International Biographical Dictionary of Central European Émigrés 1933 — 1945. Volume 2, The Arts, Sciences, and Literature* (Munich: K. G. Saur, 1999), 172.

19   Will Burtin Papers, Cary Graphic Arts Collection, Rochester Institute of Technology Libraries.

20   Martha Scotford, *Cipe Pineles: A Life of Design* (New York: Norton, 1999), 107.

21   R. Roger Remington and Robert S. P. Fripp, *Design and Science: The Life and Work of Will Burtin* (Burlington: Lund Humphries, 2007), 23.

22   Remington, 30.

23   Remington, 35–36.

24   Remington, 39–40.

25   "The American Bazaar: A picture gallery of the chief activity of Americans—selling

things to one another," *Fortune* 36 (November 1947): 109–22.

26 Will Burtin, "Integration, the new discipline in design: an exhibition by Will Burtin from November 9, 1948, to January 14, 1949." *Graphis* 27 (1949), 230-37.

27 Remington, 53.

28 Remington, 71.

29 Remington, 86.

30 Remington, 77.

31 Remington, 79.

32 Remington, 10.

33 Alan Powers, "Chermayeff, Serge," *Grove Art Online* in *Oxford Art Online,* July 28, 2014.

34 Ibid.

35 Betty J. Blum and Serge Chermayeff, "Oral History of Serge Chermayeff," Chicago Architects Oral History Project, Ernest R. Graham Study Center for Architectural Drawings, Department of Architecture, The Art Institute of Chicago, 2001.

36 Powers, "Chermayeff, Serge."

37 Betty J. Blum and Serge Chermayeff, "Oral History of Serge Chermayeff" (transcript), Chicago Architects Oral History Project, Ernest R. Graham Study Center for Architectural Drawings, Department of Architecture, The Art Institute of Chicago, 2001, 37-38.

38 Serge Chermayeff and Christopher Alexander, *Community and Privacy: Toward a New Architecture of Humanism* (New York: Doubleday, 1965); Serge Chermayeff and Alexander Tzonis, *Advanced Studies in Urban Environments: Toward an Urban Model* (New Haven: Yale University Press, 1967); Serge Chermayeff and Alexander Tzonis, *Shape of Community: Realization of Human Potential* (New York: Penguin Books, 1971).

39 "Mort and Millie Goldsholl Collection, 1942–1980: Creators," *Chicago Film Archives,* accessed September 27, 2017, http://www.chicagofilmarchives.org/collections/index.php/Detail/Object/Show/object_id/17.

40 Ibid.

41 Amy Beste, "All Roads Lead to Chicago: Encyclopaedia Britannica Films, the Institute of Design, and Nontheatrical Film," PhD dissertation, Northwestern University, 2012: 249.

42 Beste, 247.

43 Beste, 247.

44 "Mort and Millie Goldsholl," *Chicago Film Archives.*

45 Monica Penick, *Tastemaker: Elizabeth Gordon, House Beautiful, and the Postwar American Home* (New Haven: Yale University Press: 2017), 4.

46 Julie V. Iovine, "Elizabeth Gordon, 94, Dies; Was House Beautiful Editor," *New York Times,* September 17, 2000.

47 Penick, 119; Greg Castillo, *Cold War on the Home Front: The Soft Power of Midcentury Design* (Minneapolis: The University of Minnesota Press, 2010), 112–14.

48 Elizabeth Gordon, "The Threat to the Next America," *House Beautiful,* April 1953, 126; reprinted in Penick, 116-17.

49 Penick, xi.

50 Eszter Haraszty; Designer, 74," *New York Times,* December 1, 1994.

51 Mitchell Owens, "Art/Architecture; Classic Furniture Upstaged by Flower Power," *New York Times,* August 15, 1999.

52 "Knoll Designer Bios: Eszter Haraszty," *Knoll,* accessed July 2, 2017, https://www.knoll.com/designer/Eszter-Haraszty-.

53 Owens, "Art/Architecture."

54 Gordon Parks, "A House Furnished with Flowers," *Life,* July 27, 1962, 48–55.

55 Greg Castillo, "The American 'Fat Kitchen' in Europe: Postwar Domestic Modernity and Marshall Plan Strategies of Enchantment," in *Cold War Kitchen: Americanization, Technology, and European Users,* Ruth Oldenziel and Karin Zachmann, eds. (Cambridge, MA: The MIT Press, 2009), 38.

56 Greg Castillo, *Cold War on the Home Front: The Soft Power of Midcentury Design* (Minneapolis: University of Minnesota Press, 2010), 118–19.

57 "Peter Graham Harnden Dead; Architect and Designer was 58," *New York Times,* October 24, 1971.

58 "Ilonka Karasz: Rediscovering a Modernist Pioneer," *Studies in the Decorative Arts* (Fall-Winter 2000–2001): 70.

59 Ibid.

60 Ibid., 86.

61 Ibid., 74-75.

62 Ibid., 74.

63 Ibid., 84-85.

64 Katzenbach and Warren Inc., *Williamsburg Restoration Wallpaper Reproductions and Commemorative Paper Hangings* (New York: Katzenbach and Warren, 1951).

65 Leslie Jackson, *Twentieth-Century Pattern Design* (New York: Princeton Architecture Press, 2002), 88; quoting from Lois and William Katzenbach, The Practical Book of American Wallpaper (New York: J.B. Lippincott Company, 1954), 2.

66 Leslie Jackson, *Twentieth-Century Pattern Design,* 88.

67 Pepe Karmel, "Design Review; When Artwork Has a Sticky Back," *New York Times,* July 28, 1995.

68 "Alumni and Associate: Juliet Kepes (1919–1999)," University of Brighton, http://arts.brighton.ac.uk/alumni-arts/kepes,-juliet-appleby-1919-1999.

69 The Museum of Modern Art Department of Communications, "MoMA Presents *Century of the Child,* The First Large-Scale Examination Of Childhood as a Major Source for Modern Design Thinking in the 20th Century," press release.

70 Ellen Lewis Buell, "Fabulous Creatures," *New York Times,* October 2, 1955, 166.

71 "Alumni and Associate: Juliet Kepes (1919–1999)," *University of Brighton,* http://arts.brighton.ac.uk/alumni-arts/kepes,-juliet-appleby-1919-1999.

72 Virginia Lee Warren, "Woman Who Led an Office Revolution Rules an Empire of Modern Design," *New York Times,* September 1, 1964, 40.

73 Paul Goldberger, "The Cranbrook Vision," *New York Times,* April 8, 1984, 1.

74 Frederica Todd Harlow, "Knoll Associates," in *Design 1935–1965: What Modern Was: Selections from the Liliane and David M. Steward Collection,* Martin Eidelberg, ed. (New York: Harry N. Abrams, Inc. 1991), 379; and "Biographical Note," Florence Knoll Bassett papers, 1932–2000, Archives of American Art, Smithsonian Institution, accessed March 28, 2019, https://www.aaa.si.edu/collections/florence-knoll-bassett-papers-6312/biographical-note

75 For a detailed history of Knoll Inc. and its founding see Brian Lutz, "The History of Knoll," in *Knoll: A Modernist Universe* (New York: Rizzoli, 2010). For a detailed history of Knoll Textiles see Earl Martin, ed., *Knoll Textiles, 1945–2010* (New Haven: Yale University Press, 2011), which includes a Knoll Inc. chronology that dates from 1940–2010, compiled by Ann Marguerite Tartsinis.

76 The evolution of the Knoll Planning Unit and the "Knoll Look" is discussed in Bobbye Tigerman, "'I Am Not a Decorator': Florence Knoll, the Knoll Planning Unit and the Making of the Modern Office." *Journal of Design History* 20, no. 1 (2007): 61-74.

77 "The Planning Unit," accessed March 30, 2019, https://www.knoll.com/story/shop/the-planning-unit

78 Jan Logemann, "Hans Knoll," in *Immigrant Entrepreneurship: German-American Business Biographies, 1720 to the Present,* vol. 5, R. Daniel Wadhwani, ed., German Historical Institute, last modified March 25, 2014, http://www.immigrantentrepreneurship.org/entry.php?rec=63

79 Tartsinis, "Chronology," in *Knoll Textiles, 1945–2010,* 26–34.

80 "Florence Knoll Bassett: Defining Modern," Philadelphia Museum of Art, November 17, 2004–April 10, 2005, accessed March 28, 2019, https://www.philamuseum.org/exhibitions/2005/81.html

81 "Florence Knoll," The Museum of Modern Art, New York, accessed March 28, 2019, https://www.moma.org/artists/7596

82 Bernard Gallagher, "Walter Landor (1913–1995)," *Immigrant Entrepreneurship German American Business Biographies: 1720 to the Present,* November 8, 2012, accessed July 19, 2017, https://www.immigrantentrepreneurship.org/entry.php?rec=69#_edn4

83 Gallagher, "Walter Landor (1913–1995)"; "Package Design... with Meaning," *Labels and Packaging,* August 1955, Scrapbook #10: 1952–55, Series 3: Scrapbooks, Container AC0500, Landor Design Collection, ca. 1930–1994, Smithsonian National Museum of American History, Washington, DC.

84 Gallagher, "Walter Landor (1913–1995)"; Gallagher quotes from "Obituary: Walter Landor. Herald of the Corporate Image," *The Guardian,* June 16, 1995, 13.

85 Gallagher, "Walter Landor (1913–1995)."

86 Ibid. Gallagher quotes from Ken Kelley and Rick Clogher, "The Ultimate Image Maker," *San Francisco Focus,* August 1992, 67; Photographs: Industrial Design, Scrapbook #9: Landor Overview 1950s, Volume 2, Series 3: Scrapbooks, Container AC0500, Landor Design Collection, ca. 1930–1994, Smithsonian National Museum of American History, Washington, DC.

87 "Miss Josephine Martinelli Weds Walter Joseph Landor Saturday," *Madera* Tribune, June 24, 1940.

88 Walter Landor, "Inside the Studio with Walter Landor," accessed April 16, 2019 https://landor.com/thinking/inside-the-studio-with-walter-landor

89 Ibid.

90 Elaine Mayers Salkaln, "The Invisibles," *New York Times Magazine,* April 18, 2004, 54.

91 Lesley Jackson, *Twentieth-Century Pattern Design* (New York: Princeton Architectural Press, 2011), 113–14.

92 Salkaln, "The Invisibles," 50.

93 Salkaln, "The Invisibles," 51; quoting an interview with Rita Reif for the *New York Times.*

94 Jackson, Twentieth-Century Pattern Design, 113.

95 Salkaln, "The Invisibles," 54; Jackson, *Twentieth-Century Pattern Design,* 113.

96 Salkaln, "The Invisibles," 56.

97 Henry Lee, "It's in the Window," *American Artist* 5, issue 6 (1941), 15.

98 Tom Lee Biographical Materials & Photographs, ca. 1950s–1971, Sarah Tomerlin Lee and Tom Lee Collection, nysidar_2013_01, Box 12, Folder 51,

New York School of Interior Design, New York

99 "Tom Lee is Dead, Designer was 61," *New York Times*, July 16, 1971, 34.

100 Tom Lee Biographical Materials & Photographs, ca. 1950s–1971, Sarah Tomerlin Lee and Tom Lee Collection, nysidar_2013_01, Box 12, Folder 51, New York School of Interior Design, New York

101 "Correspondence & Drawings, Moscow Fashion Show, 1959, Sarah Tomerlin Lee and Tom Lee Collection, nysidar_2013_01, Box 12, Folder 26, New York School of Interior Design, New York.

102 "Tom Lee is Dead, Designer was 61," *New York Times*.

103 Ibid.

104 Alexa Griffith Winton, "None of Us Is Sentimental About the Hand: Dorothy Liebes, Handweaving, and Design for Industry," *The Journal of Modern Craft* 4, issue 3 (2011): 253–54.

105 Winton, 255.

106 Winton, 257.

107 "Raymond Loewy, FIDSA," *Industrial Designers Society of America*, 2016, accessed September 27, 2017, http://www.idsa.org/content/raymond-loewy-fidsa.

108 Gary Kulik, "Raymond Loewy: Designs for a Consumer Culture," in *Technology and Culture* 44, no. 3 (July 2003), 567.

109 Ibid.

110 Michael Beschloss, "The Man Who Gave Air Force One Its Aura," *New York Times*, August 7, 2017.

111 William Grimes, "Jack Masey, Whose Exhibitions Showed American Culture to World, Dies at 91," *New York Times*, March 21, 2016.

112 Wall Street Journal Magazine, *Wall to Wall Presents: An Interview with Jack Masey*, produced by Alastair Gordon and Randy Bell, New York: Floating Films, 2009.

113 http://www.georgenelsonfoundation.org/george-nelson/index.html.

114 "Designers: George Nelson," *Herman Miller*, 2017, accessed September 28, 2017, http://store.hermanmiller.com/our-designers/george-nelson?lang=en_US.

115 Ted Conover, "Lives Well Lived: Elizabeth Paepcke; Eve in the Garden of Aspen," *New York Times*, January 1, 1995.

116 "Biographical Note," The University of Chicago Library, Special Collections Research Center, Finding Aids, Guide to the Walter P. Paepcke Papers 1912–61, https://www.lib.uchicago.edu/e/scrc/findingaids/view.php?eadid=ICU.SPCL.PAEPCKEW.

117 Ibid.

118 Ibid.

119 Annemarie Henle Pope, oral history interview with Buck Pennington, April 21, 1981, Archives of American Art, Smithsonian Institution.

120 Memo from Annemarie Pope to Thomas M. Beggs, "Subject: Reply to AFA," October 8, 1951, Smithsonian Institution Archives, Record Unit 316, Box 14/17.

121 "Agreement between the United States Government and the American Federation of Arts," Smithsonian Institution Archives, Record Unit 316, Box 72, Folder: Exhibition Files State Department Exhibitions Correspondence 1949–51.

122 Oral history, April 21, 1981.

123 Ibid.

124 Memo from Pope to Beggs, October 8, 1951.

125 Oral history, April 21, 1981.

126 Barbara Gamarekian, "Working Profile: The 'First Lady' of a World of Art," *New York Times*, November 24, 1984, 9.

127 Richard Pearson, "Art Impresario Annemarie

Pope Dies," *Washington Post*, November 12, 2001, B6.

128 Roy Flukinger, *Fritz Henle: In Search of Beauty* (Austin: University of Texas Press, 2009) 2–3; and Herbert A. Strauss and Werner Röder, "Werner Henle," *International Biographical Dictionary of Central European Émigrés 1933–1945. Volume 2, The Arts, Sciences, and Literature* (Munich: K. G. Saur, 1999), 489.

129 "Noemi & Antonin Raymond," *Raymond Farm Center for Living Arts and Design*, 2017, http://www.raymondfarmcenter.org/theraymonds/.

130 Ibid.

131 Kurt Helfrich and William Whitaker, *Crafting a Modern World: The Architecture and Design of Antonin and Noemi Raymond* (New York: Princeton Architectural Press, 2007), 21, 25.

132 "Noemi & Antonin Raymond," *Raymond Farm Center for Living Arts and Design.*

133 Ari Seligmann, "Reviewed Works: Crafting a Modern World, the Architecture and Design of Antonin and Noemi Raymond," *Journal of the Society of Architectural Historians* 66, no. 3 (2007): 390–91.

134 Helfrich and Whitaker, *Crafting a Modern World*, 20.

135 Maura Reynolds, "Bernard Rudofsky, 82, Architect and 'Outspoken' Social Analyst," *New York Times*, March 13, 1988.

136 "Classic Sandals Sponsored For Comfort and Style," *New York Times*, April 30, 1946, 24.

137 Greg Castillo, *Cold War on the Home Front: The Soft Power of Midcentury Design* (Minneapolis: University of Minnesota Press, 2010), 146.

138 Herbert A. Strauss and Werner Röder, "Schaefer, Herwin," *International Biographical Dictionary of Central European Émigrés 1933–1945. Volume 2, The Arts, Sciences, and Literature* (Munich: K. G. Saur, 1999), 1020–21.

139 Phone conversation with Margaret Re, March 2005.

140 Herwin Schaefer, "Towards a More Useful Museum," *College Art Journal* 8, no. 2 (Winter, 1948–49), 118.

141 Ibid.

142 Herwin Schaefer, "Industrial Design in America," in *Idea 53: International Design Annual*, Gerd Hatje, ed. (New York: George Wittenborn, 1952), XV.

143 Kali Persall, "Hidden Treasures: Take Home a Masterpiece from Doe Library," *California Magazine*, May 17, 2018.

144 http://saulsteinbergfoundation.org/essay/early-years-bucharest-milan/.

145 Ibid.

146 Ibid.

147 Ian Frazier, "Saul Steinberg at One Hundred," *The New Yorker*, October 8, 2014, accessed September 29, 2017, https://www.newyorker.com/culture/cultural-comment/remembering-saul-steinberg

148 Leslie Jackson, *Twentieth-Century Pattern Design* (New York: Princeton Architecture Press, 2002) 119.

149 Peter Schjeldahl, "Life Lines: The Art of Saul Steinberg," *The New Yorker*, December 3, 2012.; Frazier, "Saul Steinberg at One Hundred."

150 Angelo Testa, "Rooted in Chicago: Fifty Years of Textile Design Traditions," in *Art Institute of Chicago Museum Studies* 23, no. 1, (1997): 13.

151 Ibid., 14.

152 Christa C. Mayer Thurman, "Angelo Testa," in *Design 1935–1965: What Modern Was* (New York: Harry N. Abrams, Inc., 1991), 147.

153 Matilda McQuaid, "American Bauhaus:

Campangna by Angelo Testa," Object of the Day, *Cooper Hewitt*, November 13, 2016, accessed September 29, 2017, https://www.cooperhewitt.org/2016/11/13/22u387/.

154 Testa, "Rooted in Chicago," 13.

155 Mary Roche, "New Fabrics in New Designs," *New York Times*, March 9, 1947, 196–97.

156 "Leslie Tillett," *Cooper Hewitt*, accessed September 29, 2017, https://collection.cooperhewitt.org/people/35459747/bio.

157 Christopher Petkanas, "When Design Burst From Cloth," *New York Times*, October 14, 2012, 12.

158 Ibid.

159 "Leslie Tillett," *Cooper Hewitt*, accessed 29 September, 2017, https://collection.cooperhewitt.org/people/35459747/bio.

160 "The World of D.D. and Leslie Tillett," *Museum of the City of New York*, accessed 29 September, 2017, http://www.mcny.org/exhibition/world-dd-and-leslie-tillett

Bibliography

Archival Sources

American Federation of Arts Records, 1895–1993. Archives of American Art. Smithsonian Institution, Washington, DC.

Bassett, Florence Knoll. Papers, 1932–2000. Archives of American Art. Smithsonian Institution, Washington, DC.

Bauhaus-Archiv/Museum für Gestaltung. Berlin, Germany.

Blase, Karl Oskar. Documenta Archiv. Kassel, Germany.

Burtin, Will. Papers. RIT Libraries, Graphic Design Archive. Rochester Institute of Technology, Rochester, NY.

Fine Arts Federation of New York. Records, 1895–2005 (bulk 1935–2002). Archives of American Art. Smithsonian Institution, Washington, DC.

General Records of the Department of State. Record Group 59. National Archives and Records Administration, College Park, MD.

Knoll Corporate Archives. Knoll Headquarters, New York and East Greenville, PA.

Office of Military Government, United States (OMGUS). Record Group 260. National Archives and Records Administration, College Park, MD.

Records of the United States Information Agency (USIA). Record Group 306. National Archives and Records Administration, College Park, MD.

Traveling Exhibition Service Records, 1950–1962. Record Unit 316. Smithsonian Institution Archives, Washington, DC.

Books and Journal Articles

Aynsley, Jeremy. *Nationalism and Internationalism.* London: Victoria & Albert Museum, 1993.

Belmonte, Laura A. *Selling the American Way: U.S. Propaganda and the Cold War.* Philadelphia: University of Pennsylvania Press, 2008.

Bergdoll, Barry and Leah Dickerman. *Bauhaus 1919–1933: Workshops for Modernity.* New York: Museum of Modern Art, 2009.

Berghahn, Volker. *America and the Intellectual Cold Wars.* Princeton: Princeton University Press, 2001.

Blaszczyk, Regina. *Imagining Consumers: Design and Innovation from Wedgwood to Corning.* Baltimore: Johns Hopkins University Press, 2002.

Brecker, Richard. "Truth as a Weapon of the Free World." *Annals of the American Academy of Political and Social Science* 278: The Search for National Security (November 1951): 1–11.

Burtin, Will. *Werbepackung in Amerika.* Eine Ausstellung der Amerika-Häuser in Deutschland. n.d.

Butler, Cornelia and Alexandra Schwartz, eds. Modern *Women: Women Artists at the Museum of Modern Art.* New York: The Museum of Modern Art, 2010

Castillo, Greg. "The Bauhaus in Cold War Germany." In *Bauhaus Culture: From Weimar to the Cold War*, edited by Kathleen James-Chakroborty, 171–93. Minnesota: University of Minnesota Press, 2006.

———. *Cold War on the Home Front: the Soft Power of Midcentury Design.* Minneapolis: University of Minnesota Press, 2010.

———. "Exhibiting the Good Life: Marshall Plan Modernism in Divided Berlin." In *Cold War Modern: Art and Design in a Divided World, 1945–1975*, edited by David Crowley and Jane Pavett. London: Victoria & Albert Museum, 2008.

———. "Domesticating the Cold War: Household Consumption as Propaganda in Marshall Plan Germany." *Journal of Contemporary History* 40, no. 2 (April 2005): 261–88.

Cockcroft, Eva. "Abstract Expressionism Weapon of the Cold War." *Artforum* 15, no. 10 (June 1974): 39–41.

Cohen, Lizabeth. *A Consumer's Republic: The Politics of Mass Consumption in Postwar America.* New York: Vintage Books, 2004.

Cull, Nicholas J. *The Cold War and the United States Information Agency: American Propaganda and Public Diplomacy, 1945–1989.* Cambridge, UK: Cambridge University Press, 2009.

De Grazia, Victoria. *Irresistible Empire: America's Advance through Twentieth-Century Europe.* Cambridge, MA: Belknap, 2006.

Diefendorf, Jeffry M. *In the Wake of War: The Reconstruction of German Cities After World War II.* New York: Oxford University Press, 1993.

Duesenberry, James S. *Income, Saving, and the Theory of Consumer Behavior.* Cambridge, MA: Harvard University Press, 1949.

Elderfield, John, ed. *The Museum of Modern Art at Mid-Century: At Home and Abroad.* New York: Harry N. Abrams, 1994.

Fermi, Laura. *Atoms for the World.* Chicago: University of Chicago Press, 1957.

Floré, Fredie and Cammie McAtee, eds. *The Politics of Furniture: Identity, Diplomacy and Persuasion in Post-War Interiors.* London: Routledge, 2017.

Franck, Klaus. *Exhibitions: A Survey of International Designs.* New York: Praeger, 1961.

Greenhalgh, Paul. *Modernism in Design.* London: Reaktion Books, 1990.

Haddow, Robert. *Pavilions of Plenty: Exhibiting American Culture Abroad in the 1950s.* Washington: Smithsonian Institution Press, 1997.

Harper, Dennis, ed. *Art Interrupted: Advancing American Art and the Politics of Cultural Diplomacy.* Athens: Georgia Museum of Art, University of Georgia, 2012.

Hoffman, Paul G. *Peace Can Be Won.* Garden City, NY: Doubleday, 1951.

Hogan, Michael J. *The Marshall Plan: America, Britain, and the Reconstruction of Western Europe, 1947–1952.* New York: Cambridge University Press, 1987.

Hunt, Michael H. *The American Ascendancy: How the United States Gained and Wielded Global Dominance.* Chapel Hill: University of North Carolina Press, 2007.

Kaufmann, Edgar, Jr. *What is Modern Design?* New York: Museum of Modern Art, 1950.

Kentgens-Craig, Margaret. *The Bauhaus in America: First Contacts 1919–1936.* Cambridge, MA: MIT Press, 1999.

Kieselbach, Burckhard, ed. *Bauhaustapete: Reklame & Erfolg einer Marke = Advertising & Success of a Brandname.* Translated by Claudia Spinner. Cologne: DuMont, 1996.

Knoll, Florence. *Textilien aus USA.* Deutschland Amerikanische Hohe Kommission, 1952.

Koelsch, Ursula. *The Amerika-Haus in Germany: The Impact of the Cold War on the Development of U.S. Information Centers during the American Occupation of Germany, 1945–1949.* Master's thesis, University of Maryland, College Park, 1991.

Krenn, Michael L. *Fall-Out Shelters for the Human Spirit: American Art and the Cold War.* Chapel Hill: University of North Carolina Press, 2005.

———. *The History of United States Cultural Diplomacy.* New York: Bloomsbury, 2017.

Kretschmer, Robert. *Window & Interior Display: The Principles of Visual Merchandising.* Scranton: Laurel Publishers, 1952.

Logemann, Jan. *Engineered Creativity: Emigrés and the Transatlantic Origins of Midcentury Marketing.* Chicago: University of Chicago Press, 2018

———. "Consumer Modernity as Cultural Translation." In *Geschichte und Gesellschaft* 43.3 (2017): 413–37.

Martin, Earl, ed. *Knoll Textiles.* Boston: Yale University Press, 2011.

Masey, Jack and Conway Lloyd Morgan. *Cold War Confrontations: US Exhibitions and Their Role in the Cultural Cold War.* Baden, Switzerland: Lars Müller Publications, 2008.

Mathews, Jane De Hart. "Art and Politics in Cold War America." *American Historical Review* 81 (October 1976): 762–87.

McDonald, Gay. "The 'Advance' of American Postwar Design in Europe: MoMA and the 'Design for Use, USA' Exhibition 1951–1953." *Design Issues* 24, no. 2 (Spring 2008): 15–27.

Merritt, Anna J. and Richard L. Merritt. *Public Opinion in Semisovereign Germany: The HICOG Surveys, 1949–1955.* Urbana: University of Illinois Press, 1970.

———. *Public Opinion in Occupied Germany: The OMGUS Surveys, 1945–1949.* Urbana: University of Illinois Press, 1979.

Meikle, Jeffrey. *Twentieth Century Limited: Industrial Design in America, 1925–1939.* Philadelphia: Temple University Press, 2001.

Mitarachi, Jane Fiske. "Design as a Political Force." *Industrial Design* 4, no. 2 (February 1957): 37–55.

Molella, Arthur and Scott Knowles, eds. *World's Fairs in the Era of the Cold War: Science, Technology, and the Culture of Progress.* Pittsburgh: University of Pittsburgh Press, 2019.

Nelson, George. *Display.* New York: Whitney Publications, 1953.

Ninkovich, Frank A. *Germany and the United States: The Transformation of the German Question Since 1945.* New York: Twayne Publishers, 1994.

———. "The Currents of Cultural Diplomacy: Art and the State Department, 1938–1947." *Diplomatic History* 1, no. 3 (Summer 1977): 215–37.

Oldenziel, Ruth and Karin Zachmann, eds. *Cold War Kitchen: Americanization, Technology, and European Users.* Cambridge, MA: MIT Press, 2011.

Osgood, Kenneth. *Total Cold War: Eisenhower's Secret Propaganda Battle at Home and Abroad.* Lawrence, KS: University of Kansas Press, 2006.

Pulos, Arthur J. *The American Design Adventure, 1940–1975.* Cambridge, MA: MIT Press, 1988.

Remington, Roger R. and Robert S. P. Fripp. *Design and Science: The Life and Work of Will Burtin.* Burlington, VT: Lund Humphries, 2007.

Riley, Terence and Edward Eigen. "Between the Museum and the Marketplace: Selling Good Design." *MoMA Journal* (1994): 151–73.

Rosenberg, Emily. *Spreading the American Dream: American Economic and Cultural Expansion, 1890–1945.* Scarborough: HarperCollins Canada, 1982.

Sager, Weston. "Apple Pie Propaganda? The Smith-Mundt Act Before and After the Domestic Dissemination Ban." *Northwestern University Law Review* (Winter 2015): 519–20.

Samuel, Laurence R. *The End of Innocence: The 1964–1965 New York World's Fair.* Syracuse, NY: Syracuse University Press, 2007.

Schaefer, Herwin. *The Roots of Modern Design: Functional Tradition in the 19th Century.* London: Studio Vista, 1970.

Slater, Don. *Consumer Culture and Modernity.* Cambridge, UK: Polity Press, 1997.

Staniszewski, Mary Anne. *The Power of Display: A History of Exhibition Installations at the Museum of Modern Art.* Cambridge, MA: MIT Press, 1998.

Steil, Benn. *The Marshall Plan: Dawn of the Cold War.* New York: Simon & Schuster, 2018.

Tigerman, Bobbye. "'I Am Not a Decorator:' Florence Knoll, the Knoll Planning Unit and the Making of the Modern Office." *Journal of Design History* 20, no. 1 (2007): 61–74.

Troy, Virginia Gardner. "Weaving Diplomacy: Textiles and Hand-Weaving at Home and Abroad at Midcentury." *Archives of American Art Journal* 53, nos. 1 & 2 (Fall 2014): 52–77.

———. *The Modernist Textile: Europe and America 1890–1940.* London: Lund Humphries, 2006.

United States Commission of Fine Arts. *Art and Government; Report to the President on Activities of the Federal Government in the Field of Art.* Washington, DC: Government Printing Office, 1953.

United States High Commissioner for Germany. *Educational and Cultural Activities in Germany Today.* Frankfurt/Main: Office of Public Affairs, 1953.

———. *The America-Houses: A Study of the U.S. Information Centers in Germany.* Frankfurt/Main: Office of Public Affairs, 1953.

United States Office of the Military Governor for Germany, U.S. Zone, Information Control Division. *Report to the Smith-Mundt Committee on Interpreting the United States to the American Zone in Occupied Germany.* Berlin, 1947.

Wagenleitner, Reinhold. *Coca-Colonization and the Cold War: The Cultural Mission of the United States after the Second World War.* Chapel Hill: University of North Carolina Press, 1994.

Weisgall, Hugo. *Advancing American Art.* Prague: United States Information Service, 1947.

Werk: Schweizer Monatsschrift für Architektur, Kunst, künstlerisches Gewerbe 43. (1956): pages unknown.

Whitfield, Stephen J. "The American Century of Henry R. Luce." In *Americanism: New Perspectives on the History of an Ideal.* Edited by Michael Kazin and Joseph A. McCartin. Chapel Hill: University of North Carolina Press, 2006.

Willett, Ralph. *The Americanization of Germany, 1945–1949.* New York and London: Routledge, 1989.

Wingler, Hans Maria. *The Bauhaus: Weimar, Dessau, Berlin, Chicago.* Cambridge, MA: MIT Press, 1976.

Wulf, Andrew James. *U.S. International Exhibitions During the Cold War.* Lanham MD: Rowman and Littlefield, 2015.